D1445790

AMERICAN
ETHNIC
LITERATURES

THE
MAGILL
BIBLIOGRAPHIES

Other Magill Bibliographies:

Biography—Carl Rollyson
Black American Women Novelists—Craig Werner
The Classical Epic—Thomas J. Sienkewicz
Classical Greek and Roman Drama—Robert J. Forman
Contemporary Latin American Fiction—Keith H. Brower
The Immigrant Experience—Paul D. Mageli
The Modern American Novel—Steven G. Kellman
Native Americans—Frederick E. Hoxie and Harvey Markowitz
Shakespeare—Joseph Rosenblum
The Vietnam War in Literature—Philip K. Jason

AMERICAN ETHNIC LITERATURES

Native American, African American, Chicano/Latino, and Asian American Writers and Their Backgrounds

An Annotated Bibliography

David R. Peck

California State University, Long Beach

SALEM PRESS

Pasadena, California   Englewood Cliffs, New Jersey

∞ The paper used in these volumes conforms to the
American National Standard for Permanence of Paper
for Printed Library Materials, Z39.48-1984.

Library of Congress Cataloging-in-Publication Data

Peck, David R.
    American ethnic literatures: Native American,
African American, Chicano/Latino, and Asian
American writers and their backgrounds / David R.
Peck
    p. cm.—(Magill bibliographies)
    Includes bibliographic references and index
    ISBN 0-89356-684-5
    1. American literature—minority authors—
Bibliography. 2. Hispanic Americans in literature—
Bibliography. 3. Asian Americans in literature—
Bibliography. 4. Afro-Americans in literature—
Bibliography. 5. Ethnic groups in literature—
Bibliography. 6. Indians in literature—Bibliography.
I. Title. II. Series.
Z1229.E87P43   1992
[PS153.M56]   92-12897
016.8109'920693—dc20   CIP

For my daughter, Sarah

EDITORIAL STAFF

CONTENTS

CONTENTS

AMERICAN
ETHNIC
LITERATURES

INTRODUCTION

The recent surge of primary work in, and secondary scholarship on, American ethnic literatures means that, after hundreds of years, Americans are coming to realize their truly multiethnic culture. Oscar Handlin first said it—American history *is* ethnic history—as Werner Sollors has more recently argued that ethnic literature is American literature, and Marcus Klein that all twentieth century American writers are, in effect if not in fact, "foreigners."[1] Many of the recent books and national news magazines devoted to the quincentennial Columbus celebration—to cite but one example—have featured the Native American cultures that existed when Columbus "discovered" North America and that were systematically destroyed in the centuries after that landfall.[2] Americans are coming to recognize this country's multiethnicity, at the same time that they are having to revise their understanding of its history.

This recent explosion of ethnic awareness has challenged people's very definitions of the national culture, and the concept of the melting pot is giving way to more accurate metaphors of the national character: a mosaic, kaleidoscope, or patchwork quilt. The last is perhaps best because it implies what is so patently true: the uneven development of the different ethnic pieces as they have come together at different times and in various shapes and sizes and colors—and as they are still being added to the national quilt.

American Ethnic Literatures is a serious effort to provide a guide to the range of creative and scholarly work in the four major American ethnic literatures. The burst of creative energies in the last thirty years among Native Americans, African Americans, Hispanic Americans, and Asian Americans has meant that many teachers have been unable to keep up with the primary literature, to say nothing of the growing secondary criticism.

American Ethnic Literatures provides a single bibliography where teachers and students alike can find listings of the major primary literatures in the four ethnic groups, plus the most important secondary criticism of those literatures, including background sources—the best treatments of slavery, immigration, and American Indian history. In short, the book lists not only primary ethnic literatures (and the scholarship that surrounds it) but the *context* for that literature: the histories of the four ethnic communities that are producing that literature in the United States today.

The reason for this predominantly American studies approach is that these literatures draw so heavily on their own ethnic history. A writer like James Baldwin, in his fiction as well as his essays, cannot be imagined free of the African American history that produced him and to which he so often returned. Likewise Luis Valdez, a playwright whose themes, forms, and language all draw heavily from the Chicano community. Maxine Hong Kingston, to cite a final example, weaves history and fiction into her works as delicate, unified tapestries. The teachers or students who do not understand that history—like the early reviewers of *Woman Warrior*—will miss the distinction and thus the real power of Kingston's prose.

Readers may understand something of American history, but until recently (and the Columbus quincentennial has highlighted this deficiency), few understood as well the ethnic story: immigration, Native American history, and the history of slavery. The two most powerful documentary series on television in the past decade were surely "The Civil War" and "Eyes on the Prize"—documentaries that gave viewers the fullest accounts of the end of slavery and the civil rights movement, which continued the struggle a century later. Similarly, Kevin Costner's popular 1990 film, *Dances with Wolves,* was a revelation of Native American life to millions of its viewers.

American Ethnic Literatures provides student and teacher alike with what I hope is an easy entrance to American ethnic literature and to the contexts out of which it rises: brief narrative histories of the four ethnic literatures, annotations to the best works of history, annotated bibliographies of the best books of criticism, and lists of the major primary literature itself.

The contents have a necessary order and are broken into two four-chapter units. The first unit could be seen as a background for teaching American ethnic literature because it provides teachers with the necessary foundations. Chapter 1, for example, annotates bibliographies on ethnic history and immigration, as well as the most important reference works for the study of Native Americans, African Americans, Hispanic Americans, and Asian Americans. I also include here the key journals in the fields of ethnic history and literature, special ethnic issues of other periodicals, and the most important journals for each of the four literatures.

Chapter 2, "The Social and Historical Record," lists the best general and theoretical works on race, ethnicity, and immigration; the major studies of ethnic American history (including the best textbooks and collections of essays); and the central volumes for understanding Native American, African American, Chicano/Latino, and Asian American history.

Chapter 3, "Teaching Ethnic Literature," lists the best journals on the subject, general guides to teaching ethnic literature, works on teaching the specific literatures of the four groups, a listing of guides to audiovisual materials, and a directory of the best anthologies of comparative ethnic literatures teachers might use in courses on ethnic literature.

The final chapter in this unit, "General Studies of American Ethnic Literature," annotates the best comparative studies of ethnic literature—that is, works dealing with more than one ethnic group—in sections on specific subjects: bibliography, autobiography, fiction, poetry, theatre, women and literature, and general literary studies.

The second and longer unit of this volume describes Native American, African American, Chicano/Latino, and Asian American literatures. Each of the four chapters in this section has the same basic shape: a brief narrative history of the literature, a selected reading list of primary works (including both annotated lists of the best anthologies and unannotated lists of the fiction, nonfiction, poetry, and drama, arranged alphabetically by author, with original dates of publication), and then an annotated secondary bibliography to the best criticism divided into specific genres: drama, poetry, fiction, and nonfiction. Thus, the reader moves from narrative history, through the primary literature, to the best secondary studies.

As with any work of this kind, it was necessary to make decisions about what to include and what to omit. I have tried to include all the relevant full-length works in each chapter, but in most cases I have been able to list recent works and omit earlier titles. (Thus, Gunnar Myrdal's classic 1944 work on Black/white relations is included because it has not yet been replaced, but a number of older works in the field—whose conclusions have been incorporated into more recent studies—are not.) I have listed only books except in the case of bibliography, where I have included several articles that have appeared only in journals or collections. Finally, I have listed only works in English, although some of the collections of Chicano/Latino criticism are in fact bilingual and include both Spanish and English pieces.

It would be useful at this point to model a typical search through the book. If a teacher assigned Leslie Marmon Silko's 1977 *Ceremony* (or inherited a course in which that book was already required), he or she might want to read or assign some background to that novel. Chapter 1 contains a section of general reference works on Native Americans and a list of major journals (one of which, *American Indian Quarterly*, had a special issue on the novel in 1979, as the annotation in Chapter 1B2 notes). Chapter 2 lists fifteen of the best works on Native American history (in a number of which the reader could learn about Silko's Laguna background). Chapter 3 has a section on teaching Native American literature listing four works that touch on Silko's novel. Chapter 4 lists a special fiction issue of *MELUS* that includes an article on the novel. Chapter 5, "Native American Literature," mentions Silko in the narrative history that opens the chapter, lists thirty-three anthologies of Indian literature (several of which contain sections of *Ceremony* or other works by her), cites all four of Silko's works in a list of primary literature (including the more recent novel *Almanac of the Dead*, which readers of *Ceremony* might move to next), describes several bibliographies of her work, lists several recent studies of Native American fiction that treat *Ceremony*, and provides a number of works in the lists of "general criticism" that also contain some analysis of it or interviews with its author (Allen, Lincoln, a special issue of *MELUS*, Velie, Vizenor, et al.) All of these references, and more, are listed in the index under Silko.

Similarly, teachers or students confronting Toni Morrison's prize-winning novel *Beloved* could make a parallel search. The index will reveal all of the different references to Morrison throughout this book, from the general reference works and journals in the opening two chapters, through the works on teaching Black literature in chapter 3, the general literary studies of ethnic literature in chapter 4 (several of which have valuable analyses of the Morrison work), to the many cross-references in chapter 6 under general literary studies, studies of African American fiction, and "Black Women Writers." The serious reader, with very little effort, can find directions to several dozen analyses of Morrison's novel.

As with any reference work, *American Ethnic Writers* is most helpful when a reader uses the index and other apparatus to locate the primary and secondary works of interest. Although a number of approaches can be taken to *American Ethnic Literatures*, the best results will be obtained by using the book for specific authors, works, ethnic genres, or literatures.

I hope that both students and teachers will find this book of some value. If they do, it is thanks to David Fine and other friends in the American Studies Program at California State University, Long Beach; Cathrine Lewis-Ida, Sharlene Laforge, and their staff at the CSULB Interlibrary Loan; and John Wilson at Salem Press. The limitations of this work may be mine, but the strengths are clearly theirs.

NOTES

1. See descriptions of Handlin, *The Uprooted*; Sollors, *Beyond Ethnicity*; and Klein, *Foreigners*, in 2B1 and 4B. (Cross-references within this book will be to chapter number and subsection letters/numbers.)

2. See, for example, the "Columbus Special Issue" of *Newsweek* (Fall/Winter, 1991): "When Worlds Collide: How Columbus's Voyages Transformed Both East and West."

Chapter 1
GENERAL BIBLIOGRAPHIES, REFERENCE WORKS, AND JOURNALS

A. Bibliographies and Reference Works

1. General

Allen, James P., and Eugene J. Turner. *We the People: An Atlas of America's Ethnic Diversity*. New York: Macmillan, 1988.
Detailed descriptions of the country's ethnic populations using maps, statistics, and readable text. Chapters contain background on the peoples of Early North American, Western European, Middle and South American, and Asian and Pacific Island origin, as well as on "General Patterns of Ethnic Identity," all based on 1980 census data. The atlas focuses "on the ethnic dimensions of the population in different places in order to illuminate something of the human geography of the country."

Buenker, John D., and Nicholas C. Burckel. *Immigration and Ethnicity: A Guide to Information Sources*. Detroit: Gale Research, 1977.
Annotates "the most significant literature on the vast subjects of immigration and ethnicity."

Cordasco, Francesco, ed. *Dictionary of American Immigration History*. Metuchen, N.J.: Scarecrow Press, 1990.
Short essays (see Mexicans, Afro-Americans, Asian Indians, Chinese, etc.) followed by brief bibliographies.

_____, comp. *The New American Immigration: Evolving Patterns of Legal and Illegal Emigration; A Bibliography of Selected References*. New York: Garland, 1987.
Annotations of the most important sources in three sections on immigration before 1986, immigration after 1986, and illegal immigrants.

Developing Library Collections for California's Emerging Majority: A Manual of Resources for Ethnic Collection Development. Oakland: Bay Area Library and Information System (BALIS), 1990.
This manual is an invaluable tool for any teacher or librarian developing a collection for one of the four major ethnic groups: African American, American Indian, Asian/Southest Asian, and Chicano/Latino.

Forster, Carol D., et al., eds. *Minorities—A Changing Role in America.* Wylie, Tex.: Information Plus, 1990.
Contains the best recent statistics on demographics, work, education, and other areas.

Hecher, Melvin, comp. *Ethnic America, 1970-1977.* Dobbs Ferry, N.Y.: Oceana, 1979.
This volume contains chronologies for thirty ethnic groups, of "important events in American history from the perspective of the ethnic community," plus bibliographies.

Ireland, Sandra L. Jones, comp. *Ethnic Periodicals in Contemporary America: An Annotated Guide.* Bibliographies and Indexes in Ethnic Studies 3. Westport, Conn.: Greenwood Press, 1990.
This bibliography is organized alphabetically. See sections on Afro-American, Black-American, and other journals.

Joramo, Marjorie K., comp. *A Directory of Ethnic Publishers and Resource Organizations.* 2d ed. Chicago: American Library Association, 1979.
Includes an annotated directory, archival and research collections, and distributors.

Kinloch, Graham C. *Race and Ethnic Relations: An Annotated Bibliography.* New York: Garland, 1984.
Describes articles and books on theory and methodology in "a fairly comprehensive overview of the most important and representative social science research on race and ethnic relations during the 1960s and 1970s."

Miller, Wayne C., with Faye Nell Vowell, eds. *Minorities in America: The Annual Bibliography (1976-1978).* 2 vols. University Park: Pennsylvania State University Press, 1985, 1986.
Republication of an annotated guide to scholarship in the humanities and social sciences in forty-four different ethnic groupings. Very useful start for any scholarly search.

Salzman, Jack, ed. *American Studies: An Annotated Bibliography, 1984-1988.* Cambridge, England: Cambridge University Press, 1990.
See "Ethnic History" (pp. 495-513) and "Native American History" (pp. 513-532) sections for annotations of recent books in American cultural studies.

Schlacter, Gail Arm, with Donna Belli. *Minorities and Women: A Guide to Reference Literature in the Social Sciences.* Los Angeles: Reference Service Press, 1977.

Dated but still useful annotations of "fact books" (encyclopedias and the like). Also contains biographical, documentary, and statistical sources and other bibliographies.

Searing, Susan, et al., eds. *Women, Race, and Ethnicity: A Bibliography*. Madison: University of Wisconsin System Women's Studies Librarian, 1991.
A "selective, annotated list of college-level print and audiovisual resources" in sections on biography and autobiography, literature (drama, fiction, history and criticism, and mixed genres), periodicals, and two dozen other categories.

Thernstrom, Stephan, et al., eds. *Harvard Encyclopedia of American Ethnic Groups*. Cambridge, Mass.: Harvard University Press, 1980.
The most useful reference work on American ethnic minorities. Essays on individual ethnic groups are followed by bibliographies. See fuller description of literary entries in 4B.

Weinberg, Meyer, comp. *Racism in the United States: A Comprehensive Classified Bibliography*. Bibliographies and Indexes in Ethnic Studies 2. Westport, Conn.: Greenwood Press, 1990.
See especially Section 47, "Literature." Entries are not annotated.

2. Native American

Haas, Marilyn L. *Indians of North America: Methods and Sources for Library Research*. Hamden, Conn.: Library Professional Publications, 1983.
The volume has three parts: library methodology and reference works (abstracts, archives, handbooks, encyclopedias); an annotated bibliography of books on topics useful in Indian studies; and an unannotated list of books on individual tribes.

Hirschfelder, Arlene B., et al., comps. *Guide to Research on North American Indians*. Chicago: American Library Association, 1983.
A bibliography "intended to serve as a basic guide to the literature for general readers, students, and scholars." Contains twenty-seven chapters in four broad subject headings; each chapter contains an essay, list of works treating the topic, and bibliography. See especially section 4, "Religion, Arts, and Literature."

Klein, Barry T. *Reference Encyclopedia of the American Indian*. 4th ed. 2 vols. New York: Todd Publications, 1986.
Volume 1 includes magazines and periodicals, annotated bibliographies in different subject areas (see fiction, poetry, and so on). The best place to start for much American Indian research.

3. African American

Bibliographic Guide to Black Studies: 1990. Boston: G. K. Hall, 1991.
A comprehensive subject bibliography. See various topics, authors in literature and language. This annual may be the best resource in which to begin many African American research subjects.

Davis, Nathaniel, comp. *Afro-American Reference: An Annotated Bibliography of Selected Resources*. Bibliographies and Indices in Afro-American and African Studies 9. Westport, Conn.: Greenwood Press, 1985.
Includes descriptions of encyclopedias, dictionaries, and biographical sources. See "Literature," pp. 131-150.

Low, W. Augustus, and Virgil A. Clift, eds. *Encyclopedia of Black America*. New York: McGraw-Hill, 1981.
This "first significant and major encyclopedic history of black Americans" contains 325 major and minor articles, 1400 biographies, and numerous cross-references.

Newman, Richard, comp. *Black Access: A Bibliography of Afro-American Bibliographies*. Westport, Conn.: Greenwood Press, 1984.
Contains lists of titles and authors of bibliographical books and articles, followed by both chronological and subject indexes.

4. Chicano/Latino

Camarillo, Albert, ed. *Latinos in the United States: A Historical Bibliography*. Santa Barbara, Calif.: ABC-CLIO, 1986.
"This bibliography contains 1382 citations expertly drawn from dozens of volumes of *America: History and Life* published between 1973 and 1985. The entries represent a diversity of disciplinary and interdisciplinary studies taken primarily from the humanities and social sciences." Includes annotated entries, subject and author indexes.

Chicano Database. Berkeley: Chicano Studies Library, 1990.
This CD-ROM data base includes more than 36,000 items on Mexican American subjects, including work printed in *The Chicano Periodical Index*, *Chicano Anthology Index*, and *Arte Chicano: An Annotated Bibliography of Chicano Art, 1965-1981*. Use "Chicanos in American Literature" as subject.

Foster, David William, ed. *Sourcebook of Hispanic Culture in the United States*. Chicago: American Library Association, 1982.
Essays containing annotated bibliographies on a range of topics. See, as the best example, Virginia Ramos Foster's essay on literature under the section on Mexican Americans, pp. 86-111.

Meier, Matt S., and Feliciano Rivera, comps. *Dictionary of Mexican American History*. Westport, Conn.: Greenwood Press, 1981.
The dictionary is followed by appendices containing bibliography, chronology, glossary, list of journals, and more.

Smith, Darren L., ed. *Hispanic Americans Information Directory, 1990-1991*. Detroit: Gale Research, 1990.
"A guide to approximately 4,700 organizations, agencies, institutions, programs, and publications concerned with Hispanic American life and culture."

5. Asian American

Kim, Hyung-Chan, comp. *Asian American Studies: An Annotated Bibliography and Research Guide*. Bibliographies and Indexes in American History 11. Westport, Conn.: Greenwood Press, 1989.
The guide is in two parts: "Historical Perspectives" and "Contemporary Perspectives." See part 1, section 4: "Culture, Communication, and Education," and part 2, section 17: "Culture, Communication, and Mass Media."

_____, ed. *Dictionary of Asian American History*. Westport, Conn.: Greenwood Press, 1986.
Contains fifteen essays on Asians in America, the dictionary, and appendices (a select bibliography, chronology, and 1980 census data).

Poon, Wei Chi, ed. *A Guide for Establishing Asian American Core Collections*. Berkeley, Calif.: Asian American Studies Library, 1989.
An annotated list of essential books, serials, sources, and subject headings.

B. Journals (including special ethnic issues)

1. General

American Quarterly. American Studies Association, four times a year (March, June, September, and December), 1949-
American Quarterly publishes articles, reviews, and review essays on American

literature and American history using interdisciplinary approaches. A number of essays have been published on ethnic topics, particularly in recent years.

American Studies International. American Studies Association, semiannual, 1962-

ASI has published several important ethnic bibliographies; see, for example, Annie O. Eysturoy and Jose Antonio Gurpegui, "Chicano Literature: Introduction and Bibliography" (7C1), and Elaine H. Kim, "Asian American Writers: A Bibliographical Review" (8C1).

The Annals of the American Academy of Political and Social Science 454 (March, 1981). Milton M. Gordon, ed.
Special issue on "America as a Multicultural Society": fifteen experts survey racial and ethnic issues.

Auto/Biography Studies 3, no. 2 (1987).
Special issue on "Multi-Cultural American Autobiography" contains essays on American Indian, Chicano, Black, and other ethnic autobiographies by A. LaVonne Brown Ruoff, Raymund A. Paredes, Richard Tuerk, SallyAnn H. Ferguson, James Robert Payne, and Amy Ling.

Cultural Critique 6 (Spring, 1987), 7 (Fall, 1987). Abdul R. JanMohamed and David Lloyd, eds. "The Nature and Context of Minority Discourse."
Theoretical essays by Barbara Christian, Henry Louis Gates, Jr., Elaine H. Kim, and others on a range of topics, including women, modernism, and Richard Wright.

Daedalus 110, no. 2 (Spring, 1981).
Special issue on "American Indians, Blacks, Chicanos, and Puerto Ricans" includes essays by John Hope Franklin, Vine Deloria, Jr., Robert Coles, Michael Dorris, and more than a dozen other writers on economic and cultural issues.

The Dispatch. The Newsletter of the Center for American Culture Studies, Columbia University, biannual, 1986-
The Dispatch has published an ongoing "Ethnicity in America" bibliography and briefly incorporated *Studies in American Indian Literatures*. (See *SAIL*, below, in 1B2.)

Ethnic Forum. Journal of Ethnic Studies and Ethnic Bibliography, Published by the Center for the Study of Ethnic Publications and Cultural Institutions, Kent State University, biannual, 1980-
A "major forum for discussion of ethnic librarianship, bibliography and archival topics." See index to volumes 1-9, compiled by Peter Muranyi, 10, nos. 1-2

(1990): 140-174; and an editorial by Lubomyr R. Wynar in the same issue, "Ten Years of *Ethnic Forum*, 1980-1989."

The Ethnic Reporter. Newsletter of the National Association for Ethnic Studies, biannual, 1986-
Absorbed the earlier *Newsletter* of the National Association of Interdisciplinary Ethnic Studies (NAIES, 1975-1986), which published short articles and reviews, often on literary subjects (e.g., Amy Ling's "Chinamerican Literature: A Partly Annotated Bibliography," 7, no. 1, May, 1982). See the index to volumes 1-10 in volume 11 (1986).

Explorations in Ethnic Studies. The Journal of the National Association for Ethnic Studies, Arizona State University, biannual, 1978-
This "multidisciplinary journal devoted to the study of ethnicity, ethnic groups, intergroup relations, and the cultural life of ethnic minorities" prints short articles and reviews. Annual Review Supplement, *Explorations in Sights and Sounds* (1981-), is a useful summary of each year's events in this field.

The Graywolf Annual Five: Multi-Cultural Literacy. Edited by Rick Simonson and Scott Walker. St. Paul, Minn.: Graywolf Press, 1988.
A collection of essays (by James Baldwin, Paula Gunn Allen, and ten other writers) plus an appendix of five hundred items of multicultural and gender literacy.

Greenfield Review 1-14 (Spring, 1970-Summer/Fall, 1987).
Some critical essays, interviews, and reviews can be found in this "eclectic magazine devoted to multicultural publishing," but mostly creative literature.

Harvard Educational Review 58, no. 3 (August, 1988).
This special issue on "Race, Racism and American Education: Perspectives of Asian Americans, Blacks, Latinos, and Native Americans" includes essays by Angela Y. Davis, June Jordan, and others.

Journal of American Ethnic History. Immigration History Society, quarterly, Fall, 1981-
Scholarly articles, reviews, and review essays primarily on historical topics.

The Journal of Ethnic Studies. Western Washington University, Bellingham, quarterly, Spring, 1973-
A "publication of interdisciplinary scholarship, opinion, and creative expression" that prints articles, reviews, and review essays on ethnic language, literature, culture, and history. See, for example, issues on Chicano fiction (Winter, 1976) and Chicano poetry (Spring, 1977).

Massachusetts Review 27, no. 2 (Summer, 1986). Jules Chametzky, ed.
Cluster of "Essays on Ethnicity and Literature"—Black poetry, American Indian, Italian-American literatures—by June Jordan, Werner Sollors, Helen Barolini, A. LaVonne Brown Ruoff, and others.

MELUS. The Journal of The Society for the Study of the Multi-Ethnic Literature of the United States, quarterly, September, 1974-
"Founded in 1973, *MELUS* endeavors to expand the definition of American literature through the study and teaching of African American, Hispanic, Native American, Asian- and Pacific-American, and ethnically specific Euro-American literary works, their authors and their cultural contexts." Notable special issues include "Literature of the Southwest," "Ethnic Images in Popular Genres and Media," "Varieties of Ethnic Criticism," "Ethnic Women Writers." Other topical issues cover specific ethnic literatures: for example, "Native American Literature," "Black American Literature."

Minority Voices: An Interdisciplinary Journal of Literature and the Arts. Paul Robeson Cultural Center, Pennsylvania State University. Vols. 1-5 (Spring, 1977-Spring/Fall, 1981); publication suspended, 1982-1988; 2d series, vol. 6 (Fall, 1989-   ); semiannual (spring and fall).
This journal "publishes original scholarly articles dealing with the arts . . . as they relate to African Americans, Chicanos, Native Americans, and Puerto Ricans." Contains articles and reviews on jazz poetry of Langston Hughes, Toni Morrison, N. Scott Momaday, Leslie Silko, and other writers and topics.

San Jose Studies 14, no. 2 (Spring, 1988). "Cultural Diversity: A Special Issue," H. Brett Melendy, guest ed.
Articles on Black Power, James Welch, Asian immigrants; also contains poetry and fiction.

2. Native American

American Indian Culture and Research Journal. American Indian Studies Center, UCLA, 1971-
This "scholarly quarterly providing an interdisciplinary forum for significant contributions to the advancement of knowledge about American Indians" publishes a wide range of essays on American Indian history, oral and written literatures, images of Indians in popular culture, etc.

American Indian Quarterly. Journal of American Indian Studies, Native American Studies Program, Berkeley, Spring, 1974-
Articles, review essays, reviews on a range of topics, including early essays on

James Welch and Mari Sandoz and an issue devoted to Leslie Marmon Silko's *Ceremony* (5, no. 1, February, 1979), as well as analyses of attitudes toward Indians in Washington Irving, John Muir, Hamlin Garland, William Faulkner, and other American writers.

SAIL: Studies in American Indian Literatures. California State University, Fullerton, quarterly, 1989-
The "only scholarly journal in the United States that focuses exclusively on American Indian literatures," *SAIL* publishes reviews, interviews, bibliographies, and creative work, including traditional oral material. Winter, 1991, and Spring, 1992, issues devoted to literature by Louise Erdrich.

3. African American

American Visions. The Magazine of Afro-American Culture, bimonthly, 1986-

This popular periodical has a number of articles on Black culture.

Black American Literature Forum. Indiana State University; official publication of The Division of Black American Literature and Culture of the MLA, quarterly, 1976-
Both creative and critical literature; see, for example, issue on "The Black Church and the Black Theatre" (25, no. 1, Spring, 1991), and "Black Film Issue" (25, no. 2, Summer, 1991).

The Black Scholar. Journal of Black Studies and Research, bimonthly, 1969-
This magazine contains a number of issues on literary matters: "Black Literature: Criticism" (12, no. 2, March/April, 1981), "Black Literature 85" (16, no. 4, July/August, 1985), "The Black Woman Writer and the Diaspora" (17, no. 2, March/April, 1986), "African Literature" (17, no. 4, July/August, 1986), "Black American Culture in the Second Renaissance, 1954-1970" (18, no. 1, January/February, 1987), and "Black Cinema" (21, no. 22 (March/April/May, 1991).

Journal of Black Studies. Quarterly, September 1970-
This journal "seeks to sustain a full analytical discussion of issues related to persons of African descent." See special issues on "African Cultural Dimensions" (8, no. 2, December, 1977), "Ebonics (Black English): Implications for Education" (9, no. 4, June, 1979), "Communication and the Afro-American" (15, no. 1, September, 1984), "The African Literary Imagination" (20, no. 4, June, 1990), and "African Aesthetics and the Diaspora" (22, no. 1, September, 1991).

Journal of Negro History. Quarterly, 1916-
A scholarly historical journal, but some articles on literary issues (Langston Hughes, "A Reading of Herman Melville on Slavery," etc.).

Phylon. The Atlanta Review of Race and Culture, quarterly, 1943-
Founded by W. E. B. Du Bois, *Phylon* includes recent special issues on "Black Press, Art and Literature" (43, no. 1, March, 1982), "Women and Blacks in Literature and Society" (44, no. 1, March, 1983), "Afro-Americans and African Literature" (47, no. 2, June, 1986), and "Race Relations Through Literature" (48, no. 3, Fall, 1987).

4. Chicano/Latino

The Americas Review (formerly *Revista Chicano-Riquena*, 1973-1985). A Review of Hispanic Literature and Art of the USA, quarterly, 1986-
Poetry, fiction, and criticism, often in special issues; see for example "A Decade of Hispanic Literature" (10, nos. 1-2, 1982), special focus on Gary Soto (11, no. 2, 1983), "Woman of Her World: Hispanic Women Write" (11, nos. 3-4, 1983), "Chicana Creativity and Criticism: Charting New Frontiers in American Literature" (15, nos. 3-4, 1987), "U.S. Hispanic Autobiography" (16, nos. 3-4, Fall-Winter, 1988), "La Prensa: Hispanic Journalism" (17, nos. 3-4, Fall-Winter, 1989).

Aztlan. A Journal of Chicano Studies. Biannual, Chicano Studies Research Center, UCLA, 1970-
Issues occasionally devoted to cultural themes; see, for example, "Mexican Folklore and Folk Art in the United States" (13, nos. 1-2, Spring-Fall, 1982).

Critica. A Journal of Critical Essays, Chicano Studies, U. of California at San Diego, annual, Spring, 1984-
Critica is a "bilingual journal that serves as a forum for critical analysis of Chicano and Latino theoretical, ideological, and historical issues." Articles in the first four issues (through Spring, 1988, vol. II, no. 1) on Carlos Fuentes, Rudolfo Anaya, Sandra Cisneros, Gary Soto, etc.

El Grito 1-7 (Fall, 1967-June/August, 1974).
This "Journal of Contemporary Mexican-American Thought" devoted a number of issues to cultural matters in its short life, e.g., "Literatura Chicana/Chicano Literature" (4, no. 2, Winter, 1971), "Contemporary Chicano Prose" (5, no. 3, Spring, 1972), "Toward a Chicano/Raza Bibliography: Drama, Prose, Poetry" (7, no. 2, December, 1973), "Chicano Drama" (7, no. 4, 1974).

Grito del Sol 1-7 (1976-1982).
Early issues printed a good deal of creative literature; see Octavio I. Romano-V.,
ed., *The Grito del Sol Collection* (Berkeley: TQS Publications, 1984), described
in 7B1b.

New Scholar. University of California, San Diego, 1-10 (1969-1986).
This irregular "Americanist Review" (1982) bills itself as "a multi-disciplinary
forum for scholars seeking a fuller understanding of the unique human condition
and experience in the Americas." Occasional cultural articles, reviews on Chicano music, theatre, Cuban literature, and so on. Recent special issues include
volume 9 on "Border Perspectives on the U.S./Mexico Relationship"; volume
10: "Voices of the First American: Text and Context in the New World."

5. Asian American

Amerasia Journal. The national interdisciplinary journal of scholarship, criticism,
and literature on Asian and Pacific Americans, Asian American Studies Center,
UCLA, three times a year, 1971-
See "Literature and Criticism" in index of volumes 1-13, 1971-1987 (1988).

Asian America: Journal of Culture and Arts. Asian American Studies Program,
University of California, Santa Barbara, 1992-
"*Asian America* will be devoted to the critical study of the changing faces of
Asian America: our claims on the physical, social, and cultural landscapes of the
United States; our communal histories; our ties to the homelands whence we
came; our changing traditions; our efforts to create a new Asian American
culture; and our contributions to, and critique of, American society."

Chapter 2
THE SOCIAL AND HISTORICAL RECORD

A. General Works: Definitions, Theories of Race, Ethnicity, Etc.

Alba, Richard D. *Ethnic Identity: The Transformation of White America*. New Haven, Conn.: Yale University Press, 1990.
A sociological study of "symbolic ethnicity" in the United States: the "irreversible decline of objective ethnic differences—in education and work, family and community—and the continuing subjective importance of ethnic origins."

Allport, Gordon W. *The Nature of Prejudice*. 25th anniv. ed. Reading, Mass.: Addison-Wesley, 1979.
Still the standard study of the origin and nature of prejudice.

Glazer, Nathan. *Affirmative Discrimination: Ethnic Inequality and Public Policy*. Reprint. Cambridge, Mass.: Harvard University Press, 1987.
Essays on affirmative action by an opponent who is of the belief that the government should instead "encourage the economic circumstances in which jobs are plentiful . . . and the economy grows."

_____. *Ethnic Dilemmas, 1964-1982*. Cambridge, Mass.: Harvard University Press, 1983.
Selected essays on issues of racial and ethnic conflict—ethnic studies, bilingualism, affirmative action, and the like.

Glazer, Nathan, and Daniel Patrick Moynihan. *Beyond the Melting Pot: The Negroes, Puerto Ricans, Jews, Italians, and Irish of New York City*. Cambridge, Mass.: MIT Press, 1963.
A landmark "effort to trace the role of ethnicity in the tumultuous, varied, endlessly complex life of New York City."

Omi, Michael, and Howard Winant. *Racial Formation in the United States: From the 1960s to the 1980s*. New York: Routledge, Chapman & Hall, 1986.
A brief work of radical critical theory. Part I is an analysis of contemporary racial theory based on ethnicity, class, and nation. Part II advances an alternative theory of race as a "fundamental organizing principle of social relationships" and as "an unstable and decentered complex of social meanings constantly being transformed by political struggle." Part III analyzes recent U.S. racial history.

Rose, Peter I. *They and We: Racial and Ethnic Relations in the United States*. New York: Random House, 1990.

One of the standard studies, originally published in 1964, by one of the foremost scholars in the field, of racial and ethnic relations.

Sowell, Thomas. *The Economics and Politics of Race: An International Perspective.* New York: William Morrow, 1983.
The "international perspective on race and ethnicity" in this book "means an opportunity to test competing beliefs and theories in a way that cannot be done in any given country."

_____. *Ethnic America: A History.* New York: Basic Books, 1981.
Perhaps the best example of the neoconservative approach to race relations. Change occurs, Sowell argues, not because of racism or affirmative action but because people pull themselves up.

Steele, Shelby. *The Content of Our Character: A New Vision of Race in America.* New York: St. Martin's Press, 1990.
Presents a conservative Black argument that the obsession with victimization by minorities since the 1960's holds people back from their potential. "Our greatest problem today is insufficient development—this more than white racism."

Steinberg, Stephen. *The Ethnic Myth: Race, Ethnicity, and Class in America.* New York: Atheneum, 1981.
The "demystification of ethnicity . . . requires an exploration of how social forces influence the form and content of ethnicity; and an examination of the specific relationships between ethnic factors on the one hand, and a broad array of historical, economic, political, and social factors on the other."

B. American Ethnic History

1. Standard Histories

Archdeacon, Thomas J. *Becoming American: An Ethnic History.* New York: Free Press, 1983.
An inclusive, comparative, "up-to-date account of the history of immigration to the United States and of the assimilation of foreign-born and foreign-stock Americans into the general society."

Bodnar, John. *The Transplanted: A History of Immigrants in Urban America.* Bloomington: Indiana University Press, 1985.
In essence, the story of immigration and industrial capitalism in nineteenth and early twentieth century America.

Cheyfitz, Eric. *The Poetics of Imperialism: Translation and Colonization from 'The Tempest' to 'Tarzan.'* New York: Oxford University Press, 1991.
An important work on language and colonization that studies, for example, "the way European invaders mapped the 'New World' according to the opposition between the *metaphoric* and the *proper*, or *literal*."

Daniels, Roger. *Coming to America: A History of Immigration and Ethnicity in American Life.* New York: HarperCollins, 1990.
A recent, comprehensive history in three parts: Colonial America (see especially chapters 3, "Slavery and Immigrants from Africa," and 5, "Ethnicity and Race in American Life"); The Century of Immigration, 1820-1924 (see chapter 9, "Minorities from Other Regions: Chinese, Japanese, and French Canadians"); and Modern Times, to the 1980's. Tables, charts, maps, and a selected bibliography.

Dinnerstein, Leonard, et al. *Natives and Strangers: Blacks, Indians, and Immigrants in America.* Reprint. New York: Oxford University Press, 1990.
The purpose of this standard history is "to emphasize—in a way that has not been done previously—the role of blacks, Indians, and immigrant minorities in the transformation of a colonial society into a behemoth of the 1990s."

Dinnerstein, Leonard, and David M. Reimers. *Ethnic Americans: A History of Immigration and Assimilation.* 3d ed. New York: Harper & Row, 1988.
A history of non-English people who came voluntarily to America, especially after 1830.

Fuchs, Lawrence H. *The American Kaleidoscope: Race, Ethnicity, and the Civic Culture.* Hanover, N.H.: University Press of New England, 1990.
A truly comprehensive (five hundred pages) history of America's "kaleidoscope" (rather than "melting pot"), a study that seeks to "provide an understanding of the historical patterns of ethnicity and the contemporary ethnic landscape."

Greeley, Andrew. *Ethnicity in the United States: A Preliminary Reconnaissance.* New York: John Wiley & Sons, 1974.
An early study of ethnic "diversity" in America that uses mainly European examples.

Green, Philip. *The Pursuit of Inequality.* New York: Pantheon Books, 1981.
Contains essays arguing against "the new individualism" and for a more egalitarian America by a leading political scientist: "the arguments of the new individualism, whether biological or ethical, are factually worthless, conceptually inadequate, and morally indefensible."

Handlin, Oscar. *The Uprooted*. Reprint. Boston: Little, Brown, 1973.
This second, "enlarged" edition drops the original subtitle ("The Epic Story of the Great Migrations That Made the American People") and adds two chapters to update this classic study of European immigration.

Higham, John. *Strangers in the Land: Patterns of American Nativism, 1860-1925*. Reprint. New York: Atheneum, 1963.
A classic 1955 study of "the hostilities of American nationalists toward European immigrants."

Horsman, Reginald. *Race and Manifest Destiny: The Origins of American Racial Anglo-Saxonism*. Cambridge, Mass.: Harvard University Press, 1981.
Analyzes the period 1800 to 1850. "My interest is in the origins of the new racial ideology and how it affected the course of American expansion."

Kessner, Thomas, and Betty Boyd Caroli. *Today's Immigrants, Their Stories: A New Look at the Newest Americans*. New York: Oxford University Press, 1981.
Includes representative narratives of the so-called new immigration, framed by an introduction, appendices, and a bibliography.

Lieberson, Stanley, and Mary C. Waters. *From Many Strands: Ethnic and Racial Groups in Contemporary America*. New York: Russell Sage Foundation, 1988.
One of a series of volumes "aimed at converting the vast statistical yield of the 1980 census into authoritative analyses of major changes and trends in American life."

McWilliams, Carey. *Brothers Under the Skin*. Boston: Little, Brown, 1964.
A new introduction to this pioneering 1943 study of race relations in the United States surveys the revolution in Black consciousness that has occurred since the first edition. It warns, however, that the economic situation of African Americans "may actually have deteriorated." The final chapter, "Beyond Civil Rights," calls for an affirmative federal policy on racial discrimination.

Mageli, Paul D., comp. *The Immigrant Experience: An Annotated Bibliography*. Pasadena, Calif.: Salem Press, 1991.
Thoughtful and thorough annotations are provided on the most important works about immigration. See especially "General Studies," "Asian Immigrants," and "Hispanic Immigrants."

Morrison, John, and Charlotte Fox Zabusky. *American Mosaic: The Immigrant Experience in the Words of Those Who Lived It*. New York: E. P. Dutton, 1980.
Contains interviews with more than 135 immigrants who arrived in the United States between 1906 and 1978.

Nash, Gary B. *Red, White, and Black: The Peoples of Early America*. Englewood Cliffs, N.J.: Prentice-Hall, 1974.
An important social history of the complex interaction of three major cultural groups: whites, African slaves, and American Indians.

Neidle, Cecyle S. *America's Immigrant Women*. Boston: G. K. Hall, 1975.
A historical account, from the first settlers through the mid-twentieth century. (See Seller, below, in 2B2.)

Portes, Alejandro, and Ruben G. Rumbaut. *Immigrant America: A Portrait*. Berkeley: University of California Press, 1990.
This is a study of recent immigration, with a focus on "the diversity of their origins and contexts of exit and in the diversity of their adaptation experiences and contexts of incorporation."

Reimers, David. *Still the Golden Door: The Third World Comes to America*. New York: Columbia University Press, 1985.
This book deals with the "major changes in policy, pressures for emigration, and the consequent migration of Third World peoples to the United States after 1945."

Ringer, Benjamin R. *"We the People" and Others: Duality and America's Treatment of Its Racial Minorities*. New York: Tavistock, 1983.
This long (more than one thousand pages) historical analysis deals with America's encounters with its minorities.

Santoli, A., comp. *New Americans: An Oral History*. New York: Viking Press, 1988.
Santoli allows "immigrants and refugees in the U.S. today"—from Africa, Asia, Europe, and Latin America—to tell their stories and prove that the American Dream is alive and well.

Saxton, Alexander. *The Rise and Fall of the White Republic: Class Politics and Mass Culture in Nineteenth-Century America*. New York: Verso, 1990.
This nineteenth century political and cultural history studies ideology and economic change. Analyses of the relation between white racial domination and ideas and attitudes about race include some literary discussions: dime novels, James Fenimore Cooper, Owen Wister, and nineteenth century drama, among others.

Takaki, Ronald. *Iron Cages: Race and Culture in 19th Century America*. New York: Alfred A. Knopf, 1979.
The author attempts "to understand how the domination of various peoples of color in America had cultural and economic bases which involved as well as

transcended race." Includes extended analyses of Bret Harte, *Moby Dick*, Twain's *Connecticut Yankee*, and other literary works.

2. Textbooks and Collections of Essays

Alba, Richard D., ed. *Ethnicity and Race in the U.S.A.: Toward the Twenty-First Century*. London: Routledge & Kegan Paul, 1985.
Contains eight papers from a 1984 conference. First published as a special issue of the British journal *Ethnic and Racial Relations* (1985).

Coppa, Frank J., and Thomas J. Curran, eds. *The Immigrant Experience in America*. Boston: Twayne, 1976.
This collection mostly concerns European immigration, but it includes essays on Hispanics, Blacks, and Asians.

Dubois, Ellen Carol, and Vicki L. Ruiz, eds. *Unequal Sisters: A Multi-cultural Reader in U.S. Women's History*. New York: Routledge, Chapman & Hall, 1990.
Thirty recent essays focus on women of color. Notable are Rayna Green's "The Image of Indian Women in American Culture" and Alma M. Garcia's "The Development of Chicana Feminist Discourse, 1970-1980."

Dunbar, Leslie W., ed. *Minority Report: What Has Happened to Blacks, Hispanics, American Indians, and Other Minorities in the 80s*. New York: Pantheon, 1984.
Essays on affirmative action, economic opportunity, the urban underclass, and related topics.

Feagin, Joe R. *Racial and Ethnic Relations*. 3d ed. Englewood Cliffs, N.J.: Prentice-Hall, 1989.
This is a standard textbook on the ethnic experience in America. Compare Parillo, *Strangers to These Shores: Race and Ethnic Relations in the United States*, below.

Liebman, Lance, ed. *Ethnic Relations in America*. Englewood Cliffs, N.J.: Prentice-Hall, 1982.
Summary essays by Stephan Thernstrom, Nathan Glazer, and others address many topics, including immigration, bilingualism, and politics in a multiethnic society.

Parillo, Vincent N., ed. *Rethinking Today's Minorities*. Contributions in Sociology 93. Westport, Conn.: Greenwood Press, 1991.
The recent assessments of contemporary race relations included here are intended to "sharpen our focus for policy development and social action in the last decade of the 20th century."

_____. *Strangers to These Shores: Race and Ethnic Relations in the United States.* 3d ed. New York: Macmillan, 1989.
One of the best textbooks on ethnic studies available. Compare Feagin, above.

Seller, Maxine Schwartz, ed. *Immigrant Women.* Philadelphia: Temple University Press, 1981.
Contains forty-seven "documents," mostly first-person accounts of how European, Asian, and Latin American women coped with immigration from 1820 to the present. (See Neidle, above, in 2B1.)

Takaki, Ronald, ed. *From Different Shores: Perspectives on Race and Culture in America.* New York: Oxford University Press, 1987.
This collection contains dialogues on questions of culture, class, and gender among radical theorists like Takaki and more conservative ethnic historians (for example, Glazer, Sowell).

Thomas, Gail E., ed. *U.S. Race Relations in the 1980s and 1990s: Challenges and Alternatives.* New York: Hemisphere, 1990.
This volume, which originated in a 1988 conference entitled "Race and Ethnic Relations in the 1990s," focuses on economics and education in terms of Blacks, Hispanics, and American Indians.

C. American Ethnic Histories

1. Native American History

Axtell, James. *The Invasion Within: The Contest of Cultures in Colonial North America.* New York: Oxford University Press, 1985.
An ethnohistory "of the colonial French, English, and Indian efforts to convert each other." It is also a prize-winning first volume of a projected trilogy on relations among the three cultures.

Berkhofer, Robert. *The White Man's Indian: Images of the American Indian from Columbus to the Present.* New York: Alfred A. Knopf, 1978.
The book represents an important effort to examine "the implications of the ideas and imagery used by Whites to understand the peoples they call Indians." See especially part 3: "Imagery in Literature, Art, and Philosophy: The Indian in White Imagination and Ideology."

Brown, Dee. *Bury My Heart at Wounded Knee: An Indian History of the American West.* New York: Henry Holt, 1970.
This is a best-selling narrative account of the settling of the American West from the perspective of the victims—the Indians who first lived there.

DeLoria, Vine, Jr. *Custer Died for Your Sins: An Indian Manifesto.* New York: Macmillan, 1969.
Part history, part call to arms, this is an important early work in the attempt to reclaim Native American history and identity.

Dippie, Brian W. *The Vanishing American: White Attitudes and U.S. Indian Policy.* Middletown, Conn.: Wesleyan University Press, 1982.
Like Berkhofer (above), this study engages literature and popular culture in its analysis of "the Vanishing American as a constant in American thinking."

Drinnon, Richard. *Facing West: The Metaphysics of Indian Hating and Empire Building.* Minneapolis: University of Minnesota Press, 1980.
This volume deals with a number of literary works (from Hawthorne and Melville to Robert Lowell) in an exhaustive examination of "deracination and extermination."

Jennings, Francis. *The Invasion of America: Indians, Colonialism, and the Cant of Conquest.* Chapel Hill: University of North Carolina Press, 1975.
One of the best accounts of the destruction wreaked on native populations by European immigrants, particularly in New England.

Josephy, Alvin M., Jr. *Now That the Buffalo's Gone: A Study of Today's American Indians.* New York: Alfred A. Knopf, 1982.
An important background study of "contemporary Native American affairs and their historical underpinnings."

Kopper, Philip. *The Smithsonian Book of North American Indians: Before the Coming of the Europeans.* Washington, D.C.: Smithsonian Institution Press, 1986.
A lavish picture book (compare Viola, below) but with a substantial printed text.

Nichols, Roger L., ed. *The American Indian: Past and Present.* 3d ed. New York: Alfred A. Knopf, 1986.
Articles deal with the white invasion of North America and the internal workings of tribal societies.

Prucha, Francis Paul. *The Great Father: The United States Government and the American Indians.* Lincoln: University of Nebraska Press, 1984.
This is a comprehensive, two-volume survey of the full scope of American Indian policy for two centuries.

Sale, Kirkpatrick. *The Conquest of Paradise: Christopher Columbus and the Columbian Legacy.* New York: Alfred A. Knopf, 1990.

The best description we have of what "Cristobal Colon" accomplished, and the legacy of that first expropriation of the Americas. Debunks the Columbus myth and shows it for the exploitation of humans and land that it actually was. Excellent coverage of the cultures thus displaced and their balanced relationships to each other and to their world; see chapter 12, "1607-25 (II) Powhatans and Others."

Snipp, C. Matthew. *American Indians: The First of This Land.* New York: Russell Sage Foundation, 1989.
Another volume in a series "aimed at converting the vast statistical analyses of major changes and trends in American life" gained from the 1980 census. (See Lieberson and Waters, 2B1.)

Spencer, Robert F., Jesse D. Jennings, et al. *The Native Americans: Ethnology and Backgrounds of the North American Indians.* 2d ed. New York: Harper & Row, 1977.
This standard one-volume history is arranged as follows: a perspective on American archaeology, language, eight chapters devoted to different regions, concluding with "American Indian Heritage: Retrospect and Prospect" and "The Urban Native Americans."

Viola, Herman J. *After Columbus: The Smithsonian Chronicle of the North American Indians.* Washington, D.C.: Smithsonian Institution Press, 1991.
A large, lavish picture book that also contains a substantial historical text (compare Kopper, above).

2. African American History

Aptheker, Herbert. *A Documentary History of the Negro People in the United States.* 2 vols. Reprint. New York: Citadel Press, 1963.
Conveys "the essence of the first 300 years of the history of the American Negro people . . . . through the words of Negro men, women and children themselves" and brings Black history up to 1910.

Berry, Mary Francis, and John W. Blassingame. *Long Memory: The Black Experience in America.* New York: Oxford University Press, 1982.
Focuses "on those themes and subjects most revealing of the complexities of the black experience in America": "Power emanating from weakness, patience and hope in the face of overwhelming odds, and the unity of masses and elites." More than most histories, this book draws on literary and folk materials.

Branch, Taylor. *Parting the Waters: America in the King Years, 1954-1963*. New York: Simon & Schuster, 1988.
A powerful, prize-winning history of the civil rights movement that focuses on Martin Luther King. Establishes Branch's thesis that King's life "is the best and most important metaphor for American history in the watershed postwar years."

Fogel, Robert William. *Without Consent or Contract: The Rise and Fall of American Slavery*. New York: W. W. Norton, 1989.
The product of a 24-year research project, this central volume has three companion volumes that provide "the evidence and procedures that underlie" the project.

Foner, Eric. *Reconstruction: America's Unfinished Revolution, 1863-1877*. New York: Harper & Row, 1988.
The best recent study of "the violent, dramatic, and still controversial era that followed the Civil War."

Franklin, John Hope, and Alfred A. Moss, Jr. *From Slavery to Freedom: A History of Negro Americans*. 6th ed. New York: Alfred A. Knopf, 1988.
Still one of the standard histories of Black Americans.

Franklin, V. P. *Black Self-Determination: A Cultural History of the Faith of the Fathers*. Westport, Conn.: Lawrence Hill, 1984.
Represents an attempt to document "Afro-American cultural meaning the nineteenth and early twentieth centuries" using slave narratives, folk songs, and other cultural evidence.

Genovese, Eugene. *The Political Economy of Slavery: Studies in the Economy and Society of the Slave South*. New York: Pantheon Books, 1965.
Studies "argue that slavery gave the South a social system and a civilization with a distinct class structure, political community, ideology, and set of psychological patterns and that, as a result, the South increasingly grew away from the rest of the nation and from the rapidly developing sections of the world."

_____. *Roll, Jordan, Roll: The World the Slaves Made*. New York: Harper & Row, 1974.
Shows the ways in which slaves "laid the foundations for a separate black national culture while enormously enriching American culture as a whole."

_____. *The World the Slaveholders Made: Two Essays in Interpretation*. New York: Pantheon Books, 1969.
Contains Marxian analyses of "The American Slave System in World Perspective" and "The Logical Outcome of the Slaveholders' Philosophy."

Gutman, Herbert. *The Black Family in Slavery and Freedom, 1750-1925*. New York: Vintage Books, 1976.
This positive examination "makes obsolete almost everything that has been written or said about the black experience in the U.S." (Charles E. Silberman).

Gwaltney, John Langston. *Drylongso: A Self-Portrait of Black America*. New York: Random House, 1980.
The "product of an anthropological field study conducted in the early 1970's in more than a dozen northeastern urban black American communities," *Drylongso* is a collection of personal narratives that provides a self-portrait of "core" Black culture in America.

Haley, Alex. *Roots*. Garden City, N.Y.: Doubleday, 1976.
Extremely popular as both a book and a television series, *Roots* is a semifictionalized recreation of Haley's African ancestry. It begins with Kunta Kinte, a Mandingo born in 1750 in Gambia, West Africa, and carried to Annapolis, Maryland, by slavers, through one hundred years and several generations of slavery in Virginia and North Carolina. Concludes with Haley's childhood in Henning, Tennessee. The last chapter describes the research and writing of the book.

Harding, Vincent. *There Is a River: The Black Struggle for Freedom in America*. New York: Harcourt Brace Jovanovich, 1981.
One of a new crop of committed, celebratory histories of the Black experience in America, "From the Shores of Africa" through the Civil War.

Jones, Jacqueline. *Labor of Love, Labor of Sorrow: Black Women, Work, and the Family from Slavery to the Present*. New York: Basic Books, 1985.
A history of Black working women from slavery up to 1980.

Jordan, Winthrop. *White Over Black: American Attitudes toward the Negro, 1550-1812*. Chapel Hill: University of North Carolina Press, 1968.
Winthrop attempts to answer "a simple question: What were the attitudes of white men toward Negroes during the first two centuries of European and African settlement in what became the United States of America?"

Lemann, Nicholas. *The Promised Land: The Great Black Migration and How It Changed America*. New York: Alfred A. Knopf, 1991.
This prize-winning volume "explores the movement of 5 million blacks to the northern cities between the early 1940s—when the mechanical cotton picker went into mass production—and the late 1960s. It concludes that the 20-year migration turned race relations into an issue affecting the texture of life in nearly every city and suburb in the nation" (*Los Angeles Times*).

Levine, Lawrence W. *Black Culture and Black Consciousness: Afro-American Folk Thought from Slavery to Freedom*. New York: Oxford University Press, 1977.
This book attempts "to present and understand the thought of people who, though quite articulate in their own lifetimes, have been rendered historically inarticulate by scholars who have devoted their attention to other groups and other problems." Discusses slave tales, songs, and more.

Lieberson, Stanley. *A Piece of the Pie: Blacks and White Immigrants since 1880*. Berkeley: University of California Press, 1980.
Study of why Blacks were less successful than late nineteenth century European immigrants who arrived twenty years after slavery ended.

Meier, August. *Negro Thought in America, 1880-1915*. Ann Arbor: University of Michigan Press, 1963.
Subtitled "Racial Ideologies in the Age of Booker T. Washington," this is still one of the crucial studies of the years following Reconstruction and the ideas of Washington, W. E. B. Du Bois, and others.

Myrdal, Gunnar. *An American Dilemma: The Negro Problem and Modern Democracy*. 20th anniv. ed. New York: Harper & Row, 1962.
Arnold Rose's "Postscript 20 Years Later" outlines the social changes since the Swedish sociologist's exhaustive, pioneering study of Black/white relations in the United States.

Wilson, William. *The Declining Significance of Race*. Chicago: University of Chicago Press, 1978.
Analysis of the increasing significance of class in Black/white relations from slavery to the present.

Woodward, C. Vann. *The Strange Career of Jim Crow*. 3d ed. New York: Oxford University Press, 1974.
Still the best short history of segregation in the South since the Civil War.

3. Chicano/Latino History

Acosta-Belén, Edna, and Barbara R. Sjostrom, eds. *The Hispanic Experience in the United States: Contemporary Issues and Perspectives*. New York: Praeger, 1988.
Contains demographic and socioeconomic profiles and essays on immigration, assimilation, and cultural identity.

Acuña, Rudolfo. *Occupied America: A History of Chicanos*. 2d ed. New York: Harper & Row, 1981.

There are two parts to this standard history: "Conquest & Colonization" and "A Radical View of the Twentieth-Century Chicano."

Boswell, Thomas D., and James R. Curtis. *The Cuban-American Experience: Culture, Images, and Perspectives*. Totowa, N.J.: Rowman & Allanheld, 1984. The best brief account of Cuban immigration, with sections on linguistic and cultural expression.

Camarillo, Albert. *Chicanos in a Changing Society: From Mexican Pueblos to American Barrios in Santa Barbara and Southern California, 1848-1930*. Cambridge, Mass.: Harvard University Press, 1979.
A "social history of the Mexican/Chicano people who have resided in the towns and cities of southern California" between the Mexican War and the Great Depression.

Daniel, Cletus E. *Bitter Harvest: A History of California Farm Workers, 1870-1941*. Ithaca, N.Y.: Cornell University Press, 1981.
A "history of the powerlessness of an occupational group: the men, women, and children who worked for wages in the fields and orchards of California from the late 19th century to the end of the 1930s."

Davis, Marilyn P., comp. *Mexican Voices/American Dreams: An Oral History of Mexican Immigration to the United States*. New York: Henry Holt, 1990.
Contains the stories of ninety informants.

Fitzpatrick, Joseph P. *Puerto Rican Americans: The Meaning of Migration to the Mainland*. 2d ed. Englewood Cliffs, N.J.: Prentice-Hall, 1987.
The second edition of this volume in the Ethnic Groups in American Life Series is intended "to help both Puerto Ricans and New Yorkers to perceive the migration in the perspective of the long and turbulent history of newcomers to New York" through chapters on religion, education, the family, and other topics.

Langley, Lester D. *America and the Americas: The United States in the Western Hemisphere*. Athens: University of Georgia Press, 1989.
A "general volume in a projected series on the relations between the United States and Latin America—a series intended to provide students and general readers with an accessible, up-to-date assessment of the inter-American experience."

_____. *MexAmerica: Two Countries, One Future*. New York: Crown, 1988.
An "impressionistic and personal account" of Hispanic culture in the United States, arguing that it is "heavily influenced by its Mexican American content and that MexAmerica from Chicago to Mexico City is shaping its values." Shows

how "the Mexican presence in the United States has shaped what we are and what we want to be."

_____. *The United States and the Caribbean in the 20th Century*. 4th ed. Athens: University of Georgia Press, 1989.
A mainstream assessment, from the Spanish-American War through the more recent crises in Central America.

McWilliams, Carey. *North from Mexico: The Spanish-Speaking People of the United States*. 2d ed. Westport, Conn.: Greenwood Press, 1968.
An introduction by the author outlines changes since the 1949 first edition of this landmark study of Mexican immigration.

Mirandé, Alfredo. *The Chicano Experience: An Alternative Perspective*. Notre Dame, Ind.: University of Notre Dame Press, 1985.
Provides "a coherent framework or perspective on Chicano sociology" in chapters on economy, education, religion, family, and so on.

Pastor, Robert A., and Jorge G. Castaneda. *Limits to Friendship: The United States and Mexico*. New York: Alfred A. Knopf, 1988.
Fresh cross-cultural perspectives that "shed new light on the rapidly changing ties and the new tensions between the two nations."

Steiner, Stan. *La Raza: The Mexican Americans*. New York: Harper & Row, 1970.
An early and lively narrative history.

Weyr, Thomas. *Hispanic USA: Breaking the Melting Pot*. New York: Harper & Row, 1988.
This is a work of journalism rather than scholarship. Much of it is based on three hundred interviews Weyr conducted in an attempt to describe the disparate Spanish culture of the U.S.—not an immigrant group but twenty million people who "have been here for 450 years and for 45 seconds." Chapters on education, politics, religion, among other topics.

4. Asian American History

Bulosan, Carlos. *America Is in the Heart*. Reprint. Seattle: University of Washington Press, 1973.
The introduction by Carey McWilliams to the reprinted edition describes it as a "social classic" that "reflects the collective life experience of thousands of Filipino immigrants who were attracted to this country by its legendary promises of a better life." (See listing in 8B2d.)

Chen, Jack. *The Chinese of America*. San Francisco: Harper & Row, 1980.
Attempts a "coherent picture of the historical record" of Chinese immigration from 1785 to 1980.

Daniels, Roger. *Asian America: Chinese and Japanese in the United States Since 1850*. Seattle: University of Washington Press, 1988.
A scholarly treatment that "attempts to synthesize the history of Chinese and Japanese in this country and to treat their lives as integral to the American mosaic."

Houston, James D., and Jeanne Wakatsuki Houston. *Farewell to Manzanar*. Boston: Houghton Mifflin, 1973.
The book describes the second author's incarceration with her family in a California relocation camp for Japanese Americans during World War II. (See listing in 8B2b.)

Fawcett, James T., and Benjamin V. Carino, eds. *Pacific Bridges: The New Immigration from Asia and the Pacific Islands*. Staten Island, N.Y.: Center for Migration Studies, 1987.
A comprehensive assessment of contemporary immigration patterns in the Asian and Pacific region, including movement to the United States.

Fessler, Loren W., ed. *Chinese in America: Stereotyped Past, Changing Present*. New York: Vantage Press, 1983.
Material compiled by the China Institute in America, Inc., was put together to create a book that would "be both interesting to general readers and useful to historians and other scholars."

Kwong, Peter. *The New Chinatown*. New York: Hill and Wang, 1987.
A study of New York's Chinatown that provides "insights into the nature of other Chinatowns as well."

Mangiafico, Luciano. *Contemporary American Immigrants: Patterns of Filipino, Korean, and Chinese Settlement in the United States*. New York: Praeger, 1988.
A highly statistical study that hopes "to lay the groundwork for future studies on these three immigrant groups."

Melendy, H. Brett. *Asians in America: Filipinos, Koreans, and East Indians*. Boston: Twayne, 1977.
A history of three immigrant groups often overlooked in other accounts, written "in order to understand their motivations for migrating and to observe their similar encounters with white America."

Nee, Victor, and Brett de Bary. *Longtime Californ': A Documentary Study of an American Chinatown*. New York: Pantheon, 1972.
A standard, if dated, study of San Francisco's Chinatown.

Perrin, Linda. *Coming to America: Immigrants from the Far East*. New York: Delacorte Press, 1981.
A "juvenile" study that could be useful to most students needing an overview. (See, for example, Perrin's appendix on "A Brief History of U.S. Immigration Laws," pp. 172-174.)

Takaki, Ronald. *Strangers From a Different Shore: A History of Asian Americans*. Boston: Little, Brown, 1989.
This best recent account of Asian immigration includes histories of Chinese, Japanese, Koreans, Asian Indians, and Filipinos, as well as the more recent influx of Vietnamese, Cambodians, and Laotians. Takaki combines scholarly analysis with immigrant narratives and effectively balances traditional Eurocentric ethnic history with a powerful story of those who arrived in America "from a different shore."

Tsai, Henry Shin-Shan. *The Chinese Experience in America*. Bloomington: Indiana University Press, 1986.
This book studies the "evolutionary patterns of Chinese-American interaction" through three different groups: the "sojourners" of the nineteenth century, American-born Chinese, and student immigrants.

Wilson, Robert A., and Bill Hosokowa. *East to America: A History of the Japanese in the United States*. New York: William Morrow, 1980.
A concise scholarly history with photographs.

Chapter 3
TEACHING ETHNIC LITERATURE

A. Journals

ADE Bulletin. Association of Departments of English.
This quarterly journal has run a series of clusters on "Multicultural Literature" in the 1980's (listed separately in chapters 5-8).

College English. National Council of Teachers of English (NCTE), monthly September through April.
Occasionally prints articles on the multicultural writing classroom, revising the canon, related ethnic issues; See for example the clusters on "The New Black Aesthetic Critics," 50, no. 4 (April, 1988), and "African-American Criticism," 52, no. 7 (November, 1990).

English Journal. NCTE, monthly September through April.
This journal has published a number of issues devoted to multiethnic concerns for high school and junior high school teachers. Examples include articles on cross-cultural literacy and English for the minority learner in 77, no. 5 (September, 1988); "When Minority Becomes Majority" and "Chicano Literature for Young Adults: An Annotated Bibliography," 79, no. 1 (January, 1990); and "Reclaiming the Canon: A Celebration of Diversity," 79, no. 4 (April, 1990).

Radical Teacher (Boston Women's Teachers' Group, Inc., triannually).
Frequently publishes articles and entire issues on racial and ethnic subjects for teachers at all levels and in all disciplines. See cluster on "Combatting Campus Racism," 34 (January, 1988); article by Ruth Hsiao on teaching Asian-American literature, 41 (Spring, 1992), 20-25.

B. Teaching Guides

1. General

Baker, Houston A., Jr., ed. *Three American Literatures: Essays in Chicano, Native American, and Asian-American Literature for Teachers of American Literature.* New York: Modern Language Association of America, 1982.
This "single-volume work offering overviews of the literary traditions of selected minority groups" includes an introduction by Walter J. Ong, two essays on Chicano literature, two on Native American literatures, and three on Asian American writers.

Banks, James A. *Teaching Strategies for Ethnic Studies.* 5th ed. Boston: Allyn & Bacon, 1991.
One of the best resources for secondary teachers and education courses. Contains three major parts. Part I presents a rationale for teaching comparative ethnic studies; part II contains chapters on major ethnic groups in the United States (including Indochinese Americans), with bibliographies for both teachers and students; and part III "illustrates how the teacher can use the information and strategies in parts I and II to develop and teach multiethnic units and curricula that focus on two or more ethnic groups." Appendices include "Ethnic Groups in U.S. History: A Chronology of Key Events," "Videotapes and Films on U.S. Ethnic Groups," and "Books about Women of Color."

Buttlar, Lois, and Lubomyr R. Wynar. *Building Ethnic Collections: An Annotated Guide for School Media Centers and Public Libraries.* Littleton, Colo.: Libraries Unlimited, 1977.
Includes five basic categories under individual listings for American Indians, Asian Americans, and others: reference sources, teaching methodology and curriculum materials, nonfiction titles, literature and fiction titles, and audiovisual materials.

Candelaria, Cordelia, ed. *Multiethnic Literature of the United States: Critical Introductions and Classroom Resources.* Boulder: Multiethnic Literature Project, University of Colorado, 1989.
A collection of essays, poems, and syllabi aimed at overcoming the "Eurocentric partiality" in American scholarship and at helping to recover ethnic diversity. The first part includes articles on Chicana feminist writing, "The Japanese American Literature of Internment," and "Reflections of Otherness in Ethnic Literature." The second part, "Classroom Resources," contains three course syllabi (e.g., "Literature of Black American Women"). Useful bibliographies throughout.

Daniels, Harvey A., ed. *Not Only English: Affirming Multilingual Heritage.* Urbana, Ill.: NCTE, 1990.
Twelve essays give the history of and responses to the English-only movement. The first of four sections "describes the nature, development, and extent of the contemporary English-only movement; the second looks at the potential impact of the proposed federal English Language Amendment; the third analyzes the causes· and motivations of language protectionism; and the fourth suggests political and professional responses to the English-only movement."

"Ethnicity and Pedagogy." Special issue of *MELUS* 16, no. 2 (Spring, 1989-1990).
Contains both psychological and political overviews of the pedagogy of ethnicity and more specific examinations of teaching particular pieces of ethnic literature

(Richard Wright and Zora Neale Hurston, Leslie Marmon Silko and N. Scott Momaday).

Fiedler, Leslie, and Houston A. Baker, Jr., eds. *English Literature: Opening up the Canon.* Selected Papers from the English Institute, 1979. Baltimore: The Johns Hopkins University Press, 1981.
Essays on language and literature teaching contained here "raise critical questions about the study of literature in the university, limited as it is by unconscious assumptions . . . rooted in race, class, and gender."

Fisher, Dexter, ed. *Minority Language and Literature: Retrospective and Perspective.* New York: Modern Language Association of America, 1977.
These published papers presented at a national symposium on minority literature and language cover Black, Chicano, Puerto Rican literatures; Black dialect; a Navajo literacy program; oral culture; and related issues.

Kelly, Ernece B., ed. *Searching for America.* Urbana, Ill.: NCTE, 1972.
An early but still valuable report of the NCTE Task Force on Racism and Bias in the Teaching of English. Includes critical evaluations of a dozen American literature textbooks, plus four essays "commenting on the literature, culture, or history of those racial and ethnic groups which have been systematically excluded from American literature collections."

Lauter, Paul. *Canons and Contexts.* New York: Oxford University Press, 1991.
Contains previously published essays on two contemporary struggles within the academy: the issue of changing the American literary canon (including the introduction to *Reconstructing American Literature*, below), and the question of the institutional purpose of the university itself.

_____, ed. *Reconstructing American Literature: Courses, Syllabi, Issues.* Old Westbury, N.Y.: Feminist Press, 1983.
Sixty-seven course syllabi are collected here that "change the teaching of American literature and . . . the definition of what we call American culture" by incorporating "the fruits of two decades of scholarship in minority and women's history, art, literature, and culture." See especially "Immigrant, Ethnic, and Minority Writing" under "Thematic Courses," pp. 165-184. (See also Lauter et al., eds., *Heath Anthology of American Literature*, 3D1, below.)

Ruoff, A. LaVonne Brown, and Jerry W. Ward, Jr., eds. *Redefining American Literary History.* New York: Modern Language Association of America, 1990.
This crucial volume includes sections on revising the canon, oral dimensions of American literature, critical and historical perspectives on American ethnic literatures, extensive bibliographies of major ethnic literatures (African American,

American Indian, Asian American, Chicano, and Puerto Rican), and lists of selected journals and presses. One of the best introductions to multiethnic American literatures for college teachers.

See also: "Multicultural Literature" (8C2)

2. Teaching American Indian Literature

"American Indian Literatures and Teaching." Special issue of *SAIL: Studies in American Indian Literatures* 43, no. 2 (Summer, 1991). Lawrence Abbott, ed.
Articles on teaching American Indian autobiography, D'Arcy McNickle, and related subjects, at the secondary and college levels.

Bataille, Gretchen M. *American Indian Literature: A Selected Bibliography for Schools and Libraries*. Pomona, Calif.: National Association of Interdisciplinary Ethnic Studies (NAIES)/California State Polytechnic University, 1981.
Aimed at precollege levels, this bibliography has a number of resources college teachers and students could find useful (for example, "Resources on American Indian Literature," "Bibliographies," "Resources on Films and Filmstrips").

Ruoff, A. LaVonne Brown, and Karl Kroeber, comps. *American Indian Literatures in the United States: A Basic Bibliography for Teachers*. New York: Association for the Study of American Indian Literatures, 1983.
This brief bibliography has sections on oral literatures; personal narratives and autobiographies; fiction, poetry, prose, and drama; and selected periodicals.

Stensland, Anna Lee, and Aune M. Fadum, comps. *Literature by and About the American Indian: An Annotated Bibliography*. Urbana, Ill.: NCTE, 1979.
An excellent resource in two sections. Part I, "Teaching the Literature of the American Indian," includes an introduction (themes, stereotypes, and so on), teaching aids (for example, "A Basic Library of Indian Literature"). Part II is a bibliography that lists literary works as well as resources in "Traditional Life and Culture," "Modern Life and Problems," and more.

See also: Allen and "Multicultural Literature" (5C5)

3. Teaching African American Literature

Fisher, Dexter, and Robert B. Stepto, eds. *Afro-American Literature: The Reconstruction of Instruction*. New York: Modern Language Association of America, 1979.

Sections on Afro-American literary history, Black figurative language, Afro-American literature and folklore, with essays by Henry-Louis Gates, Jr., Sherley Anne Williams, Robert Hemenway, and others. "Theory in Practice" presents three discussions of Frederick Douglass' narrative (1845). The final section includes three "Afro-American Literature Course Designs."

Fontenot, Chester, ed. *Writing About Black Literature*. Lincoln: University of Nebraska Press, 1976.
This collection contains "Polemical Introduction" by the editor and model essays on Black fiction, poetry, and drama by both student and professional critics.

Graham, Maryemma, et al. *The Afro-American Novel: A Study Guide*. 2d ed. Jackson: Afro-American Studies Program, University of Mississippi, 1988.
This brief study guide has ten chapters on different periods of the Afro-American novel. Also includes an appendix containing "An Outline for Reading the Afro-American Novel," "The Twenty-Five Novels Most Frequently Taught," and "Selected Bibliography."

Scafe, Suzanne. *Teaching Black Literature*. London: Virago, 1989.
A British work that "examines the role of literature in a multicultural curriculum," with examples from the Caribbean, Africa, and America.

Stanford, Barbara Dodds, and Karima Amin. *Black Literature for High School Students*. Urbana, Ill.: NCTE, 1978.
Part I, "Black American Literature," has five chapters, including a twenty-page bibliography. Part II, "Classroom Uses of Black American Literature," contains syllabi for a number of high school courses centered on Afro-American literature.

Turner, Darwin T., and Barbara Dodds Stanford. *Theory and Practice in the Teaching of Literature by Afro-Americans*. Urbana, Ill.: NCTE, 1971.
A brief (ninety-seven pages), early volume aimed at high school English teachers. Part I, "Theory, Teaching Literature by Afro-Americans," includes "A Selected Reading List of Literature by Afro-Americans for the Teacher of Grades 7-12." In part II ("Practice"), literary analyses for junior, senior high school students can be found, including different literature units.

See also: Sekora and Turner (6C3a)

C. Audiovisual Materials

Chu, Bernice, ed. *The Asian American Media Reference Guide*. New York: Asian CineVision, 1986.

This pamphlet is described as "a catalog of more than five hundred Asian American audio-visual programs for rent or sale" in the United States.

Duran, Daniel Flores. *Latino Materials: A Multimedia Guide for Children and Young Adults.* New York: ABC-Clio, 1979.
Major sections include four essays exploring "the background of Latino life and literature" in the United States, "as well as library services to Latinos"; "critical annotations of print materials and 16mm films . . . suitable as a basis for a core collection in either a public school or school library"; and a directory of publishers and distributors of Latino materials. Both Mexican American and Puerto Rican materials (in Spanish and English) are listed for elementary and secondary levels.

Johnson, Harry A., ed. *American Ethnic Minorities: A Guide to Media and Materials.* New York: R. R. Bowker, 1976.
Annotated entries for films, slides, recordings, and the like for the four major ethnic groups.

Wynar, Lubomyr R., and Lois Buttlar. *Ethnic Film and Filmstrip Guide for Libraries and Media Centers: A Selective Filmography.* Littleton, Colo.: Libraries Unlimited, 1980.
A "comprehensive annotated guide to films and filmstrips related to the experience of individual American ethnic groups as well as ethnic topics in general."

See also: Banks, Buttlar and Wynar (3B1); Bataille (3B2)

D. Comparative Ethnic Literature Collections

1. General

Beaty, Jerome, and J. Paul Hunter, eds. *New Worlds of Literature.* New York: W. W. Norton, 1989.
The thematic organization in this anthology was arranged "for an introductory course in the study of literature or as a reader for a course in composition." Includes sections of readings on "Home," "Family Devotion," "Heritage," and seven other general subjects.

Brown, Wesley, and Amy Ling, eds. *Imagining America: Stories from the Promised Land.* New York: Persea Books, 1991.
Thirty-seven stories in this collection address the themes of immigration and migration. Organized into sections on "Arriving" (Nicholasa Mohr, Bharati Mukherjee, Helena Maria Viramontes, et al.), "Belonging" (Toshio Mori, Toni

Cade Bambara, others), "Crossing" (Leslie Marmon Silko, Louise Erdrich, Sandra Cisneros), and "Remembering" (Alice Walker, Oscar Hijuelos, Paule Marshall).

Butcher, Philip, ed. *The Ethnic Image in Modern American Literature: 1900-1950.* 2 vols. Washington, D.C.: Howard University Press, 1984.
Selections were chosen "to portray the realities of ethnic participation in American culture as well as the stereotypes that have stigmatized . . . all Americans of ancestry" other than White Anglo-Saxon Protestant. The anthology thus has excerpts from ethnic authors as well as descriptions of minorities by other American writers.

_____, ed. *The Minority Presence in American Literature, 1600-1900.* Washington, D.C.: Howard University Press, 1977.
An early anthology on "the other American" in American life for three hundred years. Although the collection includes some minority selections (for example, Phillis Wheatley and Paul Laurence Dunbar), the bulk of this "Reader and Course Guide" is given over to white writers (Cooper and Twain on Indians, Melville on Blacks, and others).

Colombo, Gary, et al., eds. *Rereading America: Cultural Contexts for Critical Thinking and Writing.* New York: St. Martin's Press, 1989.
One of a number of recent anthologies aimed at freshman composition courses (see Rico and Mano, below), this collection of "readings on personal and cultural identity in a pluralistic society" has short selections from a number of ethnic writers.

Faderman, Lillian, and Barbara Bradshaw, eds. *Speaking for Ourselves: American Ethnic Writing.* 2d ed. Glenview, Ill.: Scott, Foresman, 1974.
Out of print but one of the best collections of ethnic writers. Substantial sections on Native American, Black American, Asian American, Chicano/Latino, Jewish American, and "White Ethnic Writers" begin with introductions and include essays, stories, and poems.

Freedman, Morris, and Carolyn Banks, eds. *American Mix: The Minority Experience in America.* Philadelphia: J. B. Lippincott, 1972.
Contains documents about immigration, assimilation (for example, Lincoln's Emancipation Proclamation, the 1954 U.S. Supreme Court decision on *Brown v. Board of Education*), as well as writings by American immigrants. This was one of a number of such anthologies to appear in the early 1970's (among which are collections by Miller, Newman, Simon, and others in this section).

Haslam, Gerald W., ed. *Forgotten Pages of American Literature*. Boston: Houghton Mifflin, 1970.
This early "supplement" to mainstream American literature anthologies includes selections from American Indian, Asian-American, Latino-American, and Afro-American literatures.

Lauter, Paul, et al., eds. *Heath Anthology of American Literature*. 2 vols. Lexington, Mass.: D. C. Heath, 1990.
This was the first anthology of American materials with a substantial ethnic presence. "A major principle of selection has been to represent as fully as possible the varied cultures of the United States": "25 individual Native American authors (as well as 17 texts from tribal origins), 53 African-Americans, 13 Hispanics (as well as 12 texts from earlier Spanish originals and two from French), and 9 Asian-Americans"—plus the standard white American authors. See Lauter, ed., *Reconstructing American Literature*, in 3B1, above, for the genesis of this anthology.

Miller, Wayne Charles, ed. *A Gathering of Ghetto Writers: Irish, Italian, Jewish, Black, and Puerto Rican*. New York: New York University Press, 1972.
An early anthology that seeks to remind "Americans of their pasts by making available some of the creative literature that provides insights into those pasts" from all five groups.

Newman, Katharine D., ed. *The American Equation: Literature in a Multiethnic Culture*. Boston: Allyn and Barr, 1971.
This early, partly multicultural, reader of "poems, short stories, and a play by forty-three representative American authors, from Philip Freneau to LeRoi Jones," is organized by "the four basic ways in which Americans have looked at themselves, at each other, and at America": in self-definition, as the attractive alternative, as the complementary self, and as the American metaphor.

Reed, Ishmael, and Al Young, eds. *Yardbird Lives!* New York: Grove Press, 1978.
Contains selections from *Yardbird Reader*, an early multiethnic magazine, including pieces by Ntozake Shange, Claude Brown, Jeffery Paul Chan, Amiri Baraka, Leslie Marmon Silko, Victor Hernandez-Cruz, and Simon Ortiz.

Rico, Barbara Roche, and Sandra Mano, eds. *American Mosaic: Multicultural Readings in Context*. Boston: Houghton Mifflin, 1991.
Another good college anthology (see Colombo, above), *American Mosaic* has selections of short readings on "Early Immigrants," seven ethnic groups, and "Contemporary Voices."

Simon, Myron. *Ethnic Writers in America*. New York: Harcourt Brace Jovanovich, 1972.
This early collection contains essays, poems, and short stories by Black and European ethnic writers.

2. Ethnic Women Writers

Anzaldúa, Gloria, ed. *Making Face, Making Soul = Haciendo Caras: Creative and Critical Perspectives by Women of Color*. San Francisco: Aunt Lute Foundation Books, 1990.
"This book aims to make accessible to others our struggle with all our identities, our linkage-making strategies and our healing of broken limbs." Includes both essays on sexism and racism, creative pieces by women of color.

Bankier, Joanna, and Deirdre Lashgari, eds. *Women Poets of the World*. New York: Macmillan, 1983.
This collection "reaches back in time from our own century to 2300 B.C., and embraces over 70 cultures," including women poets from what the editors term "North America" (selections from Euro-American, Afro American, Asian/Pacific American, and Chicana writers), and "Native America."

Blicksilver, Edith, ed. *The Ethnic American Woman: Problems, Protests, Lifestyle*. Dubuque, Iowa: Kendall, 1978.
This anthology is arranged thematically, with twelve units on "Growing up Ethnic," "The Immigrant Experience," family, education, and other topics. Includes selections from Asian-American, Hispanic, Jewish American, and "White-Ethnic-American Women."

Cochran, Jo, et al., eds. "Bearing Witness/Sobreviviendo: An Anthology of Native American/Latina Art and Literature." Special issue of *Calyx: A Journal of Art and Literature by Women* (8, no. 2, Spring, 1984).
This issue contains poetry and fiction by Cherríe Moraga, Pat Mora, Wendy Rose, Paula Gunn Allen, and many others.

_____ et al., eds. *Gathering Ground: New Writing and Art by Northwest Women of Color*. Seattle: Seal Press, 1984.
Focuses on Pacific Northwest poems, stories, and essays by Japanese American, Native American, Filipina, Black, and other women writers and artists.

Fisher, Dexter, ed. *The Third Woman: Minority Women Writers of the United States*. Boston: Houghton Mifflin, 1980.
An anthology of contemporary American Indian, Black, Chicana, and Asian American women writers.

Moraga, Cherríe, and Gloria Anzaldúa, eds. *This Bridge Called My Back: Writings by Radical Women of Color.* Watertown, Mass.: Persephone Press, 1981.

"The selections in this anthology range from extemporaneous stream of consciousness journal entries to well-thought-out theoretical statements; from intimate letters to friends to full-scale public addresses. In addition, the book includes poems and transcripts, personal conversations and interviews. The works combined reflect a diversity of perspectives, linguistic styles, and cultural tongues." Appendix: "Third World Women in the United States—By and About Us: A Selected Bibliography."

Chapter 4
GENERAL STUDIES OF
AMERICAN ETHNIC LITERATURE

A. Bibliographies

Etulain, Richard W., comp. *A Bibliographical Guide to the Study of Western American Literature*. Lincoln: University of Nebraska Press, 1982.
See unannotated citations in the "Special Topics" section for "Indian Literature and Indians in Western Literature" and "Mexican-American Literature and Chicanos in Western Literature." Also notable for its bibliographies of particular ethnic writers; see "Works on Individual Authors."

Taylor, J. Golden, and Tom Lyon, eds. *A Literary History of the American West*. Sponsored by the Western American Literature Association. Fort Worth: Texas Christian University Press, 1987.
This massive (more than thirteen hundred pages) encyclopedia of the American West has articles with short bibliographies on a number of ethnic literatures. See the essay, "Native Oral Traditions," in part I. See also section 1 ("Earth Tones: Ethnic Expression in American Literature") in part III, which includes an introduction by Gerald W. Haslam, three articles on American Indian literature (by A. LaVonne Brown Ruoff, Paula Gunn Allen, and Patricia Clark Smith), two on Mexican American literature (Raymund A. Paredes), and essays on Asian American (Jeffery Paul Chan and Marilyn Alquiloza) and Afro-American literatures (James W. Byrd).

B. General Literary Studies

Boelhower, William. *Through a Glass Darkly: Ethnic Semiosis in American Literature*. New York: Oxford University Press, 1987.
As Werner Sollors' foreward states, "Applying semiotics . . . to the study of American ethnicity, Boelhower breaks new ground and provides a new model for an understanding of American texts . . . [and] encourages American writers, teachers, students, and general readers to abandon the idea that 'mainstream' and 'ethnic' can be meaningfully separated: the ethnic sign is everywhere, and ethnic writing is American writing."

Gates, Henry Louis, Jr., ed. *"Race," Writing, and Difference*. Chicago: University of Chicago Press, 1986.
Originally an issue of *Critical Inquiry* (1985), this volume contains essays by Edward Said, Jacques Derrida, Mary Louise Pratt, Barbara Johnson, and others on theoretical issues of the terms.

Karrer, Wolfgang, and Hartmut Lutz, eds. *Minority Literatures in North America: Contemporary Perspectives*. Frankfurt: Peter Lang, 1990.
Papers from the First International Symposium on Minority Literatures in North America, at the University of Osnabruck, Germany, in 1988. The symposium covered Asian American, Black, Chicano, Indian, Inuit, and Metis literatures.

Klein, Marcus. *Foreigners: The Making of American Literature, 1900-1940*. Chicago: University of Chicago Press, 1981.
All twentieth century American writers, Klein argues, are "foreigners," or outside the mainstream: "Children of the Mayflower tended to invent Western culture, and children of the immigrants, who seem to me to present the more interesting case, tended to invent America." See especially chapter 5, "Tales from the Ghetto" (about 1930's New York and novels about Chicago) and chapter 8, "Black Boy and Native Son" (on Richard Wright).

Sollors, Werner. *Beyond Ethnicity: Consent and Descent in American Culture*. New York: Oxford University Press, 1986.
This is a crucial work for both social scientists and teachers of literature. Ethnic literature, Sollors argues convincingly, is "prototypically American literature" for it is "an expression of a persistent conflict between consent and descent" in American life. A multidisciplinary approach uses literature to examine notions of ethnicity and the melting pot, and vice versa.

_____, ed. *The Invention of Ethnicity*. New York: Oxford University Press, 1989.
The notion of ethnicity as a strategy and process, rather than as a fixed value in American life, informs this "collection of new essays and interpretations, all of which pursue the subject of ethnicity in a historical and dynamic context." Among the contributors are Sollors, Ishmael Reed, Richard Rodriguez, William Boelhower, and Mary V. Dearborn.

Thernstrom, Stephan, et al., eds. *Harvard Encyclopedia of American Ethnic Groups*. Cambridge, Mass.: Harvard University Press, 1980.
See Werner Sollors, "Literature and Ethnicity" and essays on Afro-American (Robert Stepto), Mexican American (Raymund A. Paredes), and Asian American (Elaine H. Kim) literatures.

Tibor, Frank, ed., *The Origins and Originality of American Culture*. Budapest: Akademiai Kiado, 1984.
Includes a section on "Native vs. Ethnic," with papers on slave narratives, the Black aesthetic, and American ethnicity and ideology.

Varieties of Ethnic Criticism. Series of special issues in *MELUS*: 9, no. 1 (Spring, 1982); 9, no. 4 (Winter, 1982); 10, no. 3 (Fall, 1983); 11, no. 2 (Summer, 1984); 13, nos. 3-4 (Fall/Winter, 1986); and 15, no. 2 (Summer, 1988).
Issues include a number of practical critical applications on a broad range of ethnic texts. For example, in *Varieties of Ethnic Criticism* 15, no. 2, see articles on Ralph Ellison, Toshio Mori, "Steinbeck and the American Indian," and an interview with Ann Petry.

Zyla, Wolodymyr T., and Wendell M. Aycock, eds. *Ethnic Literatures Since 1776: The Many Voices of America.* Part 1. Lubbock: Texas Tech Press, 1978.
This proceedings of a 1976 comparative literature symposium include papers on Black, Chicano, Chinese-American, and Japanese-American literary topics.

See also: special ethnic issues (*The Graywolf Annual Five, Massachusetts Review*) (1B1); Baker (3B1)

C. American Literary History

Bercovitch, Sacvan, ed. *Reconstructing American Literary History.* Cambridge, Mass.: Harvard University Press, 1986.
A good example of the new American literary history, which deals more inclusively with ethnic literary history. See, for example, Eric Sundquist's "Benito Cereno and New World Slavery," Werner Sollors's "A Critique of Pure Pluralism," and Robert B. Stepto's "Distrust of the Reader in Afro-American Narratives."

Elliott, Emory, ed. *Columbia Literary History of the United States.* New York: Columbia University Press, 1987.
Includes entries on various American ethnic literatures and their development. See Werner Sollors, "Immigrants and Other Americans"; N. Scott Momaday, "The Native Voice"; and essays on Afro-American (Robert Stepto), Asian-American (Elaine H. Kim), and Mexican-American (Raymund A. Paredes) literatures.

Reising, Russell J. *The Unusable Past: Theory and the Study of American Literature.* New York: Methuen, 1986.
This is a useful theoretical discussion of canon issues. For example, see chapter 6, "Conclusion: The Significance of Frederick Douglass," which argues that "Douglass's life, his works, the institution of slavery, and the struggle against slavery waged by Black and white alike are the material, social, and political basis on which the works of other major writers of the American Renaissance are founded."

Toward a New Literary History. Special issue of *MELUS*, 11, no. 1 (Spring, 1984).
This issue contains essays by Wayne Charles Miller, Paul Lauter, Rudolfo A.
Anaya, Ronald Gottesman, Jules Chametzky, Werner Sollors, and others, on the
canon and multicultural American literary history. Also includes an interview
with Ishmael Reed.

D. Genres

1. Theatre

Ethnic Theatre. Special issue of *MELUS*, 16, no. 3 (Fall, 1989-1990).
"Selected Proceedings from the 10th Anniversary of the New World Theater
Conference" reprints addresses by Jessica Hagedorn, David Henry Hwang,
Woodie King, and others. Articles and interviews.

Seller, Maxine Schwartz, ed. *Ethnic Theatre in the United States*. Westport, Conn.:
Greenwood Press, 1985.
This is a comprehensive survey of the ethnic theatre. See especially essays on
Black theatre, Mexican-American theatre, Native American theatre, and "Puerto
Rican Theatre on the Mainland."

2. Poetry

Harris, Marie, and Kathleen Aguero, eds. *A Gift of Tongues: Critical Challenges
in Contemporary American Poetry*. Athens: University of Georgia Press, 1987.
These essays were "compiled to celebrate and evaluate" the diversity of American poetry (by Joseph Bruchac, Bruce-Novoa, others) and discuss Puerto Rican,
Japanese American, Chicano, Black, and Native American poetry "by women
of color." See also Paul Lauter's "Class, Caste, and Canon".

Nelson, Cary. *Repression and Recovery: Modern American Poetry and the Politics
of Cultural Memory, 1910-1945*. Madison: University of Wisconsin Press, 1989.
This Marxist, poststructuralist study is "an effort to revise our notion of the
social function of poetry, an effort grounded in a series of rereadings of margin-
alized or forgotten poets—particularly women, Blacks, and writers on the
left—and in a theoretical discussion of poetry's cultural status as a discourse
among others."

3. Fiction

The Ethnic Novel: Appalachian, Chicano, Chinese, and Native American. Special
issue of *MELUS*, 10, no. 4 (Winter, 1983).

The issue includes essays on Harriette Arnow, Maxine Hong Kingston, Leslie Silko, "Ritual Process and the Family in the Chicano Novel," as well as an interview with N. Scott Momaday.

4. Autobiography

Ethnic Autobiography. Special issue of *MELUS*, 14, no. 1 (Spring, 1987).
Included here are "Native American Autobiography," "Autobiographies of Japanese-American Women," and "Metaphors and Myths of Cross-Cultural Literacy." See also an earlier special issue of *MELUS* (9, no. 2, Summer, 1982), "Ethnic Biography and Autobiography."

Holte, James Craig. *The Ethnic I: A Sourcebook for Ethnic-American Autobiography.* Westport, Conn.: Greenwood Press, 1988.
This "attempt to provide an overview of the genre and examination of the work of representative writers from a variety of ethnic backgrounds and historical periods" includes chapters on the autobiographical writings of Maya Angelou, Black Elk, Carlos Bulosan, Nicky Cruz, Zora Neale Hurston, Maxine Hong Kingston, Malcolm X, Richard Rodriguez, Piri Thomas, Booker T. Washington, Jade Snow Wong, Richard Wright, and seventeen other ethnic Americans.

Payne, James Robert, ed. *Multicultural Autobiography: American Lives.* Knoxville: University of Tennessee Press, 1992.
Collection establishes both the importance of autobiography in American literature and the centrality of multicultural voices to that genre in essays on European-American, as well as Native American, African American, Asian American, and Chicano/Latino self-writing.

See also: *Auto/Biography Studies* (1B1)

E. Women and Literature

Dearborn, Mary V. *Pocahontas's Daughters: Gender and Ethnicity in American Culture.* New York: Oxford University Press, 1986.
"Literature produced by American ethnic women presents in dramatically high relief aspects not only of the female or ethnic experience in America, but of American culture itself." This study of "the distinctly female ethnic literary tradition" in this country includes essays on American Indian and Black women writers.

Ethnic Women Writers. Series of special issues in *MELUS*: 7, no. 3 (Fall, 1980); 7, no. 4 (Winter, 1980); 9, no. 3 (Fall, 1982); 12, no. 3 (Fall, 1985); and 15, no. 1 (Spring, 1988).
Issues include articles, reviews, and interviews with a number of ethnic women writers. *Ethnic Women Writers V* (15, no. 1), for instance, contains articles on Maxine Hong Kingston, Lorraine Hansberry, Cathy Song, Sonia Sanchez, and Leslie Marmon Silko, as well as an interview with Mitsuye Yamada.

Chapter 5
NATIVE AMERICAN LITERATURE

A. A Brief Narrative History

American Indian literature was the first to be created on this continent and almost the last to be recognized. As late as 1963, Robert Spiller could open the third edition of his standard *Literary History of the United States* by declaring, "The literature of this nation began when the first settler from abroad of sensitive mind paused in his adventure long enough to feel he was under a different sky, breathing a new air, and that a New World was all before him with only strength and Providence for guides."[1]

The Eurocentric—to say nothing of sexist—assumptions of this view of American literary history are by now all too clear. Only a few years later, N. Scott Momaday won the Pulitzer Prize for fiction with *The House Made of Dawn* (1968), a novel that marks the beginning of both a renaissance in contemporary American Indian literature and the recognition of the centuries of that literature. For in the decades since 1968, not only have a number of important American Indian writers emerged—Paula Gunn Allen, Louise Erdrich, Leslie Marmon Silko, and James Welch, to name a few—but American Indian literature has entered the canon of American literature, and major scholarly work on that literature has begun.

Anthologies of American literature tell the story. As late as 1979, *The Norton Anthology of American Literature* carried no Native American writers in its two volumes of 4,951 pages. In the decade since its publication, major corrections have been made in those omissions, culminating in the 1989 *Heath Anthology of American Literature*, which has hundreds of pages of American Indian writers in the first truly multiethnic anthology of American literature.[2]

Anthologies devoted to Native American writers tell a similar story. A third of the thirty-three anthologies listed immediately below represent that first surge of interest in Native American materials after Momaday's success—and after an increase in political consciousness following the occupation of Wounded Knee, South Dakota, by members of AIM in 1973. The other two thirds, however, have appeared in the decade since, and almost half of that in the last two or three years. The recent interest in Native American literatures is thus great and still growing.

The literatures of North America are conveniently arranged into three periods. American literature of the first thousands of years can be called traditional tribal literature: myths, songs, ritual chants, and so forth. Most of this literature was oral, and so has been lost. What has been preserved—a great deal of it published in forty-seven volumes from the Bureau of American Anthropology, Department of the Smithsonian, from 1881 to 1932—is still being studied and reevaluated today. That literature provides glimpses into the lives of Native American peoples from before this continent was "discovered" by Europeans through the nineteenth century.

The second organizational period is what is referred to as *transitional culture*: the transformation of this continent from the vast Indian lands of the early nineteenth century to the restricted reservation life of the twentieth, or from the westward expansion of the United States at the beginning of the nineteenth century through the Indian Wars of the 1860's to the massacre at Wounded Knee in 1890. This transitional literature incorporates much of the oral literature noted earlier but also includes the orations of Indian leaders (such as Chief Joseph) and the memoirs (often told to white writers or anthropologists) by Native Americans like Geronimo and Chief Joseph. Although there are often authenticity problems with this literature (for example, what does "as told through John G. Neihardt" on the title page of *Black Elk Speaks* mean?), it is still an important literature both for itself and for what it tells about the lives of whites and Indians in the nineteenth century.

Finally, there is twentieth century American Indian literature, and particularly the renaissance of that literature in the last twenty years, when a number of important Native American writer-scholars emerged both to create the primary literature and to interpret Indian history and culture. (Note the number of writers from the primary bibliography below who also appear in the secondary.) Certainly American fiction and American poetry have been revitalized in the last two decades by writers such as Scott Momaday, Gerald Vizenor, Duane Niatum, Paula Gunn Allen—and the list keeps growing.

A word about forms. Recent scholarship is showing how much of the oral literature of the first period is a poetry of intricate structure and verbal subtlety and how it has influenced later literatures (see Hymes, Tedlock, et al., below, in 5C3 and 5C5). Similarly, scholarship on the literature of the second period has revealed the importance of Native American oratory and autobiography in the development of all American literatures. Indians were recognized as speakers of real eloquence early in American history (both Franklin and Jefferson commented on this fact in 1784). Likewise, American autobiography has been influenced strongly by the numerous accounts of Native American lives. In some ways, autobiography is the ultimate ethnic genre because it is in stories of immigration and assimilation that American ethnic writers often describe the painful truths of what it means to be—or to become—American. From the stories of Black Elk through contemporary Native American memoirs, one reads again and again the history of the nation, as well as the lives and deaths of its first citizens.

A final thought on themes. American Indian literature is important not only because it reveals this story of the country's growth but also because it iterates many of the concerns of American literature—or anticipates themes that have since become important. The spirituality of life and the sacredness of nature—and the interconnectedness between them—are ideas that contemporary Americans in great numbers have only recently discovered, but they are ideas that have been at the center of American Indian literature since the beginning of time. Likewise, the search for self (the many initiation stories of American Indian youth), the significance of the tribe (or community), and the importance of women in culture (Pocahontas, Sacajawea).

The modern deconstructionist world can find value in the ideas of the power of words and the organic nature of language found in numerous Native American texts. Finally, at a time when many Americans feel a loss of cultural wholeness, they are tapping into American cultures hundreds and even thousands of years old and are only beginning to experience their strength and to learn their lessons.

B. A Selected List of Primary Works

1. Anthologies

a. *General (including traditional oral literature)*

Bierhorst, John, ed. *Four Masterworks of American Indian Literature.* Tucson: University of Arizona Press, 1974.
  Intended "as a first step toward establishing a body of standard works, a canon of native American literature," this collection contains "Quetzalcoatl" (an Aztec hero myth), "The Ritual of Condolence" (an Iroquois ceremonial), "Cuceb" (a Maya prophecy), and "The Night Chant" (a Navajo ceremonial). Works are presented as outstanding examples "of the bardic, oratorical, prophetic, and incantatory styles characteristic of the cultures that produced them."

_____, ed. *In the Trail of the Wind: American Indian Poems and Ritual Orations.* New York: Farrar, Straus and Giroux, 1971.
  Contains songs, speeches, prayers, incantations, and legends from more than forty Indian languages of North and South America, from Mayan and Aztec cultures to twentieth century Eskimo poetry. Entries are arranged thematically to emphasize similar ideas: the power of words, significance of dreams, dualism of nature, and so on.

_____, ed. *The Red Swan: Myths and Tales of the American Indians.* New York: Farrar, Straus and Giroux, 1976.
  Sixty-four myths and tales are arranged into fifteen groups in four subject areas: "Setting the World in Order" (creation myths), "The Family Drama," "Fair and Foul" (trickster tales), and "Crossing the Threshold" (five types of passage from one state of being to another, such as initiation rites, death). Bierhorst's goal in the collection "is to present a comprehensive view of the world—the world of humanity—as perceived through the lens of American myth."

_____, ed. *The Sacred Path: Spells, Prayers, and Power Songs of the American Indians.* New York: William Morrow, 1983.
  A collection of traditional Indian poems, many in recent translations. Notes are assigned to the appendix, which means that little gets between the reader and the

poetry, and the poems are arranged into thematic groups to underline connections among them.

Brandon, William, ed. *The Magic World: American Indian Songs and Poems*. New York: William Morrow, 1971.
Another excellent short collection of primitive poetry, from Mayan hymns to Eskimo songs, "presented here not as ethnological data but strictly as literature." Includes a brief introduction, "Postface: The Sources," but otherwise no editorial apparatus.

Erdoes, Richard, and Alfonso Ortiz, eds. *American Indian Myths and Legends*. Albuquerque: University of New Mexico Press, 1984.
Some 166 legends from dozens of North American tribes are arranged into ten thematic units, from "Tales of Human Creation" to "Visions of the End." Includes stories from both "classic accounts," including several from nineteenth century sources, and versions collected by the authors but never before printed.

Hamilton, Charles, ed. *Cry of the Thunderbird: The American Indian's Own Story*. Norman: University of Oklahoma Press, 1977.
"Here the last men of the Stone Age describe their heroic struggle with the first men of the Machine Age, their incredible customs and rites, adventures in hunting and on the warpath, and finally their pathetic efforts to accept the strange ways of the white invader." Includes brief selections by Indian writers in nine thematic sections. Illustrated.

Kroeber, Theodora, ed. *The Inland Whale: Nine Stories Retold from California Indian Legends*. Berkeley: University of California Press, 1963.
Contains a selection of stories from the Native Indian literature of California, plus background, tribal origin, and use of each story.

Momaday, Natachee Scott, ed. *American Indian Authors*. Boston: Houghton Mifflin, 1972.
An early anthology of selections from Chief Joseph and Black Elk through James Welch and Vine Deloria, Jr.

Peyer, Bernd C., ed. *The Singing Spirit: Early Short Stories by North American Indians*. Tucson: University of Arizona Press, 1989.
"The purpose of this anthology is to introduce some of the major Indian authors of the late nineteenth and early twentieth centuries by way of one of the more elusive genres in the history of Indian writing: the short story." Contains eighteen stories by eleven writers covering the years from 1880 to about 1930.

Roscoe, Will, ed. *Living the Spirit: A Gay American Indian Anthology*. New York: St. Martin's Press, 1988.
Organized into three parts. "Artists, Healers, and Providers" contains articles on and stories about the berdache tradition. "Gay American Indians Today" includes some two dozen stories and poems. "Resources" includes a list of "North American Tribes with Berdache and Alternative Gender Roles," "Sources and Suggested Reading."

Rothenberg, Jerome, ed. *Shaking the Pumpkin: Traditional Poetry of the Indian North Americas*. New York: Doubleday, 1972.
A collection of translations of "classical" American poetry by contemporary American poets (including Edward Field, Denise Levertov, and William Merwin). Commentaries on some of the poems may be found on pages 403-475.

Sanders, Thomas E., and Walter W. Peek, eds. *Literature of the American Indian*. Beverly Hills, Calif.: Glencoe Press, 1976.
This abridged version of the 1973 edition has seven chapters that are organized into topics from religion, poetry, and oratory to "Anguished, Angry, Articulate: Current Voices in Poetry, Prose, and Protest."

Turner, Frederick W., ed. *The Portable North American Indian Reader*. New York: Viking Press, 1974.
This collection, intended "to introduce the general American reader to the traditions and the historical realities of the North American Indian," contains sections on myths and tales, poetry and oratory, "Culture Contact" (explorers' diaries, captivity narratives, Indian autobiographies), and "Image and Anti-Image" (popular images of the Indian, as well as self-images by N. Scott Momaday, Vine Deloria, James Welch, Simon J. Ortiz, and others).

Velie, Alan R. *American Indian Literature: An Anthology*. Norman: University of Oklahoma Press, 1979.
A collection that represents the three stages of American Indian literature, from traditional tribal culture (tales and songs), through so-called transitional literature (nineteenth century oration and memoirs), to modern poetry and fiction (N. Scott Momaday, James Welch, and Simon Ortiz, among others).

Witt, Shirley Hill, and Stan Steiner, eds. *The Way: An Anthology of American Indian Literature*. New York: Alfred A. Knopf, 1972.
This collection presents two kinds of writing: "ancient speeches of honored leaders and orators" and contemporary speeches, essays, and poetry in an effort to show Indian thought and logic in their original forms.

b. Contemporary Native American Literature

Bruchac, Joseph, ed. *New Voices from the Longhouse: An Anthology of Contemporary Iroquois Writing*. Greenfield Center, N.Y.: Greenfield Review Press, 1989. A selection of poems and stories from thirty northeastern Native American writers.

Chambers, Leland H., ed. *Native American Literature*. Special issue of *Denver Quarterly* 14 (1980).
Includes articles (by Elaine Jahner, Carter Revard, Linda Hogan, and others), fiction (Charles Brashers), poetry (Simon J. Ortiz, Jim Barnes, others), and book reviews.

"From This World: Contemporary American Indian Literature." *World Literature Today* 66, no. 2 (Spring, 1992).
This seventy-five-page cluster includes poetry and fiction by Carter Revard, Gerald Vizenor, Lance Henson, and critical essays on Native American writers (Vizenor, Louise Erdrich, Joy Harjo) by A. LaVonne Brown Ruoff, Alan R. Veloe, Andrew Wiget, and others.

Highwater, Jamake, ed. *Words in the Blood: Contemporary Indian Writers of North and South America*. New York: New American Library, 1984.
Essentially an anthology of twentieth century Native American writers, from Charles A. Eastman and D'Arcy McNickle through Duane Niatum, Joy Harjo, and Peter Blue Cloud. The collection is unique for including representative mestizo writers of South America: Cesar Vallejo, Pablo Neruda, Octavio Paz, and others.

Hobson, Geary, ed. *The Remembered Earth: An Anthology of Contemporary Native American Literature*. Albuquerque: University of New Mexico Press, 1981.
This collection is divided into writers from the Northeast (Peter Blue Cloud, Joseph Bruchac, et al.), Southeast (Joy Harjo, Linda Hogan, N. Scott Momaday, others), Southwest (for example, Paula Gunn Allen, Simon J. Ortiz), and Northwest (Ray A. Young Bear, Elizabeth Cook-Lynn, among others).

Lerner, Andrea, ed. *Dancing on the Rim of the World: An Anthology of Contemporary Northwest Native American Writing*. Tucson: Sun Tracks/University of Arizona Press, 1990.
This volume, intended "as a celebration of the creativity, enthusiasm, and craft that marks literary efforts in the region," contains stories and poems by James Welch, Jo Cochran, Duane Niatum, Nila Northsun, and thirty other northwestern Native American writers.

1. Poetry

Bruchac, Joseph, ed. *Songs from This Earth on Turtle's Back: Contemporary American Indian Poetry.* Greenfield Center, N.Y.: Greenfield Review Press, 1983.
An anthology of poetry by fifty-two writers from more than thirty-five different "Native American nations."

Foss, Phillip, ed. *The Clouds Threw This Light: Contemporary Native American Poetry.* Santa Fe, N.M.: Institute of American Arts Press, 1983.
This is a "poet's choice" collection of seventy-eight writers in which "the poets were invited to contribute what they believed to be their best work."

Niatum, Duane, ed. *Carriers of the Dream Wheel: Contemporary Native American Poetry.* New York: Harper & Row, 1975.
This important early collection contains poetry by Jim Barnes, Joseph Bruchac, Lance Henson, N. Scott Momaday, Simon J. Ortiz, Wendy Rose, Leslie Silko, James Welch, Ray A. Young Bear, and seven other writers.

_____, ed. *Harper's Anthology of Native American Poetry.* San Francisco: Harper, 1988.
This excellent anthology of contemporary American Indian poetry contains the work of thirty-six writers. An informative introduction by Brian Swann discusses themes of American Indian literature, the importance of the oral tradition, and related issues.

2. Fiction

Lesley, Craig, ed. *Talking Leaves: Contemporary Native American Short Stories.* New York: Dell Books, 1991.
Includes short fiction by Paula Gunn Allen, Carter Revard, Debra Earling, Gerald Vizenor, James Welch, and others.

Ortiz, Simon J., ed. *Earth Power Coming: Short Fiction in Native American Literature.* Traile, Ark.: Navajo Community College Press, 1983.
Stories in this collection are grounded in the oral tradition, but in a range of forms, by Leslie Marmon Silko, Gerald Vizenor, Louise Erdrich, Gerald Haslam, Paula Gunn Allen, and thirty-four other Native American writers.

Velie, Alan R., ed. *The Lightning Within: An Anthology of Contemporary American Indian Fiction.* Lincoln: University of Nebraska Press, 1991.
Stories by N. Scott Momaday, James Welch, Leslie Marmon Silko, Gerald

Vizenor, Simon J. Ortiz, Louise Erdrich, and Michael Dorris are contained in "a selection of some of the best pieces of contemporary Indian fiction to serve as an introduction to the principal Indian novelists and short-story writers of the past twenty years."

c. Native American Women

Allen, Paula Gunn. *Grandmothers of the Light: A Medicine Woman's Sourcebook.* Boston: Beacon Press, 1991.
A retelling of twenty-one Native American feminist creation myths: of the Cherokee Spider Woman, the Quiche Maya grandmother Xmucane, and the Navajo goddess Changing Woman, to name a few.

_____, ed. *Spider Woman's Granddaughters: Traditional Tales and Contemporary Writing by Native American Women.* Boston: Beacon Press, 1989.
Contains both traditional Native American oral models (some retold by Humishima [Mourning Dove] and E. Pauline Johnson) and modern stories by Louise Erdrich, Linda Hogan, Leslie Marmon Silko, and others.

Brant, Beth, ed. *A Gathering of Spirit: Writing and Art by North American Indian Women.* 2d ed. Rockland, Maine: Sinister Wisdom Books, 1984.
Originally a special issue of *Sinister Wisdom* (1983), this collection includes photographs, drawings, poems, and narratives by Paula Gunn Allen, Wendy Rose, Elizabeth Cook-Lynn, and other contemporary Native American women.

Green, Rayna, ed. *That's What She Said: Contemporary Poetry and Fiction by Native American Women.* Bloomington: University of Indiana Press, 1984.
Paula Gunn Allen, Louise Erdrich, Joy Harjo, Wendy Rose, and a dozen other contemporary Native American women writers are represented here. The collection also contains an introduction, glossary of terms, and bibliography.

Hogan, Linda, ed. *Native American Women.* Special issue of *Frontiers: A Journal of Women's Studies* 6 (1981).
Includes articles, poetry (by Wendy Rose, Rayna Green, Paula Gunn Allen, and others), and Lyle Koehler's "Native Women of the Americas: A Bibliography."

See also: Chapman (5C5)

2. Individual Writers[3]

a. Nineteenth, Early Twentieth Century Memoirs, Speeches, etc.

Apes, William
   Eulogy on King Philip, as Pronounced at the Odeon, in Federal Street, Boston, by the Rev. William Apes, an Indian (nonfiction, 1836)
   A Son of the Forest: The Experience of William Apes, a Native of the Forest, Comprising a Notice of the Pequod Tribe of Indians (autobiography, 1831)

Blackbird, Andrew J.
   History of the Ottowa and Chippewa Indians of Michigan; a Grammar of Theirr [sic] Language, and Personal and Family History of the Author (nonfiction, 1887)

Black Elk (as told to John G. Neihardt)[4]
   Black Elk Speaks (autobiography, 1932)

Black Hawk (as told to Antoine LeClaire and John B. Patterson)
   Black Hawk: An Autobiography (1833)

Blowsnake, Sam (as told to Paul Radin)
   The Autobiography of a Winnebago Indian (1926)

Chona, Maria (as told to Ruth M. Underhill)
   The Autobiography of a Papago Woman (1936)

Clarke, Peter Dooyentate
   Origin and Traditional History of the Wyandotts, and Sketches of Other Indian Tribes of North America: True Traditional Stories of Tecumseh and His League, in the Years 1811 and 1812 (nonfiction, 1870)

Copway, George
   The Life, History, and Travels of Kah-ge-ga-gahbowh (George Copway) . . . (autobiography, 1847)
   Running Sketches of Men and Places, in England, France, Germany, Belgium, and Scotland (nonfiction, 1851)
   The Traditional History and Characteristic Sketches of the Ojibway Nation (nonfiction, 1850)

Eastman, Charles A.
   From the Deep Woods to Civilization: Chapters in the Autobiography of an Indian (1916)
   Indian Boyhood (autobiography, 1902)

Old Indian Days (fiction, 1907)
Red Hunters and the Animal People (fiction, 1904)
The Soul of the Indian: An Interpretation (nonfiction, 1911)

Jones, Peter
History of the Ojibway Indians. With Especial Reference to Their Conversion to Christianity (nonfiction, 1861)

La Flesche, Francis
The Middle Five: Indian Schoolboys of the Omaha Tribe (autobiography, 1900)

Maugwudaus [pseud. George Henry]
An Account of the Chippewa Indians, Who Have Been Travelling Among the Whites, in the United States, England, Ireland, Scotland, France, and Belgium (autobiography, 1848)

Occum, Samson
A Sermon Preached at the Execution of Moses Paul, an Indian Who Was Executed at New-Haven, on the 2d of September 1772 (nonfiction, 1772)

Ridge, John Rollin
The Life and Adventures of Joaquin Murieta, the Celebrated California Bandit (fiction, 1854)

Warren, William Whipple
History of the Ojibway, Based upon Traditions and Oral Statements (nonfiction, 1885)

Winnemucca, Sarah [Hopkins]
Life Among the Piutes: Their Wrongs and Claims (autobiography, 1883)

b. Twentieth Century Fiction, Nonfiction, Drama, and Poetry

Allen, Paula Gunn
Shadow Country (poetry, 1982)
Skins and Bones: Poems: 1979-87 (poetry, 1988)
The Woman Who Owned the Shadows (fiction, 1983)

Anauta (as told to Heluiz Chandler Washburne)
Land of the Good Shadows: The Life Story of Anauta, an Eskimo Woman (autobiography, 1940)

Arnett, Caroll [pseud. Gogisgi]
  Tsalagi (poetry, 1976)

Barnes, Jim
  The American Book of the Dead (poetry, 1982)
  La Plata Cantata: Poems (1989)

Blue Cloud, Peter
  Elderberry Flute Song: Contemporary Coyote Tales (poetry and short fiction, 1982)

Bruchac, Joseph
  Entering Onondaga (poetry, 1978)
  The Dreams of Jesse Brown (fiction, 1978)

Burns, Diane
  Riding the One-Eyed Ford (poetry, 1981)

Bush, Barney
  Inherit the Blood (poetry and fiction, 1985)
  My Horse and a Jukebox (poetry, 1979)
  Petroglyphs (poetry, 1982)

Carter, Forrest
  The Education of Little Tree (fiction, 1976)
  Josey Wales: Two Westerns by Forrest Carter (fiction, 1989)

Conley, Robert J.
  The Rattlesnake Bank and Other Poems (poetry, 1984)
  The Witch of Goingsnake and Other Stories (1988)

Cook-Lynn, Elizabeth
  At the River's Edge (fiction, 1991)
  The Power of Horses and Other Stories (1990)
  Seek the House of Relatives (poetry, 1983)

Dorris, Michael
  A Yellow Raft on Blue Water (fiction, 1987)

Downing, [George] Todd
  The Case of the Unconquered Sisters (fiction, 1935)
  The Lazy Lawrence Murders (fiction, 1941)
  The Mexican Earth (fiction, 1940)

Erdrich, Louise
 Baptism of Desire: Poems (1989)
 Beet Queen (fiction, 1986)
 Love Medicine (fiction, 1984)
 Tracks (fiction, 1988)

Geigogamah, Hanay
 New Native American Drama: Three Plays (drama, 1980)

Griffis, Joseph
 Tahan: Out of Savagery into Civilization (autobiography, 1915)

Hale, Jane Campbell
 Custer Lives in Humboldt County (poetry, 1978)
 The Jailing of Cecilia Capture (fiction, 1987)
 Owl Song (fiction, 1974)

Harjo, Joy
 In Mad Love and War (poetry, 1991)
 She Had Some Horses (poetry, 1983)
 What Moon Drove Me to This? (poetry, 1979)

Henson, Lance
 Selected Poems: 1970-1983 (poetry, 1985)

Hogan, Linda
 Calling Myself Home (poetry, 1980)
 Daughters, I Love You (poetry, 1981)
 Mean Spirit (fiction, 1990)

Johnson, Emily Pauline
 Flint and Feather (poetry, 1912)
 The Moccasin Maker (fiction and nonfiction, 1913)
 The Shagganappi (fiction, 1913)

Kenny, Maurice
 Between Two Rivers: Selected Poems, 1956-84 (1987)
 Humors and/or Not So Humorous (poetry, 1988)

King, Thomas
 Medicine River (fiction, 1990)

Least Heat-Moon, William
  Blue Highways (nonfiction, 1982)
  PrairyErth (a deep map) (nonfiction, 1991)

Long, Sylvester
  Long Lance: The Autobiography of a Blackfoot Indian (fiction, 1928)

Louis, Adrian C.
  Fiore Water World (poetry, 1989)
  Muted War Drums (poetry, 1977)
  Sweets for the Dancing Bear (poetry, 1979)

Mathews, John Joseph
  Sundown (fiction, 1934)
  Talking to the Moon (autobiography, 1945)
  Wah'Kon-Tah: The Osage and the White Man's Road (fiction, 1932)

McNickle, D'Arcy
  Runner in the Sun: A Story of Indian Maize (fiction, 1954)
  The Surrounded (fiction, 1936)
  Wind from an Enemy Sky (fiction, 1978)

Mitchell, Frank (as told to Charlotte Johnson Frisbie and David P. McAllester)
  Navajo Blessingway Singer: The Autobiography of Frank Mitchell, 1881-1967
  (nonfiction, 1978)

Momaday, N. Scott
  The Ancient Child (fiction, 1989)
  The Gourd Dancer: Poems (1976)
  The House Made of Dawn (fiction, 1968)
  The Way to Rainy Mountain (nonfiction, 1969)

Mountain Wolf Woman (as told to Nancy Oestreich Lurie)
  Mountain Wolf Woman, Sister of Crashing Thunder: The Autobiography of a
  Winnebago Indian (nonfiction, 1961)

Mourning Dove
  Cogewea, the Half-Blood: A Depiction of the Great Montana Cattle Range
  (fiction, 1927)

Niatum, Duane
  Digging Out the Roots (poetry, 1977)
  Drawings of the Song Animals: New and Selected Poems (1990)

Songs for the Harvest of Dreams (poetry, 1981)

Oandasan, William
A Branch of California Redwood (poetry, 1980)

Ortiz, Simon J.
Fightin': New and Collected Stories (1983)
Going for the Rain (poetry, 1976)
A Good Journey (poetry, 1977)
Howbah Indians (fiction, 1978)
From Sand Creek (poetry, 1981)

Oskison, John Milton
Black Jack Davy (fiction, 1926)
Brother's Three (fiction, 1935)
Wild Harvest (fiction, 1925)

Pokagon, Simon
O-gi-maw-kwe Mit-i-gwa-ki (Queen of the Woods) (fiction, 1899)

Posey, Alexander
The Poems of Alexander Lawrence Posey (1910)

Revard, Carter
Ponca War Dancers (poetry, 1980)

Riggs, Lynn
The Cherokee Night (drama, 1936)
Green Grow the Lilacs (drama, 1931)
The Iron Dish (poetry, 1930)

Rogers, Will
Complete Works (nonfiction, in progress)

Rose, Wendy
The Halfbreed Chronicles (poetry, 1985)
Lost Copper (poetry, 1980)

Salisbury, Ralph
Going to the Water: Poems of Cherokee Heritage (1983)
Spirit Beast Chant (poetry, 1982)

Sanchez, Carol Lee
Message Bringer Woman (poetry, 1976)

Savala, Refugio (as told to Kathleen Mullen Sands)
The Autobiography of a Yaqui Poet (nonfiction, 1980)

Seals, David
The Powwow Highway (fiction, 1979)

Sekaquaptewa, Helen (as told to Louise Udall)
Me and Mine: The Life Story of Helen Sekequaptewa (nonfiction, 1969)

Sewid, James (as told to James P. Spradley)
Guests Never Leave Hungry: The Autobiography of James Sewid, a Kwakiutl Indian (nonfiction, 1969)

Shaw, Anna Moore
A Pima Past (autobiography, 1974)

Silko, Leslie Marmon
Almanac of the Dead (fiction, 1991)
Ceremony (fiction, 1977)
Laguna Woman (poetry, 1974)
Storyteller (fiction and poetry, 1981)

Smith, Martin Cruz
Gorky Park (fiction, 1981)
Gypsy in Amber (fiction, 1982)
Nightwing (fiction, 1977)
Polar Star (fiction, 1989)
Stallion Gate (fiction, 1986)

Standing Bear, Luther (as told to E. A. Brininstool)
Land of the Spotted Eagle (autobiography, 1933)
My People, the Sioux (autobiography, 1928)

Stands in Timber, John (as told to Margot Liberty)
Cheyenne Memories (autobiography, 1967)

Storm, Hyemeyohsts
Seven Arrows (fiction, 1972)
The Song of Heyoekhah (fiction, 1981)

Strete, Craig Kee
Death Chants (short fiction, 1988)

Talayesva, Don C. (as told to Leo W. Simmons)
Sun Chief: The Autobiography of a Hopi Indian (1942)

Tapahonso, Luci
A Breeze Swept Through (poetry, 1987)

Tucker, James
Stone: The Birth (fiction, 1981)
Stone: The Journey (fiction, 1981)

Vizenor, Gerald
Darkness in Saint Louis Bearheart (fiction, 1978)
Earthdivers (fiction and nonfiction, 1981)
The Everlasting Sky: New Voices from the People Named the Chippewa (nonfiction, 1972)
Griever: An American Monkey in China (fiction, 1990)
The Heirs of Columbus (fiction, 1991)
Landfill Meditation: Crossblood Stories (1991)
Matsushima: Pine Islands (poetry, 1984)
The People Named the Chippewa: Narrative Histories (fiction and nonfiction, 1984)
The Trickster of Liberty: Tribal Heirs to a Wild Baronage (fiction, 1988)
Wordarrows: Indians and Whites in the New Fur Trade (fiction and nonfiction, 1978)

Walker, Bertrand N. O.
Yon-Doo-Shah-We-Ah (Nubbins) (poetry, 1924)

Walsh, Marnie
A Taste of the Knife (poetry, 1976)

Welch, James
The Death of Jim Loney (fiction, 1979)
Fools Crow (fiction, 1986)
Riding the Earthboy 40 (poetry, 1976)
Winter in Our Blood (fiction, 1974)

White Bull, Chief Joseph (as told to James H. Howard)
The Warrior Who Killed Custer: The Personal Narrative of Chief Joseph White Bull (autobiography, 1968)

Whiteman, Roberta Hill
  Star Quilt (poetry, 1984)

Williams, Ted
  The Reservation (autobiography, 1976)

Young Bear, Ray
  Black Eagle Child: The Facepaint Narratives (autobiography, 1992)
  The Invisible Musician (poetry, 1990)
  Winter of the Salamander: The Keeper of Importance (poetry, 1980)

Zitkala-Sa
  American Indian Stories (fiction and nonfiction, 1921).

C. Secondary Bibliography

1. Bibliography

Brumble, H. David, III., comp. *An Annotated Bibliography of American Indian and Eskimo Autobiographies*. Lincoln: University of Nebraska Press, 1981.
A detailed description of more than five hundred autobiographical narratives (one hundred of them book-length), from the eighteenth century to the present, arranged alphabetically by subject: *Black Elk Speaks* (1932), *Geronimo* (1906), N. Scott Momaday's *The Way to Rainy Mountain* (1973), and more. (See Brumble, below, in 5C2.)

Clements, William M., and Frances M. Malpezzi, comps. *Native American Folklore, 1879-1979: An Annotated Bibliography*. Athens, Ohio: Swallow Press, 1984.
Valuable listings for Native American oral literatures are arranged into one section of general works (anthologies and collections, theory and commentary) and eleven regional sections (for example, Northeast, California, Northwest Coast).

Colonnese, Tom, and Louis Owens, comps. *American Indian Novelists: An Annotated Critical Bibliography*. New York: Garland, 1985.
Twenty-one novelists are listed alphabetically, with brief biographical sketches and primary and secondary sources: Paula Gunn Allen, Jamake Hightower, N. Scott Momaday, Leslie Marmon Silko, Gerald Vizenor, James Welch, and others.

Hirschfelder, Arlene B., comp. *American Indians and Eskimo Authors: A Comprehensive Bibliography.* New York: Association of American Indian Affairs, 1973. A revised and enlarged edition of the 1970 bibliography, this volume contains almost four hundred titles written or narrated by nearly three hundred authors.

Jacobson, Angeline, comp. *Contemporary Native American Literature: A Selected and Partially Annotated Bibliography.* Metuchen, N.J.: Scarecrow Press, 1977. Contains detailed listings of poetry, fiction, autobiography, interviews, and more covering the years 1960 to 1976.

Littlefield, David F., Jr., and James W. Parins, comps. *A Biobibliography of Native American Writers, 1772-1924.* Native American Bibliography Series 2. Metuchen, N.J.: Scarecrow Press, 1981. See the annotation for *A Biobibliography of Native American Writers 1772-1924.*

_____, comps. *A Biobibliography of Native American Writers 1772-1924: A Supplement.* Native American Bibliography Series 5. Metuchen, N.J.: Scarecrow Press, 1985. "This supplement contains the works of some 1192 writers. Works of 250 of these were included in the first biobibliography; 942 new writers were represented here." Most bibliographic entries (unlike the original volume) have been annotated. Lists "not only literary works of fiction, drama, and poetry, but also political essays and addresses, published letters, dialect pieces, historical works, myths and legends, and other genres." Includes authors known only by pen names.

Marken, Jack W., comp. *The American Indian: Language and Literature.* Arlington Heights, Ill.: AHM, 1978. This important early bibliography contains almost 3700 listings in sections, first on general literature and language and then by geographical area (California, Northeast, and so on). Not annotated.

Rock, Roger O., comp. *The Native American in American Literature: A Selectively Annotated Bibliography.* Bibliographies and Indexes in American Literature 3. Westport, Conn.: Greenwood Press, 1985. More than three hundred bibliographies are listed (one hundred annotated), nearly four hundred "Indian in Literature" citations, and nine hundred "Native American Literature" items.

Ruoff, A. LaVonne Brown, comp. "American Indian Literature." In *Redefining American Literary History,* edited by A. LaVonne Brown Ruoff and Jerry W. Ward, Jr. New York: Modern Language Association of America, 1990. Annotated sections of bibliographies, anthologies, primary and secondary works.

_____. "American Indian Literatures: Introduction and Bibliography."
American Studies International 24, no. 2 (October, 1986): 3-52.
A very useful resource containing a thirty-page introduction and a twenty-page
bibliography to the primary and secondary literatures.

Wiget, Andrew O. "Native American Literature: A Bibliographic Survey of American Indian Literary Traditions." *Choice* 23 (June, 1986): 1503-1512.
This bibliographic essay discusses major works in the history of American Indian
literatures. Works cited at end.

See also: Etulain, Taylor (4A); Ruoff (5C5)

2. Autobiography (including interviews)

Bataille, Gretchen M., and Kathleen Mullen Sands. *American Indian Women: Telling
Their Lives*. Lincoln: University of Nebraska Press, 1984.
"If the roles of American Indian women in their own societies and society at
large are to be analyzed with fairness and accuracy, we must take a closer look,
not from an outsider's viewpoint, but through modes of expression within tribal
society. Indian women's autobiographies offer, in both methodology and content,
an intimate look into the lives of these women." Includes a fifty-page annotated
bibliography.

Bruchac, Joseph, ed. *Survival This Way: Interviews with American Indian Poets*.
Tucson: Sun Tracks/University of Arizona Press, 1987.
Paula Gunn Allen, Louise Erdrich, N. Scott Momaday, James Welch, and
seventeen other contemporary American Indian writers talk about their lives and
work and about "continuance and renewal." More and more, Bruchac argues,
"in response to destruction of both language and life, Native American poets have
concerned themselves with the themes of survival."

Brumble, H. David. *American Indian Autobiography*. Berkeley: University of
California Press, 1988.
Essays toward a history of the genre, from "Preliterate Traditions of American
Indian Autobiography" to N. Scott Momaday. Appendix of autobiographies
updates the Brumble list in 5C1. Also see "Bibliography of Other Sources Used."

Coltelli, Laura. *Winged Words: American Indian Writers Speak*. Lincoln: University
of Nebraska Press, 1990.
Ten poets and novelists—Paula Gunn Allen, Louise Erdrich, Michael Dorris, N.
Scott Momaday, Leslie Marmon Silko, and James Welch among them—talk about
their careers, recurring themes in their work, and related issues.

Krupat, Arnold. *For Those Who Come After: A Study of Native American Autobiography*. Berkeley: University of California Press, 1985.
Two theoretical chapters ("An Approach to Native American Texts" and "Indian Autobiography: Origins, Type, and Function") are followed by literary analyses of several nineteenth and twentieth century American Indian autobiographies.

Swann, Brian, and Arnold Krupat, eds. *I Tell You Now: Autobiographical Essays by Native American Writers*. Lincoln: University of Nebraska Press, 1987.
Pieces by Gerald Vizenor, Paula Gunn Allen, Simon J. Ortiz, Joseph Bruchac, and fourteen other writers take a variety of forms in this "small contribution to the growing critical appreciation of Native American literary expression in its traditional and—most particularly—contemporary forms."

Wong, Hertha Dawn. *Sending My Heart Back Across the Years: Tradition and Innovation in Native American Autobiography*. New York: Oxford University Press, 1991.
Studies the transformation of Native American autobiography from early oral and pictographic personal narrative, through nineteenth century and early twentieth century life histories, to contemporary works.

3. Poetry

Hymes, Dell. *"In Vain I Tried to Tell You": Essays in Native American Ethnopoetics*. Studies in Native American Literature 1. Philadelphia: University of Pennsylvania Press, 1981.
Essays are organized in three sections: Part 1, "Unsuspected Devices and Designs," uncovers some of the forms of traditional Indian verbal art (songs, narratives, and speeches). Part 2, "Breakthrough to Performance," "presents the main record of discovery of verse-form" in the literature of the Indians of the North Pacific Coast. Part 3, "Titles, Names and Natures," "subordinates verse analysis to analysis of genre and meaning." Essential essays by a scholar who combines linguistics, anthropology, and literary analysis.

Sherzer, Joel, and Anthony C. Woodbury, eds. *Native American Discourse: Poetics and Rhetoric*. Cambridge Studies in Oral and Literature Culture 13. New York: Cambridge University Press, 1987.
This collection of essays is intended "to advance a new perspective on the presentation, philology, analysis, and interpretation of oral literature and verbal art." Part of the recent extension of discourse analysis into linguistics that has enhanced the study of Native American literature and language, it includes chapters by the editors, Dell Hymes, Virginia Hymes, and Dennis Tedlock.

See also: Kroeber, Swann, Swann and Krupat, Tedlock (5C5)

4. Fiction

Hanson, Elizabeth I. *Forever There: Race and Gender in Contemporary Native American Fiction.* New York: Peter Lang, 1989.
A critical study of the relationship between gender and race in the twentieth century fiction of D'Arcy McNickle, N. Scott Momaday, James Welch, Leslie Marmon Silko, Paula Gunn Allen, Louise Erdrich, and Michael Dorris.

Larson, Charles R. *American Indian Fiction.* Albuquerque: University of New Mexico Press, 1978.
A critical history of the twentieth century American Indian novel: N. Scott Momaday, Leslie Marmon Silko, James Welch, and others.

"Native American Fiction: Myth and Criticism." Special issue of *MELUS* 17, no. 1 (Spring, 1991-1992).
Articles discuss James Welch's *Fool's Crow* and *Winter in the Blood,* Leslie Marmon Silko's *Ceremony,* Gerald Vizenor and Henry Berry Lowry, and the Native American Trickster.

5. General Criticism

Allen, Paula Gunn, ed. *Studies in American Indian Literature: Critical Essays and Course Designs.* New York: Modern Language Association of America, 1983.
This indispensable volume has five parts: "Oral Literature"; "Personal Narrative, Autobiography, and Intermediate Literature"; "American Indian Women's Literature"; "Modern and Contemporary American Indian Literature"; and "The Indian in American Literature." Also contains a resources section. Each part contains essays by various hands on aspects of that topic, plus plans for literature courses in that area. Thus, "American Indian Women's Literature" has essays by Paula Gunn Allen, Gretchen Bataille, and others on Leslie Marmon Silko, autobiography, other topics, plus three course designs (e.g., "Life Stories and Native Traditions").

_____, ed. *The Sacred Hoop: Recovering the Feminine in American Indian Traditions.* Boston: Beacon Press, 1986.
A collection of essays exploring the role of women in Indian culture and literature (Leslie Marmon Silko, et al.)

Bright, William. *American Indian Linguistics and Literature.* Hawthorne, N.Y.: Mouton, 1984.
The first half of this short work focuses on "Studies in American Indian Linguistics," but part 2 ("Studies in American Indian Oral Literatures") contains a useful

overview (see chapter 5, "Literature: Written and Oral") and several applications of linguistic theory to Indian literature, both myth (chapter 7, "Coyote's Journey") and poetry (chapter 8, "Poetic Structure in Oral Narrative"). Bright's work is part of a recent scholarly effort to study Native American oral tradition as literature. (Compare Hymes, Sherzer and Woodbury, under poetry in 5C3.)

Chapman, Abraham, ed. *Literature of the American Indian: Views and Interpretations*. New York: New American Library, 1975.
This "Gathering of Indian Memories, Symbolic Contexts, and Literary Criticism" contains selections from both primary and secondary literature; "first, traditional and contemporary Indian views and interpretations of the Indian cultures, literature, and symbolism from older and recent writings"—from legends and tales, up to essays by Paula Gunn Allen, N. Scott Momaday, and Vine Deloria. Then follows "a historical sequence of older and contemporary non-Indian interpretations of Indian literature and the cultures out of which it grew by American writers and anthropologists outside the Indian cultures"—among them, Frank Boas, Constance Rourke, Mary Austin, Jorge Luis Borges, and William Bevis.

Jahner, Elaine, ed. *American Indians Today: Their Thought, Their Literature, Their Art*. Special issue of *Book Forum* 5, no. 3 (1981): 310-432.
Includes essays on literature by Paula Gunn Allen, Wendy Rose, Linda Hogan, Gerald Vizenor, Ward Churchill, and others. Also contains an interview with Leslie Marmon Silko; bibliographies.

Kroeber, Karl, ed. *Traditional American Indian Literature: Texts and Interpretations*. Lincoln: University of Nebraska Press, 1981.
A collection of essays "intended to introduce nonspecialists to traditional American Indian literatures." Includes pieces by Jarold Ramsey, Dennis Tedlock, Dell Hymes, and other scholars on American Indian myth, narrative, and poetry.

Krupat, Arnold. *Ethnocriticism: Ethnography, History, Literature*. Berkeley: University of California Press, 1991.
Krupat considers the ways in which Indians have attempted to "write back," producing an oppositional or parallel discourse to those of ethnography, history, and literature.

_____. *The Voice in the Margin: Native American Literature and the Canon*. Berkeley: University of California Press, 1989.
Theoretical discussion of canon issues (inclusivity/ exclusivity, for example) that concludes: "we will never comprehend American civilization or culture . . . until we comprehend the European component of it in historical relation to the Afro-American and the Indian, and, increasingly, in relation to those cultural others whose Otherness is nonetheless deeply American."

Lincoln, Kenneth. *Native American Renaissance.* Berkeley: University of California Press, 1983.
An interdisciplinary examination of contemporary American Indian literature, including essays on poetry, N. Scott Momaday, James Welch, and Leslie Marmon Silko.

"Multicultural Literature: Part I." *ADE Bulletin* 75 (Summer, 1983): 35-52.
This cluster contains Jarold Ramsey, "American Indian Literatures and American Literature: An Overview"; A. LaVonne Brown Ruoff, "Teaching American Indian Authors, 1772-1968"; Larry Evers, "Continuity and Change in American Indian Oral Literature"; and Ruoff, "Selected Bibliography of American Indian Literatures."

Murray, David. *Forked Tongues: Speech, Writing, and Representation in North American Indian Texts.* London: Pinter, 1991.
Sophisticated theoretical analysis shows "the complex and various ways in which the process of translation, cultural as well as linguistic, is obscured or effaced in a wide variety of texts which claim to be representing or describing Indians, and what cultural and ideological assumptions underlie such effacement." Chapters on eighteenth and nineteenth century American Indian autobiography, speeches, and so forth.

Native American Literature. Special issue of *MELUS* 12, no. 1 (Spring, 1985).
This issue includes essays on Black Elk, Leslie Marmon Silko, and James Welch, as well as an interview with N. Scott Momaday.

Ramsey, Jarold. *Reading the Fire: Essays in the Traditional Indian Literatures of the Far West.* Lincoln: University of Nebraska Press, 1983.
Three groups of essays are contained in this collection: (1) "general accountings of creation and origin myth-narratives and of one crucial mythic character (the Trickster)"; (2) "a central section consisting of four detailed 'practical' interpretations of individual narratives"; and (3) five essays on the "question of how the native literary imagination has responded to contact with Anglo culture."

Ruoff, A. LaVonne Brown. *American Indian Literature: An Introduction, Bibliographic Review, and Selected Bibliography.* New York: Modern Language Association of America, 1990.
A recent, comprehensive study of American Indian literatures. Part 1, "Introduction to American Indian Literatures," is a narrative history of more than one hundred pages. Part 2, "Bibliographic Review," is an analytical description of major primary and secondary works. Part 3, "A Selected Bibliography of American Indian Literatures," gives unannotated information for the works cited in part 2. Indispensable for any work with American Indian literature.

Scholer, Bo, ed. *Coyote Was Here: Essays on Contemporary Native American Literary and Political Mobilization*. Special issue of *The Dolphin* (University of Aaarhus, Denmark) 9 (1984).
"The essays in this anthology represent critical views on some of the themes in contemporary Native American literature" by Wendy Rose, Duane Niatum, Simon J. Ortiz, Kenneth Lincoln, Paula Gunn Allen, Joseph Bruchac, and other writers and scholars.

Swann, Brian, ed. *On the Translation of Native American Literatures*. Washington, D.C.: Smithsonian Institution Press, 1992.
Essays by Arnold Krupat, William M. Clements, John Bierhorst, Dell Hymes, Dennis Tedlock, Joel Sherzer, and eighteen other scholars. The collection is arranged as follows: an "introductory section, a largely historical overview of Native American translation; then Section Two, the largest section, devoted to North America, essays grouped by language and geography; and finally Section Three on Central and South America."

_____, ed. *Smoothing the Ground: Essays on Native American Oral Literature*. Berkeley: University of California Press, 1983.
Essays by Kenneth Lincoln, Dennis Tedlock, John Bierhorst, Karl Kroeber, Dell Hymes, Arnold Krupat, H. David Brumble, and others in four sections: "Context and Overview," "The Question of Translation and Literary Criticism," "Focus on Stories," and "Native American Culture and the 'Dominant' Culture." Part of the recent scholarly effort to systematize and enhance the study of traditional oral literatures.

Swann, Brian, and Arnold Krupat, eds. *Recovering the Word: Essays on Native American Literature*. Berkeley: University of California Press, 1987.
"In this book . . . linguists and poets, folklorists and literary theorists, anthropologists and professors of English meet on the common ground of concern for the appreciation and elucidation of Native American song and story. . . . It seems high time to bring such interdisciplinary sophistication to bear on Native American literatures." Sections on "Mythographic Presentation: Theory and Practice" (essays by Dell Hymes, Anthony Mattina, Joel Sherzer, Andrew Wiget, and others), and "Interpreting the Material: Oral and Written" (William Bright, Carter Revard, Dennis Tedlock, Paula Gunn Allen, Duane Niatum, and H. David Brumble III, among others).

Tedlock, Dennis. *The Spoken Word and the Work of Interpretation*. Philadelphia: University of Pennsylvania Press, 1983.
Sixteen chapters in sections on "Transcription and Translation," "Poetics," "Hermeneutics," and "Toward Dialogue." Many of the examples are drawn from Zuni and Mayan (Quiche) linguistic cultures.

Velie, Alan R., ed. *Four American Indian Literary Masters*. Norman: University of Oklahoma Press, 1982.
Has chapters on N. Scott Momaday, James Welch, Leslie Marmon Silko, and Gerald Vizenor.

Vizenor, Gerald, ed. *Narrative Chance: Postmodern Discourse on Native American Indian Literatures*. Albuquerque: University of New Mexico Press, 1989.
Includes contemporary critical essays by Karl Kroeber, Arnold Krupat, Alan Velie, Vizenor, and others. "The critical essays in this postmodern collection focus on translation and representation in tribal literatures, comic and tragic world views, trickster discourse," as well as on the work of N. Scott Momaday, Leslie Marmon Silko, Louise Erdrich, and other contemporary Native American authors.

Wiget, Andrew. *Native American Literature*. Boston: Twayne, 1985.
A brief, one-volume history of American Indian literatures that includes chapters on oral narrative and poetry, through the beginnings of written literature in the nineteenth century to contemporary poetry and fiction. Excellent introduction to Native American literatures.

_____, ed. *Critical Essays on Native American Literature*. Boston: G. K. Hall, 1985.
This collection has an introduction by Wiget, essays in sections on "Historical and Methodological Perspectives" (reprinted articles by Boas, Levi-Strauss, Krupat, et al.), "On Traditional Literatures," and "On Literature in English" (original essays by A. LaVonne Brown Ruoff, Dexter Fisher, and others).

See also: *Massachusetts Review* (1B1); Baker and Ruoff and Ward (3B1); "Teaching American Indian Literature" section (3B2); Elliott (4C); Chambers, "From This World" (5B1b); Anaya (7C6)

NOTES

1. "Address to the Reader," *LHUS* (New York: Macmillan, 1963), p. xvii.
2. See Harold F. Kolb's "Defining the Canon," in Ruoff and Ward, *Redefining American Literary History* (3B1), for a useful analysis of this information. The Heath Anthology is listed in 3D1.
3. Most useful recent listings of primary literature are to be found in Ruoff, *American Indian Literature* (5C5).
4. Second names denote "as told to" writers of autobiography.

Chapter 6
AFRICAN AMERICAN LITERATURE

A. A Brief Narrative History

African American literature comprises the largest single body of ethnic literature in this country. The scholarship it has generated, particularly in the last few decades, is immense. Yet the recognition of the contributions of Black writers to American literature has been relatively recent and is still clearly in progress.

In the introduction to his pioneering collection *Black Voices* in 1968, Abraham Chapman wrote that "much of the literature created by black American writers in the twentieth century is unknown to the general reading public and little known even to students of American literature." "You will search in vain in definitive up-to-date American literary histories," Chapman complained, "for some of the elementary facts about Negro American writers and writing."[1]

The change in less than a quarter century is remarkable. As even a cursory glance at the list of primary literature below will show, African American works have become standard texts in almost every age and area of American literature, and most teachers and readers recognize the centrality of Black writing to the canon of American literature. Not only are Black writers paramount in all genres, but African American forms are inextricably woven into the fabric of American literature, as the themes and ideas of Black literature are themselves at the heart of American culture.

The essay in America—to take but one example—has never had a more powerful spokesman than James Baldwin in *Nobody Knows My Name* (1961) and *The Fire Next Time* (1963), yet he was at only one end of a nonfictional spectrum stretching back through Richard Wright's *Black Boy* (1943), W. E. B. Du Bois's *The Souls of Black Folks* (1903), and Booker T. Washington's *Up From Slavery* (1901) in this century, to the classic *Narrative of the Life of Frederick Douglass* of 1845.

Likewise, students cannot discuss American poetry today without considering the contributions of Claude McKay, Langston Hughes, Robert Hayden, Gwendolyn Brooks (who won the Pulitzer Prize for poetry in 1949), Nikki Giovanni, and Sonia Sanchez. Nor can they write of the theatre without considering the contributions of Amiri Baraka (LeRoi Jones), Lorraine Hansberry, August Wilson, and Ntozake Shange in recent years.

The American novel is only the most visible example of this African American presence. It would be misleading to say that Black writers have influenced the American novel; rather, the twentieth century American novel is unthinkable without their contributions. Richard Wright's *Native Son* (1940) was one of the most powerful examples of urban realism to come out of the Depression decade; a dozen years later, Ralph Ellison produced *Invisible Man* (1952), which many critics consider the finest novel produced in the United States after World War II. The revival of the American novel since the 1960's has seen Black women writers emerge as its preeminent practitioners; Alice Walker won the Pulitzer Prize for fiction with *The Color Purple* in 1982, and Toni Morrison took the award five years later for her *Beloved* (1987). Other Black writers continue to contribute to the form as well: Ishmael Reed, Gloria Naylor, Ernest J. Gaines, Jamaica Kincaid, and a number of new and emerging novelists.

One might legitimately ask, however, why African American writers are so visibly at the forefront of all genres of American literature today. The most obvious answer is that the ideas and issues that have been at the center of Black writing almost since its beginnings have increasingly become the subjects of mainstream American writing in the twentieth century: the loss of self, the sense of entrapment within a world beyond one's control (or the feeling of being forced outside it), the search for community, and so on. Fueled by what Blyden Jackson has accurately called their "keen consciousness of color caste,"[2] Black writers in America have produced a social protest literature that many other Americans are writing and reading these days—about the loss of national community, about the fragile future, about the threatened environment. The Black experience has become—one wants to say unfortunately—the preeminent American experience.

If the themes of Black writing are at the core of American social thought, so too are its forms: the centrality of jazz and the blues in American music is one example of the ways in which indigenous Black forms have been influential on all American culture. Likewise in prose and poetry: Black writers often express a feeling for language that other writers can only emulate. Baldwin's ability to move between the vernacular and formal elegance is one example, the sermons and essays of Martin Luther King another, of this ability to work the language for all its poetry and power. Imagine American literature free of Black folk tales and spirituals; it is like imagining the American idiom without Black music or Black English. Black voices are everywhere in the American land.

In spite of this dominance, African American writers have often had a difficult relationship with mainstream American literature. In part it is what Robert Bone recognized some years ago, in his pioneering study of *The Negro Novel in America*:

> The Negro novel, like Negro life in America, is at once alike and different from the novels of white Americans. While it follows, usually after a short lag, the main historical development of the American novel, it has in addition a life of its own, which springs from the soil of a distinctive minority culture.[3]

In a study of that novel some thirty years later, Bernard Bell only confirms this view in arguing that "the Afro-American novel is not merely a branch of the Euro-American novel but also a development of the Afro-American oral tradition." Bell describes in his study how the Black novel has emerged from this "bicultural tradition—oral and literary, Eurocentric and Afrocentric."[4]

It is this bifocal view—this looking at the whole culture and yet affirming the African roots—that characterizes much of the African American contribution and underlies not a few of its difficulties. In one sense, this bifocal view characterizes all ethnic literatures—the yearning for acculturation and the simultaneous need for a separate cultural community. In that sense, the literary split is only a metaphor for the American ethnic experience itself: the constant tension between assimilation and separatism.

The difference in the African American experience is Black history. Black writers have a particular background that no other writers in America can claim (or would want to): they emerged from American history as slaves. (Alex Haley has documented this literary heritage most poignantly in his popular 1976 *Roots*.) Slavery, however, is not merely this horrible past all Americans cannot avoid; rather, slavery has become the central moral touchstone of American history, precisely as one hundred years after its end, the civil rights struggles of the 1960's became the focus of a similar issue. In both cases, the question was the same: What do freedom and democracy mean in a society that enslaves its own citizens? Put more positively, what *is* to be the relationship among all ethnic communities in America?

Black writers, in short, because of their history with slavery, have always been at or near the center of American moral discussions. They may not have more answers, but they have asked the questions more often, and more personally. All the crucial debates of the 1980's and the 1990's—about women's rights, gay rights, the rights of the poor—have as their fundamental moral basis the questions raised in any study of Black history. Black writers have been using these questions as the foundations of their art for centuries. Obviously, one cannot read African American writers today—John E. Wideman or Paule Marshall, Maya Angelou or Toni Cade Bambara—without some awareness of this history.

The most convenient division of the long history of African American literature into discrete, manageable periods is one that Blyden Jackson provides:[5]

1746-1830: The Age of Apprenticeship, which would include the early slave narratives and the poetry of Phillis Wheatley, one of America's first poets.

1830-1895: The Age of Abolitionists, which includes the bulk of the more than 6000 extant slave narratives, the first black novel (William Wells Brown's *Clotel* in 1853), and some of the most important works of black nonfiction (Frederick Douglass) and Afro-American folklore (best known, perhaps, in the Uncle Remus stories of Joel Chandler Harris).

1895-1920: The Age of the Negro Nadir, with the poetry of Paul Laurence Dunbar and James Weldon Johnson, the fiction of Charles Chesnutt, the essays and autobiographies of W. E. B. Du Bois, Booker T. Washington, and other turn-of-the-century black writers.

1920-1930: The Age of the Harlem Renaissance, the fertile period which, until recently, was overshadowed by the Lost Generation of Paris, but which saw the major writings of Jean Toomer, Claude McKay, Zora Neale Hurston, Countée Cullen, and many others.

1930-1960: The Age of Richard Wright—but also the age of Langston Hughes, Ralph Ellison, and the early James Baldwin, and, given the perspective from the 1990s, what may be seen as a transition period from the Harlem Renaissance to the second, more recent black renaissance in the arts (the accomplishments of Amiri Baraka, Gwendolyn Brooks, etc.)

1960-   : The Age of the Black Militant, an age that continues today, with the contributions of Alice Walker, Toni Morrison, and many other writers just emerging.

The secondary bibliography below reveals the great number of major studies and reference works that have appeared in the last decade to examine African American literature. There have been serious reevaluations of the whole history of African American literature, as well as important studies of individual genres and periods. This renaissance in African American scholarship, like the contributions in its creative literature, continues.

B. A Selected List of Primary Works

1. Anthologies

a. Bibliographies

Kallenbach, Jessamine S., comp. *Index to Black American Literary Anthologies.* Boston: G. K. Hall, 1979.
Designed "to aid students in locating Black American literature which has been published in collections," this resource has a detailed author index (to anthologies where individual works may be found) and a second "Title Index."

b. General Collections

Adams, William, ed. *Afro-American Authors.* Boston: Houghton Mifflin, 1972.
This collection of twenty-one major black writers, from Frederick Douglass and Paul Laurence Dunbar, through Langston Hughes, Richard Wright, and Ralph Ellison, to Amiri Baraka, was still available in paperback in 1991.

Brown, Sterling A., Arthur P. Davis, and Ulysses Lee, eds. *The Negro Caravan.* Reprint. New York: Arno, 1969.
A reprint of the classic, comprehensive volume aiming "to collect in one volume certain key literary works that have greatly influenced the thinking of American Negroes, and to a lesser degree, that of Americans as a whole."

Chapman, Abraham, ed. *Black Voices: An Anthology of Afro-American Literature.* New York: New American Library, 1968.
This popular paperback collection of mainly twentieth century Black fiction, autobiography, poetry, and literary criticism was still in print in 1991.

_____, ed. *New Black Voices: An Anthology of Contemporary Afro-American Literature.* New York: New American Library, 1972.
Also in print in 1991, this "companion volume" to *Black Voices* collects fiction, poetry, and criticism from the 1960's and early 1970's.

Davis, Arthur P., and Michael W. Peplow, eds. *The New Negro Renaissance: An Anthology.* New York: Holt, Rinehart and Winston, 1975.
This collection, which "represents the richness and diversity of the New Negro Renaissance (1910-1940)," is arranged thematically: among the themes are protest literature and the critical debate.

Emanuel, James A., and Theodore L. Gross, eds. *Dark Symphony: Negro Literature in America.* New York: Free Press, 1968.
This early, comprehensive collection has selections from Frederick Douglass and W. E. B. Du Bois through Mari Evans and LeRoi Jones.

Harper, Michael S., and Robert B. Stepto, eds. *Chant of Saints: A Gathering of Afro-American Literature, Art, and Scholarship.* Urbana: University of Illinois Press, 1979.
Originally published in the fall and winter issues of *The Massachusetts Review,* this collection contains both primary and secondary selections, including interviews with Toni Morrison, Derek Walcott, Gayl Jones, and Ralph Ellison.

Hill, Herbert, ed. *Soon, One Morning: New Writing by American Negroes, 1940-1962.* New York: Alfred A. Knopf, 1968.
Includes sections of essays, fiction, and poems. "The purpose of this book, beyond giving pleasure to the readers, is to display the range of contemporary writing by American Negroes."

Long, Richard A., and Eugenia W. Collier, eds. *Afro-American Writing: An Anthology of Prose and Poetry.* 2 vols. 2d enlarged ed. University Park: Pennsylvania State University Press, 1985.
This edition adds part 5: "The Seventies and Beyond," with selections from Toni Morrison, Maya Angelou, and other contemporary writers.

Olney, James, ed. *Afro-American Writing Today.* Baton Rouge: Louisiana State University Press, 1989.
Originally published as an anniversary issue of the *Southern Review* (Summer,

1985), this collection contains poetry, fiction, and drama, essays on Black writers, and interviews with James Baldwin and Ishmael Reed.

See also: Locke, Huggins (6C3c)

c. Collections of Plays

Bigsby, C. W. E., ed. *Three Negro Plays*. New York: Penguin, 1969.
Among the contents are *Mulatto* by Langston Hughes; *The Slave* by LeRoi Jones; and *The Sign in Sydney Brustein's Window* by Lorraine Hansberry.

Brasmer, William, and Dominick Consolo, eds. *Black Drama: An Anthology*. Columbus, Ohio: Merrill, 1970.
Includes Ossie Davis, *Purlie Victorious*; Paul Green, *Native Son*; Langston Hughes, *Mulatto*; and four other plays.

Couch, William, ed. *New Black Playwrights: An Anthology*. Baton Rouge: Louisiana State University Press, 1968.
Contains plays by Douglas Turner Ward, Adrienne Kennedy, Lonne Elder III, Ed Bullins, and William Wellington Mackey.

Harrison, Paul Carter, ed. *Kuntu Drama: Plays of the African Continuum*. New York: Grove Press, 1974.
Includes Jean Toomer, *Kabnis*; Amiri Baraka, *Great Goodness of Life: A Coon Show*.

Hatch, James V., ed. *Black Theater, U.S.A.: Forty-Five Plays by Black Americans, 1847-1974*. New York: Free Press, 1974.
Contains plays by James Baldwin (*The Amen Corner*), Amiri Baraka (*The Slave*), Ed Bullins, Langston Hughes, and others.

King, Woodie, and Ron Milner, eds. *Black Drama Anthology*. New York: Columbia University Press, 1972.
Includes Amiri Baraka, *Bloodrites*; Langston Hughes, *Mother and Child*; Ed Bullins, *The Corner*; twenty other plays.

Locke, Alain, and Montgomery Gregory, eds. *Plays of Negro Life: A Source-Book of Native American Drama*. 1927; New York: Harper & Row, 1969.
Some twenty plays, among them works by Paul Green, Eugene O'Neill, Jean Toomer, and other early twentieth century playwrights.

Oliver, Clinton F., and Stephanie Sills, eds. *Contemporary Black Drama, from 'A Raisin in the Sun' to 'No Place to Be Somebody'*. New York: Charles Scribner's Sons, 1971.
Also includes Baldwin, *Blues for Mister Charlie*; Bullins, *The Gentleman Caller*; LeRoi Jones, *Dutchman*.

Perkins, Kathy A., ed. *Black Female Playwrights: An Anthology of Plays Before 1950*. Bloomington: Indiana University Press, 1989.
Collects drama by Georgia Douglas Johnson, Mary P. Burrill, Zora Neale Hurston, Eulalie Spence, May Miller, and Marita Bonner. See the informative introduction by the editor.

Wilkerson, Margaret B., ed. *Nine Plays by Black Women*. New York: New American Library, 1986.
Collects drama from 1950 to 1985 by Beah Richards, Lorraine Hansberry, Alice Childress, Ntozake Shange, and five other playwrights.

See also: 6C1b, 6C4a

d. Collections of Poetry

Adoff, Arnold, comp. *Celebrations: A New Anthology of Black American Poetry*. Chicago: Follett, 1977.
"This anthology presents 240 poems by eighty-five Black American poets of this century . . . [and thus] the tradition and future of Black American poetry to young people of every race and background."

Burnett, Paula, ed. *The Penguin Book of Caribbean Verse in English*. New York: Penguin, 1986.
Following a long historical introduction, selections from both "The Oral Tradition" (slave songs, reggae) and "The Literary Tradition" (Claude McKay, Derek Walcott, others).

Hughes, Langston, ed. *New Negro Poets U.S.A.* Bloomington: Indiana University Press, 1964.
This important early collection contains poetry by Jay Wright, Julian Bond, LeRoi Jones, Mari Evans, Audre Lorde, and dozens of other Black poets.

King, Woodie, ed. *Black Spirits: A Festival of New Black Poets in America*. New York: Random House, 1972.
Poems by Amiri Baraka, Mari Evans, Nikki Giovanni, Don L. Lee, and twenty-seven other writers.

_____, ed. *The Forerunners: Black Poets in America*. Washington, D.C.: Howard University Press, 1981.
Introduction by Addison Gayle, Jr., selections from sixteen twentieth century poets.

Sherman, Joan R. *Collected Black Women's Poetry*. 4 vols. New York: Oxford University Press, 1988.
Part of the Schomburg Library of Nineteenth-Century Black Women Writers, each volume contains a general foreword, separate introduction, and poetry reprinted from original materials.

Stetson, Erlene, ed. *Black Sister: Poetry by Black American Women, 1746-1980*. Bloomington: Indiana University Press, 1981.
Works of almost sixty writers are divided into sections on "Eighteenth- and Nineteenth-Century Poets" and "Twentieth-Century Poets."

See also: 6C1c, 6C4b

e. Collections of Fiction

Hughes, Langston, ed. *The Best Short Stories by Negro Writers: An Anthology from 1899 to the Present*. Boston: Little, Brown, 1967.
Almost fifty stories—by Richard Wright, Ralph Ellison, Ernest J. Gaines, Alice Walker, and others—in a collection still available in a paperback edition in 1991.

King, Woodie, ed. *Black Short Story Anthology*. New York: Columbia University Press, 1972.
Includes an introduction by John Oliver Killens and twenty-eight examples of the genre, including stories by Nikki Giovanni, Ed Bullins, William Melvin Kelley, and Ernest Gaines.

McMillan, Terry, ed. *Breaking Ice: An Anthology of Contemporary African-American Fiction*. New York: Viking Press, 1990.
Recent stories by Samuel R. Delaney, Ernest Gaines, Gayl Jones, William Melvin Kelley, James Alan McPherson, Paule Marshall, Gloria Naylor, and fifty other writers.

Washington, Mary Helen, ed. *Memory of Kin: Stories About Family by Black Writers*. New York: Doubleday, 1991.
Stories by Ernest J. Gaines, Alice Walker, Toni Cade Bambara, Charles Chesnutt, Jamaica Kincaid, and others, followed by short commentaries.

See also: 6C1d, 6C4c

f. Autobiographies (including slave narratives)

Bontemps, Arna, ed. *Great Slave Narratives*. Boston: Beacon Press, 1969.
This early effort to rescue this important body of literature includes an introduction by Bontemps, narratives of Olaudah Equiano, James W. C. Pennington, and William and Ellen Craft.

Gates, Henry Louis, Jr., ed. *Bearing Witness: Selections from African-American Autobiography in the Twentieth Century*. New York: Pantheon, 1991.
A collection of autobiographical statements from Fannie Barrier Williams's *A Northern Negro's Autobiography* (1904) to Itabari Njeri's *Every Good-Bye Ain't Gone* (1990).

See also: Gates, Shockley (6B1h); 6C1e, 6C3a

g. Collections of Criticism

Gayle, Addison, Jr. *The Black Aesthetic*. New York: Doubleday, 1971.
This collection reflects the rise of 1960's Black cultural nationalism in sections on theory, music, poetry, drama, and fiction. The Black aesthetic, as Gayle explains it in his introduction, "is a corrective—a means of helping black people out of the polluted mainstream of Americanism, and offering logical, reasoned arguments as to why she should not desire to join the ranks of a Norman Mailer or a William Styron."

See also: 6C4d2

h. Collections of Writings by Black Women

Ammons, Elizabeth, ed. *Short Fiction by Black Women, 1900-1920*. New York: Oxford University Press, 1991.
Contained in this volume in the Schomburg Library of Nineteenth-Century Black Women Writers is fiction originally published in the monthlies *Colored American Magazine* (1900-1909) and the *Crisis* during its first decade (1910-1920). Includes stories by Pauline E. Hopkins, Jessie Redmon Fauset, and Alice Dunbar-Nelson.

Baraka, Amiri, and Amina Baraka, eds. *Confirmation: An Anthology of African American Women*. New York: William Morrow, 1983.
Fifty contemporary contributors collected in a volume whose purpose "is to draw attention to the existence and excellence of black women writers."

Gates, Henry Louis, Jr., ed. *Collected Black Women's Narratives*. New York: Oxford University Press, 1988.
Another volume in the series, The Schomburg Library of Nineteenth-Century Black Women Writers, this collection contains autobiographical narratives by Nancy Prince, Louisa Picquet, Bethany Veney, and Susie King Taylor.

Honey, Maureen, ed. *Shadowed Dreams: Women's Poetry of the Harlem Renaissance.* New Brunswick, N.J.: Rutgers University Press, 1989.
Four groups of poems—on themes of protest, heritage, love and passion, and nature—by known and unknown Black poets of the 1920's.

Shockley, Ann Allen, ed. *Afro-American Women Writers, 1746-1933: An Anthology and Critical Guide*. Boston: G. K. Hall, 1988.
This collection "seeks to record the lives and works of Afro-American women writers from the eighteenth to the early twentieth century," and thus to document "black women's contributions to Afro-American literature in particular and to American literature in general."

Washington, Mary Helen, ed. *Black-Eyed Susans/Midnight Birds: Stories By and About Black Women*. Garden City, N.Y.: Doubleday, 1990.
About half the contents are reprinted from *Midnight Birds*. The balance are new stories by Paule Marshall, Gwendolyn Brooks, others.

_____, ed. *Invented Lives: Narratives of Black Women, 1860-1960*. Garden City, N.Y.: Doubleday, 1987.
Contains narratives by Harriet Jacobs, Nella Larsen, Zora Neale Hurston, Ann Petry, Gwendolyn Brooks, and five other women.

_____, ed. *Midnight Birds: Stories by Contemporary Black Women Writers*. Garden City, N.Y.: Doubleday, 1980.
Fifteen stories by Alice Walker, Ntozake Shange, Gayl Jones, Toni Morrison, Toni Cade Bambara, and others.

See also: Perkins, Wilkerson (6B1c); 6C1f, 6C5

2. Individual Writers[6]

Albert, Octavia V. Rogers
The House of Bondage: Or, Charlotte Brooks and Other Slaves (fiction, 1890)

Andrews, Raymond
Appalachee Red (fiction, 1978)

Baby Sweet's (fiction, 1983)
Rosiebelle Lee Wildcat Tennessee (fiction, 1980)

Angelou, Maya
All God's Children Need Traveling Shoes (autobiography, 1986)
Gather Together in My Name (autobiography, 1974)
The Heart of a Woman (autobiography, 1981)
I Know Why the Caged Bird Sings (autobiography, 1969)
Singin' and Swingin' and Gettin' Merry like Christmas (autobiography, 1976)

Attaway, William
Blood on the Forge (fiction, 1941)
Let Me Breathe Thunder (fiction, 1939)

Aubert, Alvin
South Louisiana: New and Selected Poems (1985)

Baldwin, James
The Amen Corner (drama, 1954)
Another Country (fiction, 1962)
Blues for Mister Charlie (drama, 1964)
The Fire Next Time (nonfiction, 1963)
Giovanni's Room (fiction, 1956)
Going to Meet the Man (short fiction, 1965)
Go Tell It on the Mountain (fiction, 1953)
If Beale Street Could Talk (fiction, 1974)
Just Above My Head (fiction, 1979)
Nobody Knows My Name (nonfiction, 1961)
Notes of a Native Son (nonfiction, 1955)
The Price of the Ticket: Collected Nonfiction, 1948-1985 (1985)
Tell Me How Long the Train's Been Gone (fiction, 1986)

Bambara, Toni Cade
Gorilla, My Love (short fiction, 1972)
The Salt Eaters (fiction, 1980)
The Sea Birds Are Still Alive (short fiction, 1977)

Baraka, Imamu Amiri (LeRoi Jones)
The Autobiography of LeRoi Jones/Amiri Baraka (1984)
Black Magic: Sabotage, Target Study, Black Art: Collected Poetry, 1961-67 (1969)
Blues People: Negro Music in White America (nonfiction, 1980)
Daggers and Javelins: Essays, 1974-1979 (1984)

Dutchman and The Slave (drama, 1964)
Four Black Revolutionary Plays: All Praises to the Black Man (1969)
Preface to a Twenty-Volume Suicide Note (poetry, 1961)
Selected Plays and Prose of Amiri Baraka/LeRoi Jones (drama, fiction, nonfiction, 1979)
The System of Dante's Hell (fiction, 1965)
Tales (short fiction, 1967)

Beckham, Barry
Runner Mack (fiction, 1972)

Bennett, Hal
A Wilderness of Vines (fiction, 1966)

Bibb, Henry
Narrative of the Life and Adventures of Henry Bibb, an American Slave (autobiography, 1849)

Bonner, Marita
Frye Street & Environs: The Collected Works of Marita Bonner (mixed genres, 1987)

Bontemps, Arna
Black Thunder (fiction, 1936)
The Old South (short fiction, 1973)

Bradley, David
The Chaneysville Incident (fiction, 1981)
South Street (fiction, 1975)

Brooks, Gwendolyn
Blacks (poetry, fiction, nonfiction, 1987)
Report from Part One (autobiography, 1972)
Selected Poems (1963)
The World of Gwendolyn Brooks (poetry and fiction, 1971)

Brown, Claude
The Children of Ham (fiction, 1976)
Manchild in the Promised Land (autobiography, 1965)

Brown, Hallie Q.
Homespun Heroines and Other Women of Distinction (biography, 1926)

Brown, Sterling A.
The Collected Poems of Sterling A. Brown (1980)

Brown, Wesley
Boogie Woogie and Booker T (drama, 1987)
Tragic Magic (fiction, 1978)

Brown, William Wells
Clotel; Or, The President's Daughter (fiction, 1853)
Memoir of William Wells Brown, an American Bondman (autobiography, 1859)
Narrative of William Wells Brown, a Fugitive Slave (autobiography, 1847)
The Rising Sun: Or, The Antecedents and Advancement of the Colored Race (nonfiction, 1873)
Three Years in Europe: Or, Places I Have Seen and People I Have Met (autobiography, 1852)

Bullins, Ed
Five Plays (1968)

Butler, Octavia
Clay's Ark (fiction, 1984)
Dawn (fiction, 1987)
Kindred (fiction, 1979)
Mind of My Mind (fiction, 1977)
Patternmaster (fiction, 1976)
Survivor (fiction, 1978)
Wild Seed (fiction, 1980)

Cain, George
Blueschild Baby (fiction, 1970)

Campbell, Israel
An Autobiography (1861)

Chase-Riboud, Barbara
Sally Hemings (fiction, 1979)

Cheatwood, Kiarri T. H.
Bloodstorm: Five Books of Poems and Docupoems (1986)
Elegies for Patrice: A Lyrical Historical Remembrance (poetry, 1984)

Chesnutt, Charles W.
The Conjure Woman (short fiction, 1899)

The House Behind the Cedars (fiction, 1900)
The Marrow of Tradition (fiction, 1901)
The Short Fiction of Charles W. Chesnutt (1974)
The Wife of His Youth and Other Stories of the Color Line (1899)

Childress, Alice
  A Hero Ain't Nothin' but a Sandwich (fiction, 1977)
  Like One of the Family (fiction, 1956)

Cleaver, Eldridge
  Soul on Ice (autobiography, 1968)

Clifton, Lucille
  An Ordinary Woman (poetry, 1974)
  Two-Headed Woman (poetry, 1980)

Coleman, Wanda
  Heavy Daughter Blues: Poems and Stories, 1968-1986 (1987)
  Imagoes (poetry, 1983)
  Mad Dog Black Lady (poetry, 1979)

Colter, Cyrus
  The Amoralists & Other Tales (short fiction, 1988)
  The Beach Umbrella (short fiction, 1970)
  A Chocolate Soldier (fiction, 1988)
  The Hippodrome (fiction, 1973)
  Night Studies (fiction, 1979)
  The Rivers of Eros (fiction, 1972)

Cooper, Anna Julia
  A Voice from the South (nonfiction, 1892)

Cortez, Jayne
  Coagulations: New and Selected Poems (1984)
  Mouth on Paper (poetry, 1977)

Cullen, Countée
  One Way to Heaven (fiction, 1932)
  On These I Stand: An Anthology of the Best Poems of Countée Cullen (1947)

Danner, Margaret
  Iron Lace (poetry, 1968)

Davis, Angela
Angela Davis: An Autobiography (1974)

Davis, George
Coming Home (fiction, 1971)

Davis, Ossie
Purlie Victorious: A Comedy in Three Acts (1961)

Davis, Sammy, Jr., with Jane Boyar and Burt Boyar
Yes, I Can: The Story of Sammy Davis, Jr. (1965)

Delany, Martin R.
Blake: Or, The Huts of America (fiction, 1859-1861)

Delaney, Samuel R.
Dahlgren (fiction, 1975)
Driftglass (fiction, 1971)
The Motion of Light in Water: Sex and Science Fiction Writing in the East Village, 1957-1964 (autobiography, 1988)
Neveryona: Or, The Tale of Signs and Cities (fiction, 1983)
Nova (fiction, 1968)
Stars in My Pocket Like Grains of Sand (fiction, 1984)
The Tales of Neveryon (fiction, 1979)
Triton (fiction, 1976)

Demby, William
Beetlecreek (fiction, 1950)
The Catacombs (fiction, 1965)
Love Story Black (fiction, 1978)

Dent, Tom
Blue Lights and River Songs (poetry, 1982)

Dodson, Owen
The Confession Stone: Song Cycles (poetry, 1970)

Douglass, Frederick
Life and Times of Frederick Douglass: Written by Himself (autobiography, 1881)
The Life and Writings of Frederick Douglass (fiction and nonfiction, 5 vols., 1950)
My Bondage and My Freedom (autobiography, 1855)
The Narrative and Selected Writings (fiction and nonfiction, 1983)

Dove, Rita
   Fifth Sunday (fiction, 1985)
   Museum Poems (1983)
   Thomas and Beulah (poetry, 1986)
   The Yellow House on the Corner (poetry, 1980)

Du Bois, W. E. B.
   Black Folk Then and Now: An Essay in the History and Sociology of the Negro Race (nonfiction, 1939)
   Black Reconstruction in America (nonfiction, 1935)
   The Complete Published Works of W. E. B. Du Bois (1973-   )
   Dark Princess (fiction, 1928)
   Darkwater: Voices from Within the Veil (mixed genres, 1920)
   Dusk of Dawn: An Essay Toward an Autobiography of a Race Concept (nonfiction, 1940)
   The Quest of the Silver Fleece (fiction, 1911)
   The Souls of Black Folk: Essays and Sketches (fiction and nonfiction, 1903)

Dumas, Henry
   Ark of Bones and Other Stories (1970)
   Goodbye Sweetwater: New and Selected Stories (1988)
   Jonah and the Green Stone (fiction, 1976)
   Play Ebony Play Ivory (poetry, 1974)
   Rope of Wind and Other Stories (1979)

Dunbar, Paul Laurence
   The Complete Poems of Paul Laurence Dunbar (1913)
   The Sport of the Gods (fiction, 1902)
   The Strength of Gideon and Other Stories (1969)

Dunbar-Nelson, Alice
   An Alice Dunbar-Nelson Reader (poetry and prose, 1979)
   Give Us Each Day: The Diary of Alice Dunbar-Nelson (1984)
   The Works of Alice Dunbar-Nelson (fiction, nonfiction, poetry, drama, 3 vols., 1988)

Edwards, Harry
   The Struggle That Must Be: An Autobiography (1980)

Edwards, Junius
   If We Must Die (fiction, 1984)

Elder, Lonne, III
Ceremonies in Dark Old Men (drama, 1969)

Ellison, Ralph
Going to the Territory (nonfiction, 1986)
Invisible Man (fiction, 1952)
Shadow and Act (nonfiction 1964)

Equiano, Olaudah
The Interesting Narrative of the Life of Oloudah Equiano, or Gustavus Vassa, the African (autobiography, 1789)

Evans, Mari
I Am a Black Woman (poetry, 1970)
Nightstar, 1973-1978 (poetry, 1981)

Everett, Percival
Suder (fiction, 1983)
The Weather and Women Treat Me Fair (fiction, 1987)

Fabio, Sarah Webster
A Mirror: A Soul (poetry, 1969)
Rainbow Signs (poetry, 1974)

Farmer, James
Lay Bare the Heart: An Autobiography of the Civil Rights Movement (1985)

Fauset, Jessie Redmon
The Chinaberry Tree (fiction, 1931)
Plum Bun: A Novel Without a Moral (1929)
There Is Confusion (fiction, 1924)

Fields, Mamie Garvin, with Karen Fields
Lemon Swamp and Other Places: A Carolina Memoir (autobiography, 1983)

Fisher, Rudolph
The Walls of Jericho (fiction, 1928)

Flipper, Henry Ossian
The Colored Cadet at West Point (autobiography, 1878)

Forrest, Leon
The Bloodworth Orphans (fiction, 1977)

There Is a Tree More Ancient Than Eden (fiction, 1973)
Two Wings to Veil My Face (fiction, 1983)

Fuller, Charles
  A Soldier's Play (drama, 1981)

Gaines, Ernest J.
  The Autobiography of Miss Jane Pittman (fiction, 1971)
  Bloodline (short fiction, 1968)
  Catherine Carmier (fiction, 1964)
  A Gathering of Old Men (fiction, 1983)
  In My Father's House (fiction, 1978)
  Of Love and Dust (fiction, 1967)

Gibson, Althea
  I Always Wanted to Be Somebody (autobiography, 1958)

Giovanni, Nikki
  Black Feeling, Black Talk (poetry, 1968)
  Gemini: An Extended Autobiographical Statement on My First Twenty-five Years of Being a Black Poet (1971)

Gordone, Charles
  No Place to Be Somebody: A Black Comedy in Three Acts (drama, 1969)

Greenlee, Sam
  The Spook Who Sat by the Door (fiction, 1969)

Griggs, Sutton E.
  Imperium in Imperio (fiction, 1899)

Grimke, Charlotte Forten
  The Journal of Charlotte Forten: A Free Negro in the Slave Era (autobiography, 1953)
  The Journals of Charlotte Forten Grimke (autobiography, 1988)

[Grosvenor], Verta Mae
  Vibration Cooking: Or, The Travel Notes of a Geechee Girl (autobiography, 1970)

Guy, Rosa
  Bird at My Window (fiction, 1966)
  The Disappearance (fiction, 1979)

Edith Jackson (fiction, 1978)
The Friends (fiction, 1973)
A Measure of Time (fiction, 1983)
My Love, My Love: Or, The Peasant Girl (fiction, 1985)
Ruby (fiction, 1976)

Haley, Alex
Roots (autobiography-fiction, 1976)

Hammon, Briton
A Narrative of the Uncommon Sufferings and Surprizing Deliverance of Briton Hammon, a Negro Man (autobiography, 1760)

Hansberry, Lorraine
The Collected Last Plays (1983)
A Raisin in the Sun (drama, 1959)

Harper, Frances Ellen Watkins
Complete Poems (1988)
Iola Leroy: Or, Shadows Uplifted (fiction, 1892)

Harper, Michael S.
Dear John, Dear Coltrane (poetry, 1970)
Healing Song for the Inner Ear (poetry, 1984)
Images of Kin: New and Selected Poems (1977)

Hayden, Robert E.
Collected Poems (1985)
Selected Poems (1966)

Henderson, George Wylie
Ollie Miss (fiction, 1935)

Henry, George
Life of George Henry. Together with a Brief History of the Colored People in America (1894)

Herndon, Angelo
Let Me Live (autobiography, 1937)

Himes, Chester
Cotton Comes to Harlem (fiction, 1965)
If He Hollers Let Him Go (fiction, 1945)

Lonely Crusade (fiction, 1947)
My Life of Absurdity (autobiography, 1976)
The Quality of Hurt (autobiography, 1972)

Holliday, Billie, with William Dufty
Lady Sings the Blues (autobiography, 1956)

Hopkins, Pauline E.
Contending Forces: A Romance Illustrative of Negro Life North and South (fiction, 1900)
The Magazine Novels of Pauline Hopkins (1901-1903)

Hughes, Langston
The Best of Simple (short fiction, 1961)
The Big Sea (autobiography, 1940)
Five Plays (1963)
Good Morning, Revolution: Uncollected Social Protest Writings (1973)
I Wonder as I Wander: An Autobiographical Journey (1956)
The Langston Hughes Reader (poetry, fiction, nonfiction, 1958)
Not Without Laughter (fiction, 1930)
The Selected Poems of Langston Hughes (1959)
Simple Speaks His Mind (short fiction, 1950)
Simple's Uncle Sam (short fiction, 1965)
Something in Common and Other Stories (1963)
The Ways of White Folks (short fiction, 1934)

Hunter, Jane Edna
A Nickel and a Prayer (autobiography, 1940)

Hunter, Kristin
God Bless the Child (fiction 1964)

Hurston, Zora Neale
Dust Tracks on a Road: An Autobiography (1942)
I Love Myself When I Am Laughing . . . : A Zora Neale Hurston Reader (autobiography, fiction, nonfiction, 1979)
Jonah's Gourd Vine (fiction, 1934)
Moses, Man of the Mountain (fiction, 1939)
The Sanctified Church (nonfiction, 1981)
Spunk: The Selected Short Stories of Zora Neale Hurston (1985)
Tell My Horse (nonfiction, 1938)
Their Eyes Were Watching God (fiction, 1937)

Jackson, Angela
 Solo in the Boxcar Third Floor E (poetry, 1981)
 VooDoo/Love Magic (poetry, 1974)

Jackson, George
 Soledad Brother: The Prison Letters of George Jackson (1970)

Jacobs, Harriet A. Brent
 Incidents in the Life of a Slave Girl, Written by Herself (Linda Brent) (autobiography, 1861)

Jeffers, Lance
 My Blackness Is the Beauty of This Land (poetry, 1970)
 O Africa, Where I Baked My Bread (poetry, 1977)
 Witherspoon (fiction, 1983)

Johnson, Amelia
 Clarence and Corinne: Or, God's Way (fiction, 1890)
 The Hazeley Family (fiction, 1894)

Johnson, Charles R.
 Faith and the Good Thing (fiction, 1974)
 Oxherding Tale (fiction, 1982)
 The Sorcerer's Apprentice: Tales and Conjurations (short fiction, 1986)

Johnson, James Weldon
 Along This Way: The Autobiography of James Weldon Johnson (1933)
 The Autobiography of an Ex-Coloured Man (1912)
 Black Manhattan (nonfiction, 1972)
 God's Trombones: Seven Negro Sermons in Verse (1927)

Jones, Gayl
 Corregidora (fiction, 1975)
 Eva's Man (fiction, 1976)
 Song for Anninho (poetry, 1981)
 White Rat (short fiction, 1977)
 Xarque and Other Poems (1985)

Jordan, Barbara, and Shelby Hearon
 Barbara Jordan: A Self-Portrait (autobiography, 1979)

Jordan, June
 Civil Wars (nonfiction, 1981)

His Own Where (fiction, 1971)
Living Room: New Poems (1985)
On Call: Poetical Essays (nonfiction, 1985)
Passion: New Poems, 1977-1980 (1980)
Things That I Do in the Dark: Selected Poetry (1977)

Kaufman, Bob
The Ancient Rain: Poems 1956-78 (1981)
Golden Sardine (poetry, 1967)
Solitudes Crowded with Loneliness (poetry, 1965)

Keckley, Elizabeth
Behind the Scenes: Or, Thirty Years a Slave and Four Years in the White House
(autobiography, 1868)

Kelley, William Melvin
Dancers on the Shore (fiction, 1964)
dem (fiction, 1967)

Kelley-Hawkins, Emma D.
Four Girls at Cottage City (fiction, 1898)
Megda (fiction, 1891)

Kennedy, Adrienne
Adrienne Kennedy in One Act (drama, 1988)

Killens, John O.
And Then We Heard the Thunder (fiction, 1963)
The Cotillian: Or, One Good Bull Is Half the Herd (fiction, 1971)
'Sippi (fiction, 1967)
Youngblood (fiction, 1954)

Kincaid, Jamaica
Annie John (fiction, 1985)
Lucy (fiction, 1991)

King, Coretta Scott
My Life with Martin Luther King, Jr. (autobiography, 1969)

King, Martin Luther, Jr.
Strength to Love (nonfiction, 1963)
Stride toward Freedom: The Montgomery Story (nonfiction, 1958)

Why We Cant't Wait (nonfiction, 1964)
The Words of Martin Luther King, Jr. (nonfiction, 1983)

Knight, Ethridge
Born of a Woman: New and Selected Poems (1980)
The Essential Ethridge Knight (poetry)

Kounyakaa, Yusef
Copacetic (poetry, 1984)
Dien Cai Dau (poetry, 1988)

Lacy, Leslie Alexander
The Rise and Fall of a Proper Negro (autobiography, 1842)

Lane, Lunsford
Narrative of Lunsford Lane, Published by Himself (1842)

Lane, Pinkie Gordon
I Never Scream: New and Selected Poems (1985)

Langston, John Mercer
From the Virginia Plantation to the National Capitol: Or, the First and Only Negro Representative in Congress from the Old Dominion (autobiography, 1894)

Larison, Cornelius W.
Sylvia Dubois: A Biografy of the Slav Who Whipt Her Mistres and Gand Her Fredom (autobiography, 1883)

Larsen, Nella
Passing (fiction, 1929)
Quicksand (fiction, 1928)

Lee, Andrea
Russian Journal (autobiography, 1981)
Sarah Phillips (fiction, 1984)

Lee, Jarena
The Life and Religious Experiences of Jarena Lee, a Coloured Lady (1836)

Lester, Julius
Do Lord Remember Me (fiction, 1984)

Lincoln, C. Eric
  The Avenue, Clayton City (fiction, 1988)

Locke, Alain
  The Critical Temper of Alain Locke: A Selection of His Essays on Art and Culture
  (nonfiction, 1983)

Loguen, Jermain W.
  The Rev. J. W. Loguen, as a Slave and as a Freeman (autobiography, 1859)

Lorde, Audre
  The Black Unicorn (poetry, 1978)
  A Burst of Light: Essays (1988)
  The Cancer Journals (autobiography, 1980)
  Chosen Poems, Old and New (1982)
  Sister Outsider: Essays and Speeches (nonfiction, 1984)
  Zami: A New Spelling of My Name (autobiography, 1982)

Madhubuti, Haki (Don L. Lee)
  Black Pride (poetry, 1968)
  Directionscore: Selected and New Poems (1971)
  Don't Cry, Scream (poetry, 1969)
  Earthquakes and Sunrise Missions (nonfiction and poetry, 1984)
  Killing Memory: Seeking Ancestors (poetry, 1987)
  We Walk the Way of the New World (poetry, 1970)

Magee, J. H.
  The Night of Affliction and the Morning of Recovery: An Autobiography (1873)

Major, Clarence
  All-Night Visitors (fiction, 1969)
  My Amputations (fiction, 1986)
  No (fiction, 1973)
  Painted Turtle: Woman with Guitar (fiction, 1988)
  Reflex and Bone Structure (fiction, 1975)
  Such Was the Season (fiction, 1987)
  The Syncopated Cakewalk (poetry, 1974)

Malcolm X, with Alex Haley
  The Autobiography of Malcolm X (1965)

Marrant, John
  A Narrative of the Lord's Wonderful Dealings with John Marrant, a Black (autobiography, 1785)

Marshall, Paule
  Brown Girl, Brownstones (fiction, 1959)
  The Chosen Place, the Timeless People (fiction, 1969)
  Daughters (fiction, 1991)
  Praisesong for the Widow (fiction, 1983)
  Reena and Other Stories (1984)
  Soul Clap Hands and Sing (short fiction, 1961)

Mayfield, Julian
  The Hit (fiction, 1957)
  The Long Night (fiction, 1958)

McKay, Claude
  Banana Bottom (fiction, 1933)
  Banjo: A Story Without a Plot (fiction, 1929)
  Home to Harlem (fiction, 1928)
  A Long Way from Home (autobiography, 1937)
  The Passion of Claude McKay: Selected Poetry and Prose, 1912-1948 (1973)
  Selected Poems (1953)

McPherson, James A.
  Elbow Room (short fiction, 1977)
  Hue and Cry (short fiction, 1969)

Meriwether, Louise
  Daddy Was a Number Runner (fiction, 1970)

Miller, E. Ethelbert
  Season of Hunger/Cry of Rain: Poems, 1975-1980 (1982)
  Where Are the Love Poems for Dictators? (poetry, 1986)

Millican, Arthenia Bates
  Seeds Beneath the Snow: Vignettes from the South (short fiction, 1969)

Moody, Anne
  Coming of Age in Mississippi (autobiography, 1968)

Moore, Archie, and Leonard B. Pearl
  Any Boy Can: The Archie Moore Story (1971)

Morrison, Toni
  Beloved (fiction, 1987)
  The Bluest Eye (fiction, 1970)
  Jazz (fiction, 1992)
  Song of Solomon (fiction, 1977)
  Sula (fiction, 1973)
  Tar Baby (fiction, 1978)

Morrow, E. Frederic
  Forty Years a Guinea Pig: A Black Man's View from the Top (autobiography, 1980)

Mossell, Gertrude E. H. Bustill (Mrs. N. F.)
  The Work of the Afro-American Woman (nonfiction, 1894)

Motley, Willard
  Knock on Any Door (fiction, 1947)

Murray, Albert
  Train Whistle Guitar (fiction, 1974)

Naylor, Gloria
  Linden Hills (fiction, 1985)
  Mama Day (fiction, 1988)
  The Women of Brewster Place (fiction, 1982)

Neal, Larry
  Hoodoo Hollerin' Bebop Ghosts (poetry, 1974)

Northup, Solomon
  Twelve Years a Slave (autobiography, 1853)

Osbey, Brenda Marie
  Ceremony for Minneconjoux: Poems (1983)
  In These Houses (poetry, 1987)

Parks, Gordon
  A Choice of Weapons (autobiography, 1966)
  The Learning Tree (fiction, 1963)

Pennington, James W. C.
  The Fugitive Blacksmith: Or, Events in the History of James W. C. Pennington (autobiography, 1850)

Perry, Richard
   Montgomery's Children (fiction, 1984)

Petry, Ann
   Miss Muriel and Other Stories (1971)
   The Narrows (fiction, 1953)
   The Street (fiction, 1946)

Phillips, Jane
   Mojo Hand: An Orphic Tale (fiction, 1966)

Plato, Ann
   Essays, Including Biographies and Miscellaneous Pieces, in Prose and Poetry
   (1841)

Plumpp, Sterling D.
   Black Rituals (nonfiction, 1972)
   Blues: The Story Always Untold (poetry, 1989)
   Clinton (poetry, 1976)
   The Mojo Hands Call, I Must Go (poetry, 1982)
   Steps to Break the Circle (poetry, 1974)

Polite, Carlene Hatcher
   The Flagellants (fiction, 1967)

Prince, Mary
   The History of Mary Prince (autobiography, 1831)

Prince, Nancy Gardener
   A Narrative of the Life and Travels of Mrs. Nancy Prince (1850)

Randall, Dudley
   Cities Burning (poetry, 1968)
   More to Remember: Poems of Four Decades (1971)

Randolph, Peter
   From Slave Cabin to the Pulpit: The Autobiography of Rev. Peter Randolph, the
   Southern Question Illustrated and Sketches of Slave Life (1893)

Redding, J. Sanders
   No Day of Triumph (autobiography, 1942)
   Stranger and Alone (fiction, 1950)

Reed, Ishmael
 Flight to Canada (fiction, 1976)
 The Freelance Pallbearers (fiction, 1967)
 God Made Alaska for the Indians: Selected Essays (1982)
 The Last Day of Louisiana Red (fiction, 1974)
 Mumbo Jumbo (fiction, 1972)
 New and Collected Poems (1988)
 Reckless Eyeballing (fiction, 1986)
 Shrovetide in Old New Orleans (nonfiction, 1978)
 The Terrible Threes (fiction, 1989)
 The Terrible Twos (fiction, 1983)
 Writin' Is Fightin': Thirty-Seven Years of Boxing on Paper (nonfiction, 1988)
 Yellow Back Radio Broke-Down (fiction, 1969)

Reeves, Donald
 Notes of a Processed Brother (autobiography, 1971)

Rodgers, Carolyn
 The Heart as Ever Green: Poems (1978)
 How I Got Ovah: New and Selected Poems (1976)

Sanchez, Sonia
 Homecoming: Poems (1970)
 Homegirls and Handgrenades (nonfiction and poetry, 1984)
 It's a New Day: Poems for Young Brothas and Sistuhs (1971)
 I've Been a Woman: New and Selected Poems (1978)
 We a baddDDD People (poetry, 1971)

Schuyler, George
 Black No More (fiction, 1931)

Seacole, Mary
 Wonderful Adventures of Mrs. Seacole in Many Lands (autobiography, 1857)

Shange, Ntozake
 Betsey Brown (fiction, 1985)
 For Colored Girls Who Have Considered Suicide When the Rainbow Is Enuf: A Choreopoem (drama, 1977)
 Nappy Edges (poetry, 1978)
 Ridin' the Moon in Texas: Word Paintings (mixed genres, 1987)
 Sassafrass, Cypress and Indigo (fiction, 1976)

Smith, Amanda
An Autobiography: The Story of the Lord's Dealings with Mrs. Amanda Smith the Colored Evangaelist (1893)

Smith, William Gardner
Last of the Conquerors (fiction, 1948)

Stewart, Maria W.
Maria W. Stewart, America's First Black Political Writer: Essays and Speeches (1987)
Productions of Mrs. Maria W. Stewart (autobiography, 1835)

Terrell, Mary Church
A Colored Woman in a White World (autobiography, 1940)

Thomas, Lorenz
The Bathers (poetry, 1981)
Chances Are Few (poetry, 1979)

Thurman, Wallace
The Blacker the Berry (fiction, 1929)
Infants of the Spring (fiction, 1932)

Tolson, Melvin B.
A Gallery of Harlem Portraits (poetry, 1979)
Harlem Gallery (poetry, 1965)

Toomer, Jean
Cane (fiction, poetry, 1923)
The Collected Poems of Jean Toomer (1988)
The Wayward and the Seeking: A Collection of Writings by Jean Toomer (mixed genres, 1980)

Van Dyke, Henry
Ladies of the Rachmaninoff Eyes (fiction, 1965)

Walker, Alice
The Color Purple (fiction, 1982)
Good Night, Willie Lee, I'll See You in the Morning: Poems (1979)
Horses Make a Landscape More Beautiful: Poems (1984)
In Love and Trouble: Stories of Black Women (1967)
In Search of Our Mothers' Gardens: Womanist Prose (nonfiction, 1983)
Living by the Word: Selected Writings, 1973-1987 (mixed genres, 1988)

Meridian (fiction, 1976)
Possessing the Secret of Joy (fiction, 1992)
Once: Poems (1968)
Revolutionary Petunias and Other Poems (1973)
The Temple of My Familiar (fiction, 1989)
The Third Life of Grange Copeland (fiction, 1970)
You Can't Keep a Good Woman Down: Stories (1981)

Walker, Margaret
For My People (poetry, 1942)
"How I Wrote 'Jubilee'" and Other Essays on Life and Literature (autobiography, nonfiction, 1989)
Jubilee (fiction, 1966)
Prophets for a New Day (poetry, 1970)

Washington, Booker T.
Up from Slavery: An Autobiography (1901)

Wells, Ida B.
Crusade for Justice: The Autobiography of Ida B. Wells (1970)

West, Dorothy
The Living Is Easy (fiction, 1948)

Wheatley, Phillis
The Collected Works of Phillis Wheatley (poetry and nonfiction, 1988)
The Poems of Phillis Wheatley (1966)

Wideman, John E.
Brothers and Keepers (autobiography, 1984)
Fever: Twelve Stories (1989)
A Glance Away (fiction, 1967)
The Homewood Trilogy (fiction, 1985)
Hurry Home (fiction, 1970)
The Lynchers (fiction, 1973)
Reuben (fiction, 1987)

Wilkins, Roy, with Tom Mathews
Standing Fast: The Autobiography of Roy Wilkins (1982)

Williams, John A.
Captain Blackman (fiction, 1972)
!Click Song (fiction, 1982)

Jacob's Ladder (fiction, 1987)
The Junior Bachelor Society (fiction, 1976)
The King God Didn't Save: Reflections on the Life of Martin Luther King, Jr.
(nonfiction, 1970)
The Man Who Cried I Am (fiction, 1967)
Mothersill and the Foxes (fiction, 1975)
Sissie (fiction, 1963)

Williams, Sherley Anne
Dessa Rose (fiction, 1986)
The Peacock Poems (1977)
Some One Sweet Angel Chile (poetry, 1982)

Wilson, August
Fences (drama, 1986)
Joe Turner's Come and Gone (drama, 1988)
Ma Rainey's Black Bottom (drama, 1985)

Wilson, Harriet E.
Our Nig: Or, Sketches from the Life of a Free Black (fiction, 1859)

Wright, Jay
Death as History (poetry, 1967)
Dimensions of History (poetry, 1976)
The Double Invention of Komo (poetry, 1980)
Elaine's Book (poetry, 1988)
The Homecoming Singer (poetry, 1971)
Selected Poems of Jay Wright (1987)
Soothsayers and Omens (1976)

Wright, Richard
American Hunger (autobiography, 1977)
Black Boy: A Record of Childhood and Youth (autobiography, 1945)
Eight Men (short fiction, 1961)
Lawd Today (fiction, 1963)
The Long Dream (fiction, 1958)
Native Son (fiction, 1940)
The Outsider (fiction, 1953)
Richard Wright Reader (mixed genres, 1978)
Savage Holiday (fiction, 1954)
Twelve Million Black Voices: A Folk History of the Negro in the United States
(nonfiction, 1941)
Uncle Tom's Children (short fiction, 1938)

Wright, Sarah E.
This Child's Gonna Live (fiction, 1969)

ya Salaam, Kalamu
Revolutionary Love: Poems and Essays (1978)

Young, Al
Ask Me Now (fiction, 1980)
The Blues Don't Change: New and Selected Poems (1982)
Bodies and Soul: Musical Memoirs (nonfiction, 1981)
Seduction by Light (fiction, 1988)
Sitting Pretty (fiction, 1976)
Snakes (fiction, 1970)
Who Is Angelina? (fiction, 1975)

C. Secondary Bibliography

1. Bibliographies and Literary Reference Works

a. General

Bogle, Donald, ed. *Black Arts Annual 1987/88.* New York: Garland, 1989.
A yearbook containing nine essays on literature, theatre, dance, and other topics, each one covering the year's events—from September 1, 1987, to August 31, 1988—in that particular field.

Davis, Thadious M., and Trudier Harris, eds. *Afro-American Fiction Writers After 1855.* Dictionary of Literary Biography 33. Detroit: Gale Research, 1984.
The entry format consists of a list of publications, critical assessment of the writer, and "references" (bibliography of books, reviews).

_____, eds. *Afro-American Writers After 1955: Dramatists and Prose Writers.* Dictionary of Literary Biography 38. Detroit: Gale Research, 1985.

Harris, Trudier, and Thadious M. Davis, eds. *Afro-American Writers Before the Harlem Renaissance.* Dictionary of Literary Biography 50. Detroit: Gale Research, 1986.
Entries list publications, give critical assessments of each writer and "references" (bibliography of books, reviews).

_____, eds. *Afro-American Writers, 1940-1955.* Dictionary of Literary Biography 70. Detroit: Gale Research, 1988.

_____, eds. *African-American Writers from the Harlem Renaissance to 1940*. Dictionary of Literary Biography 51. Detroit: Gale Research, 1987.

Inge, M. Thomas, et al., eds. *Black American Writers: Bibliographical Essays*. 2 vols. New York: St. Martin's Press, 1978.
Volume 1 covers "The Beginnings Through the Harlem Renaissance and Langston Hughes"; volume 2, "Richard Wright, Ralph Ellison, James Baldwin, and Amiri Baraka." Each volume "is intended as an appraisal of the best biographical and critical writings about America's seminal black writers, as well as an identification of manuscript and special resources for continued study. It is also intended to give an overview of the current state of scholarly recognition of the lives and careers of these authors and an appreciation of their works."

Metzger, Linda, et al., eds. *Black Writers: A Selection of Sketches from "Contemporary Authors."* Detroit: Gale Research, 1989.
"Contains more than 400 entries on 20th-century black writers, all updated or originally written for this volume." Format: biography, critical information, plus brief bibliographies.

Newby, James Edward. *Black Authors: A Selected Annotated Bibliography*. New York: Garland, 1991.
More than 3200 titles (nearly half annotated) are arranged into ten subject areas. See especially chapters 6 and 7, "Juvenile Literature" and "Language and Literature."

Page, James A., comp. *Selected Black American Authors: An Illustrated Bio-Bibliography*. Boston: G. K. Hall, 1977.
More than four hundred authors are arranged alphabetically; each entry contains both biographical and bibliographical information.

Page, James A., and Jae Min Roh, comps. *Selected Black American, African, and Caribbean Authors: A Bio-Bibliography*. Littleton, Colo.: Libraries Unlimited, 1985.
This revised edition of the 1977 bibliography has been expanded to include 632 "African-descended authors and their works." The format is same as in the original volume.

Peavy, Charles D., comp. *Afro-American Literature and Culture Since World War II: A Guide to Information Sources*. Detroit: Gale Research, 1979.
Includes sections on "Subjects" (anthologies, bibliographies, drama, novels, poetry, and so on) and "Individual Authors" (fifty-two writers, from James Baldwin and Gwendolyn Brooks to Frank Yerby and Al Young).

Perry, Margaret, ed. *The Harlem Renaissance: An Annotated Bibliography and Commentary*. New York: Garland, 1982.
"This bibliography attempts a comprehensive, though not exhaustive, listing of works by and about black writers of what has come to be known as the Harlem Renaissance—a period extending from the early 1920s through the early 1930s." Alphabetical format by author.

Rush, Theresa Gurnels, Carol Fairbanks Myers, and Esther Spring Arata, comps. *Black American Writers Past and Present: A Biographical and Bibliographical Dictionary*. 2 vols. Metuchen, N.J.: Scarecrow Press, 1975.
Volume 1 contains "The Dictionary (A-I)"; volume 2, "The Dictionary (J-Z)," plus a general bibliography.

Southgate, Robert L. *Black Plots and Black Characters: A Handbook for Afro-American Literature*. Syracuse, N.Y.: Gaylord Professional Publications, 1979.
In four major sections. Part 1 contains concise "Plot Summaries" of some seventy novels, plays, and long poems. Part 2 is "A Short Companion for Afro-American Literature and History." Part 3 contains an author bibliography. Finally, part 4 is a general bibliography.

Turner, Darwin T., comp. *Afro-American Writers*. Northbrook, Ill.: AHM, 1970.
A useful, though unannotated, listing of both primary and secondary materials through the 1960's. Sections cover "Aids to Research" (bibliographies, periodicals, and the like), "Backgrounds" (social, historical), "Literary History and Criticism," and "Afro-American Writers" (about 140 authors)

See also: "Multicultural Literature: Part II" (6C2), Whitlow (6C3b)

b. Drama

Arata, Esther Spring, and Nicholas John Rotoli, comps. *Black American Playwrights, 1800 to the Present: A Bibliography*. Metuchen, N.J.: Scarecrow Press, 1976.
Lists of 530 Black playwrights and more than 1550 play titles are arranged in three sections: a listing of plays and playwrights, with criticism and reviews, awards; a selected, general bibliography; and an index of play titles.

Arata, Esther Spring, comp. *More Black American Playwrights: A Bibliography*. Metuchen, N.J.: Scarecrow Press, 1978.
The format is the same as in the work listed above and includes "Errata for Previous Volume."

Fabré, Genevieve E., et al., comps. *Afro-American Poetry and Drama, 1760-1975.* Detroit: Gale Research, 1979.
The volume contains two separate bibliographies: Fabré is the compiler of "Afro-American Drama, 1850-1975."

Hatch, James V., and OMANii Abdullah, comps. *Black Playwrights, 1823-1977: An Annotated Bibliography of Plays.* New York: R. R. Bowker, 1977.
More than 2700 plays by approximately 900 Black American playwrights are listed. Bibliographies, appendices.

Peterson, Bernard L., Jr., comp. *Contemporary Black American Playwrights and Their Plays: A Biographical Directory and Dramatic Index.* Westport, Conn.: Greenwood Press, 1988.
Follows the format used in the companion volume below: a five hundred-page, alphabetical "Biographical Directory" is followed by appendixes, bibliographies, and title and general index.

_____, comp. *Early Black Playwrights and Dramatic Writers: A Biographical Directory and Catalog of Plays, Films, and Broadcasting Scripts.* Westport, Conn.: Greenwood Press, 1990.
A "convenient source of information on approximately 218 pioneer black American playwrights, screenwriters, and other originators of dramatic works written and/or produced in the United States and in Europe during the 19th century and the first half of the 20th century."

Woll, Allen. *Dictionary of the Black Theatre: Broadway, Off-Broadway, and Selected Harlem Theatre.* Westport, Conn.: Greenwood Press, 1983.
Lists more than three hundred shows, from 1898-1981, with biographical entries for writers, directors, performers, and notes on major theatrical organizations. Useful appendices, bibliographies.

See also: 6B1c, 6C4a

c. Poetry

Chapman, Dorothy H., comp. *Index to Black Poetry.* Boston: G. K. Hall, 1974.
Undertakes "to bring into one volume for the first time a complete reference of black poems and poets." Three alphabetical sections: a title and first line index (including bibliographical and publication information), author and subject indexes.

_____, comp. *Index to Poetry by Black American Women.* Westport, Conn.:
Greenwood Press, 1986.
Same format as above.

Davis, Thadious M., and Trudier Harris. *Afro-American Poets Since 1955.* Dictionary of Literary Biography. Detroit: Gale Research, 1985.
Follows an essay format: list of publications, critical assessment of each writer,
and "references" (bibliography of books, reviews).

Fabré, Genevieve E., et al., comps. *Afro-American Poetry and Drama, 1760-1975.*
Detroit: Gale Research, 1979.
Contains two separate bibliographies: William P. French, Michel J. Fabre, and
Amrijit Singh have compiled the longer "Afro-American Poetry, 1760-1975,"
which opens this volume.

See also: 6B1d, 6C4b

d. Fiction

Fairbanks, Carol, and Eugene A. Engeldinger, comps. *Black American Fiction:
A Bibliography.* Metuchen, N.J.: Scarecrow Press, 1978.
"The purpose of this bibliography is to provide the user with a list of Black
American authors, their fiction and criticism. . . . A bibliography of general
criticism is included at the end for those wishing overviews of Black American
literature."

Houston, Helen Ruth. *The Afro-American Novel, 1965-1975: A Descriptive Bibliography of Primary and Secondary Material.* Troy, N.Y.: Whitston Publishing,
1977.
More than fifty novelists are listed. "For each author, there is a biographical
statement, a descriptive listing of his works since 1964 and a listing of criticism
about the author and his works."

Margolies, Edward, and David Bakish, eds. *Afro-American Fiction, 1853-1976: A
Guide to Information Sources.* Detroit: Gale Research, 1979.
Contains "Checklist of Novels," "Short Story Collections," "Major
Authors—Secondary Sources," and "Bibliographies and General Studies."

Yancy, Preston M., comp. *The Afro-American Short Story: A Comprehensive,
Annotated Index with Selected Commentaries.* Westport, Conn.: Greenwood
Press, 1986.
"The objective of this book is to provide both a comprehensive reference to

modern Afro-American short stories and some analysis and commentary on modern black short fiction. Over 850 stories by approximately 300 authors are included." In three parts: a chronology (listing of stories by year of publication), list of anthologies, and commentaries. Author and title indexes.

See also: 6B1e, 6C4c

e. Autobiography

Brignano, Russell C., comp. *Black Americans in Autobiography: An Annotated Bibliography of Autobiographies and Autobiographical Books Written Since the Civil War.* Rev. ed. Durham: N.C.: Duke University Press, 1984.
This valuable volume annotates 424 Black autobiographies and 229 "autobiographical books" (diaries, travelogues, collections of letters, essays, and so forth).

See also: 6B1f, 6C4d1

f. Women Writers

Glikin, Ronda. *Black American Women in Literature: A Bibliography, 1976 Through 1987.* Jefferson, N.C.: McFarland, 1989.
This volume lists "the poetry, short fiction, novels, essays, and plays by, and criticism on, approximately 300 women whose work has been published in periodicals and anthologies between 1976 and 1987." Alphabetical entries include both primary works and "Textual Criticism" (secondary works).

Roses, Lorraine Elena, and Ruth Elizabeth Randolph. *Harlem Renaissance and Beyond: Literary Biographies of 100 Black Women Writers, 1900-1945.* Boston: G. K. Hall, 1990.
Critical essays followed by selective bibliographies.

Werner, Craig, comp. *Black American Women Novelists.* Pasadena, Calif.: Salem Press, 1989.
Contains detailed annotations for both "General Studies" (criticism, history) and thirty-three novelists. The format for each writer includes sections on biography, commentary, and criticism of individual novels.

Yellin, Jean Fagan, and Cynthia D. Bond, comps. *The Pen Is Ours: A Listing of Writings by and about African-American Women Before 1910 with Secondary Bibliography to the Present.* New York: Oxford University Press, 1991.

This important volume in the Schomburg Library of Nineteenth-Century Black Women Writers series includes a foreword by Henry Louis Gates, Jr., an introduction by the editors, and entries for some two hundred black women writers.

See also: 6B1h, 6C5

2. General Literary Studies

Davis, Charles T. *Black Is the Color of the Cosmos: Essays on Afro-American Literature and Culture, 1942-1981*. Edited by Henry Louis Gates, Jr. New York: Garland, 1982.
Essays are arranged into sections of "Theories of Black Literature and Culture," "The Structure of the Afro-American Literary Tradition" (essays on Paul Laurence Dunbar, Jean Toomer, Robert Hayden, and the Harlem Renaissance, among others), "On Wright, Ellison, and Baldwin," plus "A Bibliography to the Writings of Charles T. Davis."

De Jongh, James. *Vicious Modernism: Black Harlem and the Literary Imagination*. New York: Cambridge University Press, 1990.
De Jongh answers the question, "Why does the idea of Harlem so pique and intrigue the literary imagination?" in sections on paired decades: 1920's/1930's, 1940's/1950's, 1960's/1970's.

Dixon, Melvin. *Ride out the Wilderness: Geography and Identity in Afro-American Literature*. Urbana: University of Illinois Press, 1987.
"Analyzes images of physical and spiritual landscapes that reveal over time a changing topography in black American quests for selfhood, from early slave songs and narratives, which first located alternative places of refuge and regeneration, to works by modern authors, which construct equally complex geographical figures leading to the discovery and the performance of identity." Detailed analyses of Jean Toomer, Claude McKay, Richard Wright, Ralph Ellison, LeRoi Jones, Zora Neale Hurston, Alice Walker, Gayl Jones, James Baldwin, and Toni Morrison.

Evans, James H., Jr. *Spiritual Empowerment in Afro-American Literature: Frederick Douglass, Rebecca Jackson, Booker T. Washington, Richard Wright, Toni Morrison*. Lewiston, N.Y.: Edwin Mellen Press, 1987.
This is a study of Afro-American religion and literature "as types of cultural expression. An underlying assumption is that there is no radical separation between the quest for beauty (aesthetics) and the quest for ultimate truth (religion) in black experience."

Fabre, Michel. *From Harlem to Paris: Black American Writers in France, 1840-1980.* Urbana: University of Illinois Press, 1991.
A detailed scholarly study from "The New Orleans Connection" through Langston Hughes, Claude McKay, Richard Wright, and James Baldwin, to Ted Joans and James Emanuel. "I have chosen to emphasize the various and shifting aspects of a vast panorama that will portray the complexity of the black dimension of the American experience in France, neglected until now, and the influence it had and continues to have in both countries."

Hedgepeth, Chester, Jr. *Theories of Social Action in Black Literature.* New York: Peter Lang, 1986.
"This study advances several theories of social action which are inextricably a part of selected works of black literature written in this century. . . . It seeks to demonstrate by an examination of both imaginative and nonfictive sources the complexity and diversity of various types of adaptive behavior employed by Blacks to achieve equality under socially repressive conditions."

Jones, Gayl. *Liberating Voices: Oral Tradition in African American Literature.* Cambridge, Mass.: Harvard University Press, 1991.
"Modern African American writers began to shape and modify their literature using models not only from European and American traditions, but also from their own distinctive oral and aural forms." Sections on poetry, short fiction, and the novel.

LaCapra, Dominick, ed. *The Bounds of Race: Perspectives on Hegemony and Resistance.* Ithaca, N.Y.: Cornell University Press, 1991.
Half of the essays here deal with African literature. Those on American issues include Henry F. Gates, Jr.'s "The Master's Pieces: On Canon Formation and the Afro-American Tradition."

Miller, R. Baxter, ed. *Black American Literature and Humanism.* Lexington: University of Kentucky Press, 1981.
Essays by Alice Childress, Michael S. Harper, Trudier Harris, and four others on Langston Hughes, Gwendolyn Brooks, and literary topics.

Moses, Wilson Jeremiah. *The Wings of Ethiopia: Studies in African-American Life and Letters.* Ames: Iowa State University Press, 1990.
This collection contains section of analyses of literature: on literary Garveyism, the novels of Sutton E. Griggs, the first novel of W. E. B. Du Bois, the literary theory of Langston Hughes, and Ralph Ellison's *Invisible Man.*

"Multicultural Literature: Part II." Special section of *ADE Bulletin* 78 (Summer, 1984): 35-42.

Includes an article on Afro-American literature and the canon by Richard Yarborough and a "Selected Bibliography of Afro-American Literature" by Jerry W. Ward, Jr.

Nelson, Emmanuel S., ed. *Connections: Essays on Black Literature.* Canberra, Australia: Aboriginal Studies Press, 1988.
Eight essays that came out of the 1986 University of Queensland Conference on Black Literatures, the first conference "to place Australian and Aboriginal and South Pacific literatures along with other conventionally black literatures of the African Diaspora."

Ostendorf, Berndt. *Black Literature in White America.* New York: Barnes & Noble Books, 1982.
"A quest for literacy, freedom, and respect characterizes the development of black culture. . . . This book focuses on the historical and structural contingencies which defined its course and which gave shape to a black aesthetic grammar; the contingencies of race, class, and poverty, and the cultural gamesmanship of affirmation, rejection, and subterfuge which make for a specific black style." Essays on nineteenth and twentieth century Black writing by a European critic.

White, Vernessa C. *Afro-American and East German Fiction: A Comparative Study of Alienation, Identity, and the Development of Self.* New York: Peter Lang, 1983.
Similarities in social problems lead to analyses of novels by Alice Walker, Toni Morrison, Guenter De Bruyn, and Hermann Kant.

See also: essays in Ruoff and Ward (3B1); Olney (6B1b)

3. Historical Studies

a. Eighteenth and Nineteenth Centuries

Bruce, Dickson D., Jr. *Black American Writing from the Nadir: The Evolution of a Literary Tradition, 1877-1915.* Baton Rouge: Louisiana State University Press, 1989.
"This book examines ways in which black Americans responded to the growing virulence of white racism in late nineteenth and early twentieth century America." Focus on Paul Laurence Dunbar and James Weldon Johnson.

Davis, Charles T., and Henry Louis Gates, Jr., eds. *The Slave's Narrative.* New York: Oxford University Press, 1985.
This collection "of essays and reviews addressing the autobiographical narratives

written or dictated by ex-slaves of African descent in the 18th, 19th, and 20th centuries" has two goals: "to demonstrate the nature and function of the interpretation of this curious genre of literature and to explicate the structure of the world these narratives represent." In three sections: "Views and Reviews, 1750-1861," "The Slave Narratives as History," and "The Slave Narratives as Literature."

Elder, Arlene A. *The "Hindered Hand": Cultural Implications of Early African-American Fiction*. Westport, Conn.: Greenwood Press, 1978.
Contains analyses of Sutton Griggs, Paul Laurence Dunbar, Charles Chesnutt. Shows "the earliest African-American authors' exploration of the social and psychological clashes between individuals and their society" and how these writers themselves "were living, breathing exempla of the dangers about which they wrote."

Foster, Francis Smith. *Witnessing Slavery: The Development of Ante-bellum Slave Narrative*. Westport, Conn.: Greenwood Press, 1979.
"This study examines not only the forms of separately published slave narratives but also the social context and literary traditions within which they changed in order to determine relationships among them." A short, general study of the genre that produced some six thousand works. Also a concluding chapter, "Post-bellum Influence," and selected bibliography.

Jackson, Blyden. *The Long Beginning, 1746-1895*. Vol. 1 in *A History of Afro-American Literature*. Baton Rouge: Louisiana State University Press, 1989.
This volume covers the first two stages in Afro-American literature as Jackson defines them: the "Age of Apprenticeship" (1746 to 1830) and an "Age of Abolitionists" (1830-1895). Future volumes will explore the remaining four ages: the Negro Nadir (1895-1920), the Harlem Renaissance (1920-1930), The Age of Richard Wright (1930-1960), and The Age of the Black Militant (1960-   ). Detailed scholarly history followed by a comprehensive bibliographical essay.

McDowell, Deborah E., and Arnold Rampersad, eds. *Slavery and the Literary Imagination*. Selected Papers from the English Institute, 1987. Baltimore: The Johns Hopkins University Press, 1989.
Seven essays on Frederick Douglass and Booker T. Washington, W. E. B. Du Bois, "The Historical Novel of Slavery," and related topics.

Sekora, John, and Darwin T. Turner, eds. *The Art of Slave Narrative: Original Essays in Criticism and Theory*. Macomb: Western Illinois University Press, 1982.
Contains ten essays on the "art" of the slave narrative (form, style, point of view), plus appendices on the slave narrative in college courses and a selective checklist of criticism.

a. Twentieth Century

Bigsby, C. W. E. *The Second Black Renaissance: Essays on Black Literature.*
Westport, Conn.: Greenwood Press, 1980.
Chapters on Richard Wright, Ralph Ellison, James Baldwin, black poetry, drama,
and more.

Cooke, Michael G. *Afro-American Literature in the 20th Century: The Achievement
of Intimacy.* New Haven, Conn.: Yale University Press, 1984.
This study "centers on the intrinsic development of this literature out of the secret
matrix of signifying and the blues into successive conditions of (1) *self-veiling*,
(2) *solitude*, (3) *kinship*, and (4) *intimacy*" in chapters on major twentieth century
writers. Covers up to "Recent Black Fiction."

Davis, Arthur P. *From the Dark Tower: Afro-American Writers, 1900-1960.* Wash-
ington, D.C.: Howard University Press, 1974.
Twenty-eight writers are treated chronologically in two sections: "The New
Negro Renaissance (1900-1940)" and "Toward the Mainstream (1940-1960)."

Gibson, Donald B., ed. *Five Black Writers: Essays on Wright, Ellison, Baldwin,
Hughes, and LeRoi Jones.* New York: New York University Press, 1970.
Essays on the five writers by various critics, plus a section on "The Writer and
Social Responsibility." Includes essays by Langston Hughes, James Baldwin,
Irving Howe, and others.

_____. *The Politics of Literary Expression: A Study of Major Black Writers.*
Westport, Conn.: Greenwood Press, 1981.
Most critics are formalists, but most Black writers "write with an eye to the
social situation of the time in which they are writing." The introduction, "Preface
to a Social Theory of Literature," spells out critical assumptions, which are then
applied to analyses of Richard Wright, Ralph Ellison, James Baldwin, Charles
Chesnutt, and Jean Toomer.

Hill, Herbert, ed. *Anger, and Beyond: The Negro Writer in the United States.* New
York: Harper & Row, 1966.
Essays by Sanders Redding, Arna Bontemps, LeRoi Jones, Robert Bone, Nat
Hentoff, and half a dozen others. Several of the essays were given at a 1964
Berkeley seminar. Includes "Reflections on Richard Wright: A Symposium on
an Exiled Native Son" (also included in Gibson, *Five Black Writers*).

Ikonne, Chidi. *From Du Bois to Van Vechten: The Early New Negro Literature,
1903-1926.* Westport, Conn.: Greenwood Press, 1981.
A study of "The New Negro Literary Awakening," which took place between

the publications of W. E. B. Du Bois's *The Souls of Black Folks* and Carl Van Vechten's *Nigger Heaven*.

Jackson, Blyden. *The Waiting Years: Essays on American Negro Literature*. Baton Rouge: Louisiana State University Press, 1976.
Collected essays on Jean Toomer and Richard Wright, the Harlem Renaissance, general subjects.

Lynch, Michael F. *Creative Revolt: A Study of Wright, Ellison, and Dostoevsky*. New York: Peter Lang, 1990.
"This study analyzes the parallel development of Dostoevsky, Wright, and Ellison away from naturalism and collectivism and toward existential freedom. It also focuses on Dostoevsky's evident influence on Wright and Ellison and on their adaptations of and responses to certain of his observations and themes."

Margolies, Edward. *Native Sons: A Critical Study of Twentieth-Century Black American Authors*. Philadelphia: J. B. Lippincott, 1968.
This early standard history of twentieth century Black writing has chapters on "The First Forty Years: 1900-1940," "Migration: William Attaway and Blood on the Forge," Richard Wright, Chester Himes, James Baldwin, Ralph Ellison, Malcolm X, William Demby, and "Prospects: LeRoi Jones?"

O'Brien, John, ed. *Interviews with Black Writers*. New York: Liveright, 1973.
Interviews with Arna Bontemps, Cyrus Colter, William Demby, Ralph Ellison, Ernest J. Gaines, Michael Harper, Robert Hayden, Ann Petry, Alice Walker, and eight other writers.

Petesch, Donald A. *A Spy in the Enemy's Country: The Emergence of Modern Black Literature*. Iowa City: University of Iowa Press, 1989.
Treatment of the qualities (e.g., *masking*) and themes (the preoccupation with identity and the self) in the writers of the early twentieth century: Charles W. Chesnutt, James Weldon Johnson, Nella Larsen, Jean Toomer, and others.

Whitlow, Roger. *Black American Literature: A Critical History*. Chicago: Nelson Hall, 1973.
An early, comprehensive history that scants the nineteenth century but includes a seventy-five-page, "1,520-title bibliography of works written by and about black Americans."

Young, James O. *Black Writers of the 30s*. Baton Rouge: Louisiana State University Press, 1973.
A scholarly study of Langston Hughes, Zora Neale Hurston, Richard Wright, and other writers who came of age in the Depression decade.

c. The Harlem Renaissance

Baker, Houston A., Jr. *Modernism and the Harlem Renaissance.* Chicago: University of Chicago Press, 1987.
This extended essay provides "a model of discursive analysis and ample examples of its interpretive method in order to recode the 'Harlem Renaissance' as a comprehensible moment in a distinctive, family modernity."

Huggins, Nathan Irvin. *Harlem Renaissance.* New York: Oxford University Press, 1971.
This standard history of the period attempts "the study of the interplay between white and black in American life, the illumination of the Afro-American experience within American culture . . . white men and black men unknowingly dependent in their work to shape American character and culture."

_____, ed. *Voices from the Harlem Renaissance.* New York: Oxford University Press, 1976.
Contains three parts: "'New Negro' Radicalism" (essays by A. Philip Randolph, Marcus Garvey, W. E. B. Du Bois, and others); "Harlem Renaissance: The Urban Setting" (fiction, poetry, visual arts, journalism); and "Reflections on the Renaissance and Art for a New Day" (poetry, commentary).

Kellner, Bruce, ed. *The Harlem Renaissance: A Historical Dictionary for the Era.* Westport, Conn.: Greenwood Press, 1984.
This four-hundred-page dictionary is amplified by numerous illustrations, appendices (including "A Chronology of Significant Events, 1917-1935"), and an extensive bibliography.

Kramer, Victor A., ed. *The Harlem Renaissance Re-Examined.* New York: AMS, 1987.
Essays in two parts: "Theory and Questions" includes works by Darwin Turner, Amrijit Singh, Bruce Kellner, and Nellie Y. McKay; "Part Two: Art and Answers" contains discussions by Jean Toomer, Langston Hughes, Sterling A. Brown, and other Renaissance writers.

Locke, Alain, ed. *The New Negro.* Reprint. New York: Atheneum, 1968.
Original documents from the Harlem Renaissance: essays, fiction, poetry, "music," bibliography. Robert Hayden's preface explains the significance of the 1925 volume.

Perry, Margaret. *Silence to the Drums: A Survey of the Literature of the Harlem Renaissance.* Westport, Conn.: Greenwood Press, 1976.
Examines the social and literary background, as well as major and minor writers.

Singh, Amrijit, et al., eds. *The Harlem Renaissance: Reevaluations*. New York: Garland, 1989.
Twenty-two essays on writers and themes of the period by Margaret Perry, Robert B. Stepto, Arnold Rampersad, Bruce Kellner, and other critics and historians.

_____. *The Novels of the Harlem Renaissance: Twelve Black Writers, 1923-1933*. University Park: Pennsylvania State University Press, 1976.
This study "focuses on the interracial issues of self-definition, class, caste, and color" in twenty-one novels of Arna Bontemps, Countée Cullen, W. E. B. Du Bois, Langston Hughes, Nella Larsen, Claude McKay, Jean Toomer, and five other Black writers.

Turner, Darwin T. *In a Minor Chord: Three Afro-American Writers and Their Search for Identity*. Carbondale: Southern Illinois University Press, 1971.
An early study that gave new estimates of Jean Toomer, Countée Cullen, and Zora Neale Hurston.

Wintz, Gary D. *Black Culture and the Harlem Renaissance*. Houston, Tex.: Rice University Press, 1988.
Not a study of individual writers but, rather, an examination of the Harlem Renaissance as a movement "within the framework of black social and intellectual history in early twentieth-century America. In particular I examine the relationship of the Renaissance to earlier Black literature and its relationship to its new urban setting."

See also: Honey (6B1h), Perry (6C1a), Roses and Randolph (6C1f), Jackson (6C3b), Hull (6C5)

d. Contemporary Literature

Fox, Robert Elliot. *Conscientious Sorcerers: The Black Postmodernist Fiction of LeRoi Jones/Amiri Baraka, Ishmael Reed, and Samuel R. Delaney*. Westport, Conn.: Greenwood Press, 1987.
A study of "three of the most important and gifted American authors to have emerged in the tumultuous period of the 1960s."

Harris, Norman. *Connecting Times: The Sixties in Afro-American Fiction*. Jackson: University of Mississippi Press, 1988.
In two sections: "Novels of the Vietnam War" and "Novels of the Civil Rights and Black Power Movements." "The central point I wish to illustrate through analyzing the impact of the activism of the sixties on Afro-American fictional

characters and Afro-Americans in the real world is that the process involved in achieving freedom and literacy increases the chances that individuals will be able to resolve conflict."

Johnson, Charles. *Being and Race: Black Writing Since 1970.* Bloomington: Indiana University Press, 1988.
A philosophical analysis of contemporary Black writers using a phenomenological approach.

Major, Clarence. *The Dark and Feeling: Black American Writers and Their Work.* New York: The Third Press, 1974.
Collected essays and reviews of contemporary Black writing by a major practitioner.

Ro, Sigmund. *Rage and Celebration: Essays on Contemporary Afro-American Writing.* Atlantic Highlands, N.J.: Humanities Press, 1984.
A Scandinavian critic writes about the dual theme in James Baldwin, William Melvin Kelley, John A. Williams, Afro-American autobiography, and 1960's writing.

Williams, Sherley Anne. *Give Birth to Brightness: A Thematic Study in Neo-Black Literature.* New York: Dial Press, 1972.
Analyzes Black writers in the 1960's who "are turning their attention inward, seeking to identify the traditions of Black people, to explore their experiences, to define themselves and their people in images which grow out of their individual quests and group explorations."

4. Genre Studies

a. Drama

Abramson, Doris E. *Negro Playwrights in the American Theatre, 1925-1959.* New York: Columbia University Press, 1969.
An early study of Black New York theatre, from "Garland Anderson's *Appearances* (the first play by a Negro to be produced on Broadway" to Lorraine Hansberry's *A Raisin in the Sun* (the climax of a realistic emphasis in plays about Negro life)."

Bigsby, C. W. E. *The Black American Writer.* 2 vols. Deland, Fla.: Everett/Edwards, 1969.
Volume 2 contains essays by Gerald Haslam, Darwin Turner, and others on Lorraine Hansberry, LeRoi Jones. Also contains an interview with Harold Cruise.

Craig, E. Quita. *Black Drama of the Federal Theatre Era: Beyond the Formal Horizon*. Amherst: University of Massachusetts Press, 1980.
A serious study of plays of the Negro Units of the Federal Theatre Project written and produced between 1935 and 1939.

Williams, Mance. *Black Theatre in the 1960s and 1970s: A Historical-Critical Analysis of the Movement*. Westport, Conn.: Greenwood Press, 1985.
Analyzes the Black Theatre Movement, which "focuses not only on the playwrights but on the important theatre companies, their formation, productions, and performers . . . [and] the role and contributions of the Black producers."

See also: 6B1c, 6C1b

b. Poetry

Bell, Bernard W. *The Folk Roots of Contemporary Afro-American Poetry*. Detroit: Broadside Press, 1974.
The main goal of the study "is to reveal why and how contemporary Afro-American poetry makes use of folk materials."

Bigsby, C. W. E. *The Black American Writer*. 2 vols. Deland, Fla.: Everett/Edwards, 1969.
Volume 2 contains essays on Langston Hughes, Gwendolyn Brooks, and other poets. (See Bigsby in 6C4a and 6C4c2.)

Gibson, Donald B., ed. *Modern Black Poets: A Collection of Critical Essays*. Twentieth Century Views. Englewood Cliffs, N.J.: Prentice-Hall, 1973.
Analyses of themes and forms among major Black poets such as Langston Hughes, Countée Cullen, Amiri Baraka, and others.

Jackson, Blyden, and Louis D. Rubin, Jr. *Black Poetry in America: Two Essays in Historical Interpretation*. Baton Rouge: Louisiana State University Press, 1974.
The essay by Rubin is on the language of Black poetry, that of Jackson on "the ways in which the black poet has explored and delineated the modes of modern black American experience."

Melham, D. H. *Heroism in the New Black Poetry: Introductions and Interviews*. Lexington: University Press of Kentucky, 1990.
Essays on and interviews with six leading Black poets: Gwendolyn Brooks, Dudley Randall, Don L. Lee, Sonia Sanchez, Jayne Cortez, and Amiri Baraka.

Miller, R. Baxter, ed. *Black American Poets Between Worlds, 1940-1960*. Knoxville: University of Tennessee Press, 1986.
Critical appraisals of poetry by six Black poets who emerged in those two
decades: Melvin B. Tolson, Robert Hayden, Dudley Randall, Margaret Esse
Danner, Margaret Walker, and Gwendolyn Brooks.

Sherman, Joan R. *Invisible Poets: Afro Americans of the 19th Century*. 2d ed.
Urbana: University of Illinois Press, 1989.
An intensive study of twenty-six nineteenth century poets. The author's goal is
"to construct for the first time certain significant profiles of their life experiences
and to appraise the qualities and import of their poetry." Appendices and bibliographies list other resources for studying nineteenth century Black poetry.

Wagner, Jean. *Black Poets of the United States: From Paul Laurence Dunbar to
Langston Hughes*. Translated by Kenneth Douglas. Chicago: University of Illinois
Press, 1973.
This is a study of a half-century of African American poetry, from 1890 to 1940,
including Paul Laurence Dunbar and his contemporaries and the major talents
of the Harlem Renaissance.

See also: 6B1d, 6C1c; Bigsby (6C3b); Nelson (4D2)

c. Fiction

1. Short Story

Bruck, Peter, ed. *The Black American Short Story in the 20th Century: A Collection
of Critical Essays*. Amsterdam: B. R. Gruner, 1977.
Contains essays on short stories by James Baldwin, Ralph Ellison, Langston
Hughes, Richard Wright, and eight other writers.

2. Novel

Bell, Bernard W. *The Afro-American Novel and Its Tradition*. Amherst: University
of Massachusetts, 1987.
Discusses more than 150 novels by 100 representative novelists. Through an
interdisciplinary approach, Bell seeks "to explain the richness of the Afro-
American novel as a hybrid narrative whose distinctive tradition and vitality are
derived basically from the sedimented indigenous roots of Black American
folklore and literary genres of the Western world."

Bigsby, C. W. E. *The Black American Writer*. 2 vols. Deland, Fla.: Everett/Edwards, 1969.

This fiction volume includes essays by Richard Gilman, Theodore Gross, Brian Lee, and others on Richard Wright, James Baldwin, general problems. Also includes interviews with Baldwin and Ralph Ellison.

Bone, Robert. *The Negro Novel in America*. 1958; New Haven, Conn.: Yale University Press, 1965.

This early standard history has four sections: "The Novel of the Rising Middle Class: 1890-1920," "The Discovery of the Folk: 1920-1930," "The Search for a Tradition: 1930-1940," and "The Revolt Against Protest: 1940-1952." Also contains a postscript on James Baldwin; an epilogue, "Freedom for the Negro Novelist"; and a bibliography that lists "Full-length Novels Written by American Negroes, 1853-1952."

Bruck, Peter, and Wolfgang Karrer, eds. *The Afro-American Novel Since 1960*. Amsterdam: B. R. Gruner, 1982.

Includes essays on Paule Marshall, Ishmael Reed, Ernest Gaines, Toni Morrison, Alice Walker, and other contemporary Black novelists by various European scholars. Two-part introduction to the subject and an appendix, "A Chronological Checklist of Afro-American Novels 1945-1980."

Byerman, Keith E. *Fingering the Jagged Grain: Tradition and Form in Recent Black Fiction*. Athens: University of Georgia Press, 1985.

In four parts: "Ralph Ellison's Invisible Man as a Paradigmatic Work for More Recent Writers"; four realistic writers (James Alan McPherson, Ernest Gaines, Toni Cade Bambara, and Alice Walker); two writers (Gayl Jones and Toni Morrison) who "exceed the boundaries of realism"; and three writers (Ishmael Reed, Leon Forrest, and Clarence Major) who represent "the experimentalist element in contemporary black fiction."

Callahan, John F. *In the African-American Grain: Call-and-Response in Twentieth-Century Black Fiction*. 2d ed. Middletown, Conn.: Wesleyan University Press, 1988.

Subtitled "The Pursuit of Voice in 20th Century Black Fiction" in its first edition, this volume traces some "of the variations and adaptations of the call-and-response pattern worked out in twentieth century black fiction." Henry Louis Gates has called this "the most sophisticated study of Black narrative published to date" (cover notes).

Campbell, Jane. *Mythic Black Fiction: The Transformation of History*. Knoxville: University of Tennessee Press, 1987.

This study "explores the ways romance has served as the predominant mode of black historical fiction writers," from William Wells Brown's *Clotel*, through Charles Chesnutt and W. E. B. Du Bois, to Ralph Ellison, James Baldwin, and Toni Morrison.

Christian, Barbara. *Black Women Novelists: The Development of a Tradition, 1892-1976*. Westport, Conn.: Greenwood Press, 1980.
Attempts "to trace the development of stereotypical images imposed on black women and [to] assess how these images have affected the work of black women artists." Chapters on Paule Marshall, Toni Morrison, and Alice Walker.

Gayle, Addison, Jr. *The Way of the New World: The Black Novel in America*. New York: Anchor Press, 1975.
One of the first surveys of Black fiction, from its beginnings to the 1960's.

Lee, A. Robert, ed. *Black Fiction: New Studies in the Afro-American Novel Since 1945*. London: Vision, 1980.
Essays on Richard Wright, Ralph Ellison, James Baldwin, Langston Hughes, Ann Petry, and their themes and structures, mainly by British critics.

Payne, Ladell. *Black Novelists and the Southern Literary Tradition*. Athens: University of Georgia Press, 1981.
A study of the Southern roots and elements in Jean Toomer, Charles Chesnutt, James Weldon Johnson, Richard Wright, and Ralph Ellison.

Rosenblatt, Roger. *Black Fiction*. Cambridge, Mass.: Harvard University Press, 1974.
An early, important study of the unique qualities and themes (e.g., consciousness of "external limitation," "the search for a grounding or cultural history"). Organized around the "cyclical conception of black American history upon which practically every American black novel and short story has been based."

Smith, Valerie. *Self-Discovery and Authority in Afro-American Narrative*. Cambridge, Mass.: Harvard University Press, 1987.
A study of the "ways in which the idea of literacy is used within the tradition of Afro-American letters. I argue here that slave narrators and the protagonist-narrators of certain twentieth-century novels . . . affirm and legitimize their psychological autonomy by telling the stories of their lives." Examines three slave narratives, *The Autobiography of an Ex-Coloured Man*, Richard Wright, Ralph Ellison, and Toni Morrison.

Stepto, Robert B. *From Behind the Veil: A Study of Afro-American Narrative*. Urbana: University of Illinois Press, 1979.
Influential essays on black narrative of the nineteenth century (four slave narra-

tives, Booker T. Washington's *Up from Slavery*, W. E. B. Du Bois's *The Souls of Black Folks*) and twentieth century (James Weldon Johnson's *The Autobiography of an Ex-Coloured Man*, Richard Wright's *Black Boy*, and Ralph Ellison's *Invisible Man*).

Thomas, H. Nigel. *From Folklore to Fiction: A Study of Folk Heroes and Rituals in the Black American Novel*. Westport, Conn.: Greenwood Press, 1988.
"This study focuses on the transposition of Afro-American folk heroes and rituals from folklore to literature." Discussions of tricksters, preachers, "Black Moses," "Superstitions and Conjure," and so on.

See also: 6B1f, 6C1d; Werner (6C1f); Awkward, Carby, Pryse and Spillers, Wade-Gayles, Walker, and Watson (6C5)

d. Nonfiction

1. Autobiography

Andrews, William L. *To Tell a Free Story: The First Century of Afro-American Autobiography, 1760-1865*. Urbana: University of Illinois Press, 1986.
"The thesis of this book, simply put, is this: the import of the autobiographies of black people during the first century of the genre's existence in the United States is that they 'tell a free story' as well as talk about freedom as a theme and goal of life." Indeed, "autobiographers demonstrate through a variety of rhetorical means that they regard the writing of autobiography as in some ways self-liberating, the final, climactic act in the drama of their lifelong quests for freedom."

Butterfield, Stephen. *Black Autobiography in America*. Amherst: University of Massachusetts Press, 1974.
"The present work is an exploration of black autobiographical writing in America from the 1830s to 1972. Our purpose is to read the books closely, to evaluate their importance, to trace the development of the genre over a period of time, to discuss the books as embodiments of the black American experience, to relate them where possible to the literature of the white mainstream. We focus specifically on the complex relationships between viewpoint, identity, audience, motive, occasion, and use of language in each book."

Dudley, David L. *My Father's Shadow: Intergenerational Conflict in African American Men's Autobiography*. Philadelphia: University of Pennsylvania Press, 1991.

From Frederick Douglass, Booker T. Washington, and W. E. B. Du Bois, to Richard Wright, James Baldwin, Eldridge Cleaver, and Malcolm X.

Smith, Sidonie. *Where I'm Bound: Patterns of Slavery and Freedom in Black American Autobiography*. Westport, Conn.: Greenwood Press, 1974.
"The earliest black American autobiographies, the slave narratives, established certain prototypical patterns, both thematic and structural, that recur again and again in subsequent black autobiographies." (Both a "successful break into a community that allowed authentic self-expression and fulfillment in a social role" and an escape "away from an enslaving community"). "This study examines the increasingly complex and ambiguous manifestations of these patterns as they find expression in succeeding generations of autobiographers."

See also: Braxton (6C5)

2. Literary Criticism

Baker, Houston A., Jr. *Afro-American Poetics: Revisions of Harlem and the Black Aesthetic*. Madison: University of Wisconsin Press, 1988.
Baker calls this a "kind of intellectual autobiography" and a panel in the triptych formed with his *Modernism and the Harlem Renaissance* and *Workings of the Spirit: The Poetics of Afro-American Women's Writing*. Subjects of the essays in this volume include Jean Toomer's *Cane*, Countée Cullen, Amiri Baraka, Larry Neal, and Hoyt Fuller.

_____. *Blues, Ideology, and Afro-American Literature: A Vernacular Theory*. Chicago: University of Chicago Press, 1984.
"The guiding presupposition of the chapters that follow is that Afro-American culture is a complex, reflexive enterprise which finds its proper figuration in blues conceived as a matrix." Critical chapters on fiction, literary criticism, a "New American Literary History," and more.

_____. *The Journey Back: Issues in Black Literature and Criticism*. Chicago: University of Chicago Press, 1980.
Baker uses the "notions of discourse, culture, and context in an attempt to reveal some of the underlying rules and conventional procedures of Black American literature and culture," and to create a kind of "anthropology of art."

_____. *Long Black Song: Essays in Black American Literature and Culture*. Charlottesville: University of Virginia Press, 1972.
The distinctiveness of Black American culture is demonstrated in essays on Black folklore, Booker T. Washington's *Up From Slavery*, W. E. B. Du Bois's *The

Souls of Black Folk, Richard Wright's *Native Son,* other works of Black expression.

_____. *Singers of Daybreak: Studies in Black American Literature.* Washington, D.C.: Howard University Press, 1974.
Essays in this collection deal "with several manifestations of the black creative spirit which have aided [the] process of cultural regeneration. They are concerned with writers, themes, and techniques that have helped to illumine the path for contemporaries and successors." Essays on James Weldon Johnson, Paul Laurence Dunbar, Gwendolyn Brooks, Jean Toomer, and George Cain.

Baker, Houston A., Jr., and Patricia Redmond, eds. *Afro-American Literary Study in the 1990s.* Chicago: University of Chicago Press, 1989.
Theoretical and critical papers (from a 1987 conference) on major genres of Afro-American literature: poetry, fiction, autobiography, and the like.

Gates, Henry Louis, Jr. *Figures in Black: Words, Signs, and the 'Racial' Self.* New York: Oxford University Press, 1987.
An account "of one critic's confrontation with the role of theory in the study of noncanonical literature." Includes sections on "The Literature of the Slave" (with chapters on Phillis Wheatley, Frederick Douglass, among others) and "Black Structures of Feeling" (chapters on Jean Toomer, Sterling A. Brown, others.)

_____. *Loose Canons: Notes on the Culture Wars.* New York: Oxford University Press, 1992.
Contains essays on cultural pluralism and the battles fought over it in the arenas of "Literature," "The Profession," and "Society."

_____. *The Signifying Monkey: A Theory of Afro American Literary Criticism.* New York: Oxford University Press, 1988.
This award-winning study "explores the relation of the black vernacular tradition to the Afro-American literary tradition." Individual analyses of Zora Neale Hurston's *Their Eyes Were Watching God,* Alice Walker's *The Color Purple,* and Ishmael Reed's *Mumbo Jumbo.*

_____, ed. *Black Literature and Literary Theory.* New York: Methuen, 1984.
This volume addresses "two audiences, one seeking to learn about contemporary theory, the other seeking to learn about the nature and function of black writing." Contains an introduction by Gates, "Criticism in the Jungle"; "Theory: On Structuralism and post-Structuralism" and "Practice" (essays on Frederick Douglass, Jean Toomer, Zora Neale Hurston, Ralph Ellison, Gwendolyn Brooks, and Toni Morrison).

Hogue, W. Lawrence. *Discourse and the Other: The Production of the Afro-American Text.* Durham, N.C.: Duke University Press, 1986.
Seeks to examine "how literary texts in general, and Afro-American texts in particular, are produced, defined, interpreted, and appropriated, how they function politically and culturally." Includes analyses of Ernest J. Gaines and Toni Morrison.

Martin, Reginald. *Ishmael Reed and the New Black Aesthetic Critics.* New York: Macmillan, 1988.
An analysis of the Black aesthetic, which Martin traces from its roots in the middle of the nineteenth century (Josiah Henson) through Douglass and Du Bois to Addison Gayle, Amiri Baraka, and Ishmael Reed in the 1960's and 1970's.

Weixlmann, Joe, and Chester J. Fontenot, eds. *Belief Versus Theory in Black American Literary Criticism.* Vol. 2 in *Studies in Black American Literature.* Greenwood, Fla.: Penkevill Publishing, 1986.
Essays by Houston A. Baker, Jr., W. Lawrence Hogue, Craig Werner, John M. Reilly, Amiri Baraka, and other critics on Richard Wright, Maya Angelou, Nikki Giovanni, Ed Bullins, Black theater and poetry, other topics.

_____, eds. *Black American Prose Theory.* Vol. 1 in *Studies in Black American Literature.* Greenwood, Fla.: Penkevill Publishing, 1984.
Essays by William L. Andrews, Chester J. Fontenot, Trudier Harris, Jerome Klinkowitz and other critics on Black fiction and autobiography, Clarence Major, Alex Haley and Toni Morrison, and other topics.

See also: Harper (6B1b); Gates, Wall (6C5).

5. Black Women Writers

Awkward, Michael. *Inspiriting Influences: Tradition, Revision, and Afro-American Women's Novels.* New York: Columbia University Press, 1989.
Contains an introduction ("Toward an Intertextual Reading of Afro-American Women's Novels"); also analyses of Zora Neale Hurston's *Their Eyes Were Watching God*, Toni Morrison's *The Bluest Eye*, Gloria Naylor's *The Women of Brewster Place*, and Alice Walker's *The Color Purple*.

Baker, Houston A. *Workings of the Spirit: The Poetics of Afro-American Women's Writing.* Chicago: University of Chicago Press, 1991.
Part of the theoretical trilogy made up by *Afro-American Poetics: Revisions of Harlem and the Black Aesthetic* and *Modernism and the Harlem Renaissance.*

Braxton, Joanne M. *Black Women Writing Autobiography: A Tradition Within a Tradition.* Philadelphia: Temple University Press, 1989.
Braxton views Black autobiography "as an attempt to define a life work retrospectively and as a form of symbolic memory that evokes the black woman's deepest consciousness." Treats representative autobiographical texts as both literature and history.

Braxton, Joanne M., and Andree Nicole McLaughlin, eds. *Wild Women in the Whirlwind: Afro-American Culture and the Contemporary Literary Renaissance.* New Brunswick, N.J.: Rutgers University Press, 1990.
Includes introductions by the two editors, sections on "Foremothers" (essays on Phillis Wheatley, Sojourner Truth, and others by Angela Y. Davis, June Jordan, other critics); "Redefining the Veil" (Calvin Hernton, Barbara Smith, and others on language and sexuality); "Visions and Re-visions" (essays on Alice Walker, Toni Morrison's *Sula*, an interview with Toni Cade Bambara and Sonia Sanchez); and "A Selected Bibliography of English-Language Works by Black Women of the Americas, 1970-1988" by Gale P. Jackson.

Carby, Hazel V. *Reconstructing Womanhood: The Emergence of the Afro-American Woman Novelist.* New York: Oxford University Press, 1987.
Chapters on "Narratives of Slave and Free Women Before Emancipation," Frances Ellen Watkins Harper, Pauline Elizabeth Hopkins, and other early Black women writers.

Christian, Barbara. *Black Feminist Criticism: Perspectives on Black Women Writers.* New York: Pergamon Press, 1985.
Essays on Alice Walker, Toni Morrison, Paule Marshall, Gwendolyn Brooks, and other Black women novelists.

Evans, Mari, ed. *Black Women Writers (1950-1980): A Critical Evaluation.* Garden City, N.Y.: Doubleday, 1984.
Essays by and about contemporary black women writers: Maya Angelou, Alice Childress, Margaret Walker, and twelve others. A statement by each writer is followed by two essays on her work and then a brief "Bio/Selected Bibliography."

Gates, Henry L., Jr., ed. *Reading Black, Reading Feminist: A Critical Anthology.* New York: Meridian, 1990.
Sections on "Constructing a Tradition" (essays by Zora Neale Hurston, Barbara Christian, Hazel V. Carby, and others); "Reading Black, Reading Feminist" (Houston A. Baker, Jr., Bell Hooks, Nellie Y. McKay, others on various writers and topics); interviews with Rita Dove and Jamaica Kincaid.

Hernton, Calvin C. *The Sexual Mountain and Black Women Writers: Adventures in Sex, Literature, and Real Life.* Garden City, N.Y.: Doubleday, 1987.
"This book examines the controversial role that black women have played and are playing in the making of Black American Literature. . . . It documents the sexist bigotry of black males and confirms that black women authors are celebrating a literary Fourth of July for the first time in America." Chapters on Alice Walker's *The Color Purple,* Ann Petry, Langston Hughes, and Black women poets.

Holloway, Karla F. C. *Moorings and Metaphors: Figures of Culture and Gender in Black Women's Literature.* New Brunswick, N.J.: Rutgers University Press, 1992.
This study "is an extended discussion of the kinds of theoretical considerations that emerge with a critical reading of black women writers' imaginative textual languages."

Hull, Gloria T. *Color, Sex and Poetry: Three Women Writers of the Harlem Renaissance.* Bloomington: Indiana University Press, 1987.
Studies of Alice Dunbar-Nelson, Angelina Weld Grimke, and Georgia Douglas Johnson.

Pryse, Marjorie, and Hortense J. Spillers, eds. *Conjuring: Black Women, Fiction, and Literary Tradition.* Bloomington: Indiana University Press, 1985.
Contains essays on slave narratives, Ann Petry, Toni Morrison, Toni Cade Bambara, and other writers by Bernard W. Bell, Gloria T. Hull, Barbara Christian, other critics.

Russell, Sandi. *Render Me My Song: African-American Women Writers from Slavery to the Present.* New York: St. Martin's Press, 1990.
The "discovery, analysis and celebration of the voice of African-American women," from slave poets through Alice Walker, Toni Morrison, and Maya Angelou.

Tate, Claudia, ed. *Black Woman Writers at Work.* New York: Continuum, 1983.
Interviews with Maya Angelou, Toni Cade Bambara, Gwendolyn Brooks, Nikki Giovanni, Gayl Jones, Audre Lorde, Toni Morrison, Sonia Sanchez, Ntozake Shange, Alice Walker, Margaret Walker, Sherley Anne Williams, and others.

Wade-Gayles, Gloria. *No Crystal Stair: Visions of Race and Sex in Black Women's Fiction.* New York: Pilgrim Press, 1984.
The "first full-length, interdisciplinary study of black women's novels in the contexts of race, sex, and class," focusing on Black women's fiction after World War II.

Walker, Melissa. *Down from the Mountaintop: Black Women's Novels in the Wake of the Civil Rights Movement, 1966-1989.* New Haven, Conn.: Yale University Press, 1991.
A study of how eighteen novels "published since the peak moments of the civil rights movement relate to the movement and to the historical contingencies that fostered it and led to its decline."

Wall, Cheryl A., ed. *Changing Our Own Words: Essays on Criticism, Theory, and Writing By Black Women.* New Brunswick, N.J.: Rutgers University Press, 1989.
Barbara Christian, Gloria T. Hull, Susan Willis, and half a dozen other critics on Black feminist discourse, theory, and culture.

Watson, Carole McAlpine. *Prologue: The Novels of Black American Women, 1891-1965.* Westport, Conn.: Greenwood Press, 1985.
A study of the prehistory of the contemporary novel, with chapters on the period 1891-1920 (Frances E. W. Harper, Pauline Hopkins), 1921-1945 (Jessie Fauset, Zora Neale Hurston), and 1946-1965 (Ann Petry, Paule Marshall, Kristin Hunter, and Mary E. Vroman). Annotated bibliography of the novels studied.

Weixlmann, Joe, and Houston A. Baker, eds. *Black Feminist Criticism and Critical Theory.* Vol. 3 in *Studies in Black American Literature.* Greenwood, Fla.: Penkevill Publishing, 1988.
"Like the essays in the first two volumes of Studies in Black American Literature, those in this third volume either establish a theoretical perspective for examining the corpus of Black literature or proceed, from a theoretical basis, to offer readings of specific texts or bodies of texts." Here are essays by Michael Awkward, Houston A. Baker, Jr., and other critics on Zora Neale Hurston, Nella Larsen, Sonia Sanchez, other writers and topics.

Willis, Susan. *Specifying: Black Women Writing the American Experience.* Madison: University of Wisconsin Press, 1987.
An intensive study of Zora Neale Hurston, Paule Marshall, Toni Morrison, Toni Cade Bambara, and the relationship of Black women writers to history.

See also: Sherman, Stetson (6B1d); 6B1g (collections); Werner, Yellin (6C1f); Christian (6C4c2)

NOTES

1. See Chapman (6B1b), pp. 25, 27.
2. *A History of Afro-American Literature* (1989), p. 8 (6C3a).
3. Bone (1958), p. 2 (6C4c2).

4. *The Afro-American Novel and Its Tradition* (1987), pp. xiii-xiv (6C4c2).

5. Introduction, *A History of Afro-American Literature*, pp. 25-26.

6. The most useful listing is A. LaVonne Brown Ruoff et al., comps., "African American Literature," in Ruoff and Ward, eds., *Redefining American Literary History* (3B1).

Chapter 7
CHICANO/LATINO LITERATURE

A. A Brief Narrative History

Hispanic Americans—Mexican Americans, Cuban Americans, Puerto Ricans, and other Spanish-speaking groups—represent the fastest-growing ethnic population in the United States today. It increased 36 percent during the 1980's, and, at twenty million, is the second-largest minority after African Americans. And, as in African American culture, Hispanic Americans have experienced a cultural renaissance in the past several decades that has produced works of art and literature establishing their presence and influence in all areas of mainstream culture. Playwrights like Luis Valdez (*Zoot Suit*); novelists like Rudolfo A. Anaya (*Bless Me, Ultima*), Oscar Hijuelos (*The Mambo Kings Play Songs of Love*), and Sandra Cisneros (*The House on Mango Street*); poets like Gary Soto (*The Tale of Sunlight*), Jimmy Santiago Baca (*What's Happening*), Lorna Dee Cervantes (*Emplumada*), and Bernice Zamora (*Restless Serpents*) have only confirmed the importance of Hispanic culture to American life and letters.

Two problems, however, confront the student of Chicano/Latino literatures at once. First, many Hispanic Americans use Spanish as a vehicle of their art. (All Hispanic writing before 1850 was in Spanish, of course, but even today a number of writers continue to use some combination of English and Spanish.) Readers who are not bilingual have difficulty reading individual works, to say nothing of grasping the whole range of Chicano/Latino literary culture.

More important for the literary scholar or historian, Chicano/Latino literature as a category incorporates a variety of literatures with different backgrounds and perspectives. The bulk of this literature is Chicano, or literature with its roots in the Mexican-American community and its history in a part of the United States that was once Spanish. (Of all Hispanic Americans living in the United States, approximately 63 percent are Chicanos.) As Chicano playwright Luis Valdez has said, "We did not in fact come to the United States at all. The United States came to us."[1] Like Native Americans, Chicanos can claim a culture that predates the United States, and its writers often have a necessarily bifocal view that looks back to Aztlan, their spiritual homeland in the American Southwest.

Hispanic, or Spanish-speaking, culture in the United States also includes Puerto Ricans (both on the island and on the mainland), who have a similarly dual relationship with dominant American culture, and Cuban Americans, especially those writers and artists who have lived in exile in this country since the 1960's. Finally, and increasingly in future years, one imagines, Chicano/Latino literature and culture in the United States will come to encompass the hundreds of thousands of Spanish-speaking immigrants from Central and South America who, for economic and/or political reasons, have chosen this country as their permanent home. One cannot begin to describe the shape that Chicano/Latino literature will take in the future.

Chicano/Latino is therefore an imprecise but inclusive title meant to gather within its broad limits all the Spanish-speaking populations of the United States. It even includes what has come to be called *Literatura Chicanesca,* or literature about Chicanos by non-Chicanos, like Jim Sagel and "Danny Santiago" (Daniel James), which has become part of the canon of Chicano/Latino literature. (James's 1983 novel *Famous All Over Town* has already become "a classic of the Chicano urban experience."[2]) At the same time, of course—and this is true of every ethnic literature—Chicano/Latino literature includes writers such as John Rechy, whose creative work (for example, *City of Night,* 1963) is not noticeably ethnic.

The history of Chicano literature, the literature of the majority of the primary and secondary works listed below, can conveniently be divided into three stages.[3]

1. *Pre-Chicano literature* (to 1848) encompasses all the literature created from the first Spanish explorers to the Southwest through the Treaty of Hidalgo, when vast areas of the American Southwest were ceded to the United States, and when in effect thousands of Spanish-speaking people suddenly became American citizens. Besides travel narratives and diaries, this period also produced a great number of religious and secular plays, romances and *corridos* (narrative ballads), and hundreds of years of literary folklore. As Raymund A. Paredes has forcefully argued, it is this oral tradition—found in the folklore and the corridos—which is most important in later literature, and which Chicano writers are still tapping today.[4]

2. *Chicano literature* (1848-1959) in fact incorporates several periods: what is known as the period of transition (1848-1910), when Mexican-Americans were created and began to define themselves, and when their literature reflected their dual status, various border struggles, and the continuing importance of the folk tradition, ballads, and the like. The period of 1910 to 1960 is divided by 1943: Heavy migration in the early decades of the century culminated in the Zoot Suit riots in Los Angeles, and the growing minority consciousness of the first half led to the increasing confrontations before 1960. This was also the period when Chicano writers mastered modern literary forms (e.g., Josephina Niggli's novel *Mexican Village* in 1945, or the poetry and fiction of Fray Angélico Chávez in the 1940's and 1950's).

3. *Contemporary Chicano literature* (1959-   ) reflects an explosion of political consciousness in the 1960's matched only by the second African American renaissance of the same period. As Chicanos gained a sense of themselves as *la raza* (the Chicano community), their art increasingly reflected that identity and the energy and commitment it carried. Luis Valdez and El Teatro Campesino turned theatre into a political forum, where everyday problems become the focus of short *actos.* Fiction went through a similar resurgence, from the first Chicano novel of Jose Antonio Villarreal (*Pocho,* 1959), through the work of Rolando Hinojosa, Tomás Rivera, Ron Arias, and others. Poetry saw perhaps the greatest flowering of all in the work of Alurista, Cherríe Moraga, and many others. Chicano writers in the past thirty years have explored all aspects of the Chicano experience, in works as varied as

Oscar Acosta's *The Autobiography of a Brown Buffalo* (1972) and Richard Rodríguez's controversial *Hunger of Memory* (1982).

Chicano writers appear in nearly every national literary forum. Although many of the cultural vehicles that fueled this literary renaissance in the 1960's and 1970's—journals such as *El Grito* (1967-1974) and *Grito del Sol* (1976-1982), and publishers such as Quinto Sol (1967-1975)—are no longer around to help, the literature itself is strong enough to continue to grow on its own.

Given the growth in Hispanic populations across the country, the possibility for the development of all Chicano/Latino literatures appears great. The literature being written by Chicanos, Puerto Ricans (for example, Piri Thomas, Victor Hernandez-Cruz, and Nicholasa Mohr), Cuban Americans (Oscar Hijuelos, to name only one), and others appears as colorful pieces in the multicultural tapestry being stitched together in this country by many hands. It is a literature that is important for the entire tapestry because, beyond its individual differences, it has a strong sense of history and it celebrates positive ethnic values and traditions—especially the importance of family and community—at the same time that it calls into question outmoded American values and attitudes. It is also a literature that has at its core the quest for identity, which is the essential ethnic story and, finally, the essential American story.

B. A Selected List of Primary Works

1. Anthologies

a. Bibliographies

García-Ayvens, Francisco, comp. *Chicano Anthology Index: A Comprehensive Author, Title, and Subject Index to Chicano Anthologies, 1965-1987.* Berkeley: Chicano Studies Library Publications Unit, University of California, 1990.
Identifies 280 anthologies containing approximately 5000 essays and other creative works. (Anthologies published after 1987 are indexed through the *Chicano Database*; see 1A4.)

b. General Collections

Alegría, Fernando, and Jorge Ruffinelli, eds. *Paradise Lost or Gained? The Literature of Hispanic Exile.* Houston, Tex.: Arte Público Press, 1990.
Includes both poetry and prose (by Cubans, other Latin American writers) and essays on the literature of exile.

Alurista, et al., eds. *Festival de flor y canto: An Anthology of Chicano Literature.*
Los Angeles: University of Southern California Press, 1976.
This collection of bilingual works was first read at a 1973 festival in Los Angeles
and contains short stories, poetry, selections from novels, and "Teatro Presenta-
tions."

Anaya, Rudolfo A., ed. *Voces: An Anthology of Nuevo Mexicano Writers.* Albuquerque, N.M.: El Norte Publications, 1987.
Fiction and poetry that demonstrates the "vital links in the oral and written
traditions" of New Mexico's literary expression, by Anaya, Sabine Ulibarri,
Jimmy Baca, Fray Angélico Chávez, and three dozen other writers.

Armas, José, et al., eds. *Mestizo: Anthology of Chicano Literature.* Albuquerque,
N.M.: Pajarito Publications, 1978.
This collection from an issue of *De Colores* (4, nos. 1-2) is aimed at presenting
"the range and diversity" of Chicano literature. Forty-three writers are represented in sections on poetry, fiction, translation, children's story, prison writings,
and more.

Babín, María Teresa, and Stan Steiner, eds. *Borinquen: An Anthology of Puerto
Rican Literature.* New York: Alfred A. Knopf, 1974.
An early collection that is the "first attempt to offer in English a representative
selection of important Puerto Rican poetry and prose writings from the sixteenth
century to the present day." An introduction by Babín is followed by selections
arranged in twenty-nine historical units.

Cárdenas de Dwyer, Carlota, ed. *Chicano Voices.* Boston: Houghton Mifflin, 1975.
Selections are arranged by the main themes of Chicano literature: the barrio, "La
Chicana," the Chicano movement, and so forth. Alurista, Luis Valdez, John
Rechy, "Danny Santiago," Tomás Rivera, Cesar Chavez, Ruben Salazar, and
thirty other Chicano writers are represented.

Carillo, Leonardo, et al., eds. *Canto al Pueblo: An Anthology of Experiences.* San
Antonio, Tex.: Penca Books, 1978.
This bilingual collection contains drawings and photography, poetry and fiction
by Lorna Dee Cervantes, Abelardo Delgado, Evangelina Vigil, Rolando Hinojosa-Smith, others.

Casteñeda-Shular, Antonia, et al., eds. *Literatura Chicana: Texto y Contexto/Chica-
no Literature: Text and Context.* Englewood Cliffs, N.J.: Prentice-Hall, 1972.
This collection has three sections of poetry and prose centering on the themes
of social protest, the essence of Chicano culture, and the experience of migration.
The fourth section—"Literatura de la Raza"—attempts to place Chicano literature

in a number of larger contexts: Mexican, Puerto Rican, and Latin American literatures (selections by Octavio Paz, Piri Thomas, Jose Marti and Pablo Neruda, etc.)

de Armas, Jose R., and Charles W. Steele, eds. and trans. *Cuban Consciousness in Literature: 1923-1974 (A Critical Anthology of Cuban Culture)*. Miami, Fla.: Ediciones Universal, 1978.
Contains a general introduction as well as introductions to each of the three groupings of poetry, essays, and short stories: "The Integrative Period of Cuban National Consciousness (1923-1940)," "Pre-Revolution (1940-1959)," and "Revolution (1959-1974)." The last part also contains a subsection entitled "Literary Production in Exile."

Harth, Dorothy E., and Lewis M. Baldwin, eds. *Voices of Aztlan: Chicano Literature of Today*. New York: New American Library, 1974.
An early paperback anthology of contemporary Chicano poetry, prose, and drama.

Hospital, Carolina, ed. *Cuban American Writers: Los Atrevidos*. Princeton, N.J.: Linden Lane Press, 1988.
A collection of Cuban American prose and poetry that shows "a mosaic of cultural traditions, as well as an underlying exile consciousness."

Kanellos, Nicolás, ed. *Decade of Hispanic Literature: An Anniversary Anthology*. Houston, Tex.: Arte Público Press, 1982.
First printed as an anniversary issue of *Revista Chicano-Riqueña* (10, nos. 1-2, 1982), this collection contains poetry, fiction, and essays by Lorna Dee Cervantes, Gary Soto, Rudolfo Anaya, Tomás Rivera, and forty other writers.

Keller, Gary D., and Francisco Jiménez, eds. *Hispanics in the United States: An Anthology of Creative Literature*. 2 vols. Ypsilanti, Mich.: Bilingual Review/Press, 1980, 1982.
These collections are intended "to provide the reader with a glimpse of the varieties of literature written today that treat the United States Hispanic experience." Poems and stories are arranged in thematic units, such as the immigrant experience, war and death, and schooling.

Ludwig, Ed, and James Santibanez, eds. *The Chicanos: Mexican American Voices*. Baltimore, Md.: Penguin, 1971.
An anthology of stories, poems, and essays by Raymond Barrio, Luis Valdez, Cesar Chavez, Joan Baez, Reies Lopez Tijerina, and others reflecting early political struggles of Chicanos.

Nosotros. Special issue of *Revista Chicano-Riqueña* 5, no. 1 (1977).
This "collection of Latino poetry and graphics from Chicago" contains contributions from Cuban American, Mexican American, and Puerto Rican poets and artists.

Ortego, Philip D., ed. *We Are Chicanos: An Anthology of Mexican American Literature*. New York: Washington Square Press, 1973. Designed "both as a text for classroom use and as a general introduction to the long-neglected body of Mexican-American literature," this collection has sections on "Perspectives" (backgrounds, folklore, etc.) and "The Creative Spirit" (poetry, fiction, drama).

Paredes, Américo, and Raymund Paredes, eds. *Mexican-American Authors*. Boston: Houghton Mifflin, 1972.
Twelve representative writers from "The Aztlan Territory" of the Southwest are represented, among whom are Josephina Niggli, Luis Omar Salinas, and Rafael Jesús González.

Romano, Octavio I., ed. *The Grito del Sol Collection*. Berkeley, Calif.: TQS Publications, 1984.
This anthology includes stories by Rudolfo A. Anaya, Sabine R. Ulibarrí, and works by eight other contemporary writers.

Romano, Octavio I., and Herminio Rios-C., eds. *El Espejo/The Mirror: Selected Chicano Literature*. Rev. ed. Berkeley, Calif.: Quinto Sol Publications, 1972.
This first anthology of "Chicano literature published by Chicanos" collects poetry as well as prose by Rudolfo Anaya, Tomás Rivera, Alurista, and other contemporary writers.

Salinas, Luis Omar, and Lillian Faderman, eds. *From the Barrio: A Chicano Anthology*. San Francisco: Canfield Press, 1973.
This early Chicano collection has two sections. "My Revolution" presents literature that seeks to make a political statement (Luis Omar Salinas, Luis Valdez, et al.); "My House" contains "literature that seeks to make a personal statement" (Leonard Adamé, Rafael Jesús González, others).

Turner, Faythe, ed. *Puerto Rican Writers at Home in the USA*. Seattle: Open Hand Publishing, 1991.
This collection contains a "Poets' Sampler" plus an anthology of seventeen Puerto Rican writers.

Valdez, Luis, and Stan Steiner, eds. *Aztlán: An Anthology of Mexican American Literature*. New York: Alfred A. Knopf, 1972.
The introduction, "La Plebe," by Valdez opens this collection of thirteen chrono-

logical/thematic sections of drama, prose, and poetry, from Mayan and Aztec roots in Mexico to contemporary Chicano struggles.

See also: Fisher, Haslam, and others (3D); Miller (7C6)

c. Drama Collections

Garza, Roberto J., ed. *Contemporary Chicano Theatre.* Notre Dame, Ind.: University of Notre Dame Press, 1976.
Includes introductions and eight plays by Luis Valdez, Alurista, Estela Portillo, and others.

Huerta, Jorge A., ed. *The Necessary Anthology: Plays of the Chicano Experience.* Houston, Tex.: Arte Público Press, 1989.
Two plays by El Teatro de la Esperanza, Luis Valdez's *The Shrunken Head of Pancho Villa,* three other dramas, each preceded by a brief biography of the author and "followed by a production history and commentary on the play."

_____. *El Teatro de la Esperanza: An Anthology of Chicano Drama.* Goleta, Calif.: El Teatro de la Esperanza, 1973.
Eight examples of the Chicano theatre group that emerged in Santa Barbara, California, in the early 1970's.

Kanellos, Nicolás, and Jorge A. Huerta, eds. *Nuevos Pasos: Chicano and Puerto Rican Drama.* Houston, Tex.: Arte Público Press, 1989.
First published as a special issue of *Revista Chicano-Riqueña* in 1979, this collection has complete scripts of plays by Ron Arias, Estela Portillo-Trambley, and half a dozen other playwrights.

Osborn, M. Elizabeth, ed. *On New Ground: Contemporary Hispanic-American Plays.* New York: Theatre Communications Group, 1987.
Six plays from the 1980's by Lynne Alvarez, Maria Irene Fornes, John Jesurun, Eduardo Machado, Jose Rivera, and Milcha Sanchez-Scott. Each play is prefaced by a brief autobiographical essay.

Romano, Octavio I., and Herminio Rios, eds. *Chicano Drama. El Grito Book* Series 7, no. 4 (June-August, 1974).
This collection contains plays by Alurista and Carlos Morton, in addition to three short pieces by Alfonso C. Hernandez.

Valdez, Luis, and El Teatro Campesino. *Actos.* San Juan Batista, Calif.: Cucaracha Press, 1971.

Nine examples of the short social dramatic form developed by this successful guerilla theatre troupe in the 1960's.

d. Poetry Collections

Adamé, Leonard, et al., eds. *Entrance: Four Chicano Poets.* Greenfield Center, N.Y.: Greenfield Review Press, 1975.
A chapbook of poems by Adamé, Luis Omar Salinas, Gary Soto, and Ernesto Trejo.

Binder, Wolfgang, ed. *Contemporary Chicano Poetry: An Anthology.* Erlangen, Germany: Palm & Enke, 1986.
A companion volume to Binder's *Partial Autobiographies* (see 7C2), this collection represents twenty contemporary poets, including Gary Soto, Alurista, Sandra Cisneros, Luis Omar Salinas, and Jimmy Santiago Baca. Includes a long analytical introduction by the editor.

Empringham, Toni, ed. *Fiesta in Aztlán: Anthology of Chicano Poetry.* Santa Barbara, Calif.: Capra Press, 1982.
Contemporary poems grouped by three constant themes in Chicano poetry: home/family, "The Streets of the Barrio," and the world.

Keller, Gary D., ed. *Triple Crown: Chicano, Puerto Rican, and Cuban-American Poetry.* Tempe, Ariz.: Bilingual Review/Press, 1987.
Three "full-length collections of poems by three important young poets": Roberto Durán, *Red on My Way to the Rose,* Judith Ortiz Cofer, *Reaching for the Mainland,* and Gustavo Perez Firmat, *Carolina Cuban.*

e. Collections of Short Fiction

Anaya, Rudolfo A., and Antonio Márquez, eds. *Cuentos Chicanos: A Short Story Anthology.* Rev. ed. Albuquerque: University of New Mexico Press, 1984.
This collection demonstrates "that the Chicano short story has reached new levels of maturity and sophistication," with examples by Anaya, Bruce-Novoa, Nash Candelaria, Ana Castillo, Denise Chávez, and sixteen other writers.

Kanellos, Nicolás, and Luis Dávila, eds. *Latino Short Fiction.* Special issue of *Revista Chicano-Riqueña* 8, no. 1 (1980).
Stories by Miguel Algarín, José Antonio Burciaga, Hugo Martínez-Serros, and six other prize-winning Chicano writers.

Simmen, Edward, ed. *The Chicano: From Caricature to Self-Portrait.* New York: New American Library, 1971.
Representative short fiction in three sections: "From the Beginnings to 1930" contains early caricatures by Bret Harte, Jack London, and others. "Through the Depression to 1940" has "Realistic Profiles" by William Saroyan, John Steinbeck, Paul Horgan. The final, and longest section, "From World War II to the Present," contains portraits and self-portraits, including stories by Mario Suarez, Nick C. Vaca, and others.

Wegenheim, Kal, ed. *Cuentos: An Anthology of Short Stories from Puerto Rico.* New York: Schocken Books , 1978.
This bilingual collection contains twelve stories by six twentieth century Puerto Rican writers. Most reflect the "critical period in the island's history—the 1940s and 1950s—when chronic poverty, coupled with vertiginous social change, caused great anguish and confusion."

f. Collections of Latina Writings

Alarcón, Norma, ed. *Third Woman: The Sexuality of Latinas.* Special issue of *Third Woman* 4, no. 2 (1989).
Poetry, prose, drama, and essays/reviews by Sandra Cisneros, Gloria Anzaldúa, Cherríe Moraga, and others. Includes a bibliography, "Chicana Writers and Critics in a Social Context."

_____, ed. *Third Woman: Texas and More.* Special issue of *Third Woman* 3, nos. 1-2 (1986).
Poetry, narratives, essays, interviews (with Pat Mora and Cherríe Moraga), and reviews, all by Hispanic-American women.

Boza, Maria del Carmen, et al., eds. *Nosotras: Latina Literature Today.* Binghamton, N.Y.: Bilingual Review/Press, 1986.
Selections from Chicana, Cuban-American, and Puerto Rican writers in six thematic categories, including imagination, family, women's rights, and love.

Gómez, Alma, et al., eds. *Cuentos: Stories by Latinas.* New York: Kitchen Table, 1983.
Stories by Gloria Anzaldúa, Aurora Levins, Rosario Morales, Roberta Fernandez, and two dozen other women.

Herrera-Sobek, María, and Helena Maria Viramontes, eds. *Chicana Creativity and Criticism: Charting New Frontiers in American Literature.* Houston, Tex.: Arte Público Press, 1988.

Originally an issue of *The Americas Review* 25, nos. 3-4 (Fall-Winter, 1987) from a 1985 University of California, Irvine, conference, this collection has poetry (Denise Chávez, Lorna Dee Cervantes, Lucha Corpi, and Evangelina Vigil-Pinon), fiction (Chávez, Viramontes, Roberta Fernandez), and criticism (Tey Diana Rebolledo, Yvonne Yarbro-Bejarano, Norma Alarcón, Julian Olivares, Herrera-Sobek).

Kanellos, Nicolás, and Luis Dávila, eds. *La Mujer: A Special Issue. Revista Chicano-Riqueña* 6, no. 2 (1978).
In this issue are poetry (María Herrera-Sobek, Omar Salinas, et al.) prose (for example, Abelardo Delgado, Norma Alarcón), criticism (Vernon E. Lattin on Rudolfo Anaya), and reviews.

Keller, Gary D., ed. *Three Times a Woman: Chicana Poetry.* Tempe, Ariz.: Bilingual Review/Press, 1989.
Full length collections of poetry by Alicia Gaspar de Alba, María Herrera-Sobek, and Demetria Martinez.

Rebolledo, Tey Diana, et al., eds. *Las Mujeres Hablan: An Anthology of Nuevo Mexicana Writers.* Albuquerque, N.M.: El Norte Publications, 1988.
This bilingual regional collection contains Chicana poetry and prose by Denise Chávez, Cordelia Candelaria, over fifty other writers.

Rios-C, Herminio, and Octavio I. Romano-V, eds. *Chicanas en la literatura y el arte. El Grito* Book Series 7, no. 1. Berkeley, Calif.: Quinto Sol Publications, 1973.
This bilingual collection represents a dozen women in poetry and prose and an excerpt from a morality play (by Estela Portillo).

Vigil, Evangelina, ed. *Woman of Her Word: Hispanic Women Write.* Houston, Tex.: Arte Público Press, 1987.
Poetry (Sandra Cisneros, Judith Ortiz Cofer, Pat Mora, others), prose (Nicholosa Mohr, Roberta Fernandez, et al.), and criticism (three essays) reveal "the vibrant imagination, talent and intelligence of Latina writers."

2. Individual Writers[5]

a. Chicano

Acosta, Aldaberto Joel
   Chicanos Can Make It (autobiography, 1971)
   From Common Clay (fiction, 1978)

Acosta, Oscar Zeta
The Autobiography of a Brown Buffalo (fiction, 1972)
The Revolt of the Cockroach People (fiction, 1973)

Acosta Torres, José
Cachito mio (short fiction, 1973)

Adamé, Leonard
Cantos pa' la memoria (poetry, 1979)

Aguilar, Ricardo
Caravana enlutada (poetry, 1975)
En son lluvia (poetry, 1980)

Aguilar-Henson, Marcela
Figura cristalina (poetry, 1983)

Alurista
A'nque (poetry, 1979)
Floricanto en Aztlán (poetry, 1971)
Nationchild Plumaroja: Poems 1969-1972 (1972)
Return: Poems Collected and New (1982)
Spik in Glyph? (poetry, 1981)
Timespace Huracán: Poems 1972-1975 (1976)

Alvarado, Arturo Roca
Crónica de Aztlán: A Migrant's Tale (short fiction, 1977)

Amezquita, Ricardo
Eating Stones (poetry, 1977)

Anaya, Rudolfo A.
The Adventures of Juan Chicaspatas (poetry, 1985)
Bless Me, Ultima (fiction, 1972)
Heart of Aztlán (fiction, 1976)
The Legend of La Llorona: A Short Novel (1984)
Lord of the Dawn: The Legend of Quetzalcoatl (fiction, 1987)
The Silence of the Llano: Short Stories (1982)
Tortuga (fiction, 1979)

Anzaldúa, Gloria
Borderlands/La Frontera: The New Mestiza (poetry, prose, 1987)

Apodaca, Rudy
  The Waxen Image (fiction, 1977)

Aranda, Charles
  Dudes or Dud (fiction, 1984)

Arellano, Juan
  Palabras de la vista (poetry, 1984)

Argüelles, Iván
  Captive of the Vision of Paradise: Poems (1982)
  Instamatic Reconditioning (poetry, 1976)
  The Invention of Spain: Poems (1978)
  Manicomio: Poems (1984)
  The Tattooed Heart of the Drunken Sailor: Poems (1983)

Arias, Ron
  The Road to Tamazunchale (fiction, 1978)

Avedaño, Fausto
  El Corrido de California: A Three Act Play (1979)

Baca, Jimmy Santiago
  Immigrants in Our Own Land (poetry, 1979)
  Swords of Darkness (poetry, 1981)
  What's Happening (poetry, 1982)

Baez, Joan
  Daybreak (autobiography, 1968)

Baptiste, Victor
  Unos Pasos (poetry, 1968)

Bernal, Vincente
  Las primicias (poetry, 1916)

Barrio, Raymond
  The Plum Plum Pickers (fiction, 1969)

Barrios, Gregg
  Puro rolo (poetry, 1982)

Blea, Irene
Celebrating Crying and Cursing (poetry, 1980)

Bornstein-Somoza, Miriam
Bajo cubierta (poetry, 1976)

Brawley, Ernest
The Alamo Tree (fiction, 1984)
Selena (fiction, 1979)

Brinson-Pineda, Barbara
Nocturno (poetry, 1978)
Vocabulary of the Dead (poetry, 1984)

Brito, Aristeo
El diablo en Texas (fiction, 1976)

Bruce-Novoa, Juan D.
Inocencia perversa/Perverse Innocence (poetry, 1977)

Burciaga, José
Drink Cultura Refrescante (poetry, 1978)
Restless Serpents (poetry, 1976)

Burk, Ronnie
En el jardin de nos nopales: Poems 1976-1977 (1983)

Calderón, Tomás
Think of This Situation (poetry, 1977)

Campa, Arthur Leon
Los Comanches: A New Mexican Folk Drama (1942)

Campbell, Roberto
Poems from My Notebook (1978)

Campbell, Trini
Canto indio mexicano (poetry, 1977)

Candelaria, Cordelia
Ojo de la Cueva/Cave Springs (poetry, 1984)

Candelaria, Nash
  The Day the Cisco Kid Shot John Wayne (short fiction, 1987)
  Inheritance of Strangers (fiction, 1985)
  Memories of the Alhambra (fiction, 1977)
  Not by the Sword (fiction, 1982)

Cardenas, Leo
  Return to Ramos (fiction, 1970)

Cárdenas, Reyes
  Chicano Territory: Poems (1984)
  I Was Never a Militant Chicano (poetry, 1986)
  Survivors of the Chicano Titanic (poetry, 1981)

Castaño, Wilfredo
  Cast Small Stones upon the Tender Earth (poetry, 1981)

Castellano, Olivia
  Blue Mandolin, Yellow Field (poetry, 1980)
  Blue Horse of Madness (poetry, 1982)

Castillo, Ana
  I Close My Eyes (To See) (poetry, 1976)
  The Mixquiahuala Letters (fiction, 1986)
  My Father Was a Toltec (poetry, 1988)
  Otro canto (poetry, 1975)
  Women Are Not Roses (poetry, 1984)
  Zero Makes Me Hungry (poetry, 1975)

Catalcos, Rosemary
  Again for the First Time (poetry, 1984)

Cervantes, Irma
  Sparks, Flames and Cinders (poetry, 1982)

Cervantes, Lorna Dee
  Emplumada (poetry, 1981)

Chacon, Eusebio
  El hijo de la tempestad: Tras la tormenta la calma (fiction, 1892)

Chacón, Felipe Maximiliano
  Obras de Felipe Maximiliano Chacón, "el Cantor neomexicano": Poesia y prosa

(poetry, 1924)
Short Stories (1980)

Chávez, Denise
  The Last of the Menu Girls (fiction, 1986)
  Face of an Angel (fiction, 1988)

Chávez, Fray Angélico
  Clothed with the Sun (poetry, 1939)
  Eleven Lady Lyrics and Other Poems (1945)
  From an Altar Screen: Tales from New Mexico (short fiction, 1943)
  La Conquistadora: The Autobiography of an Ancient Statue (fiction, 1954)
  The Lady from Toledo (fiction, 1960)
  New Mexico Triptych (short fiction, 1976)
  Selected Poems (1969)
  The Short Stories of Fray Angélico Chávez (1987)
  The Single Rose: Poems of Divine Love (1948)
  The Virgin of Port Lligat (poetry, 1959)

Chávez, Mario
  When It Rains in Cloves (poetry, 1980)

Cisneros, Sandra
  Bad Boys (poetry, 1980)
  The House on Mango Street (fiction, 1983)
  My Wicked, Wicked Ways (poetry, 1986)
  Woman Hollering Creek, and Other Stories (1991)

Corpi, Lucha
  Delia's Song (fiction, 1988)
  Palabras de mediodia: Noon Words (poetry, 1980)

Cota-Cárdenas, Margarita
  Noches despertando inconciencias (poetry, 1977)
  Puppet (fiction, 1985)

Cuellar Jiminez, Ben
  Gallant Outcast (poetry, 1963)

De Casas, Celso
  Pelón Drops Out (fiction, 1982)

De France, Gary
  Seascapes (poetry, 1979)

de Hoyos, Angela
  Arise, Chicano! and Other Poems (1975)
  Chicano Poems for the Barrio (1975)
  Selecciones (poetry, 1976)
  Selected Poems (1979)
  Woman, Woman (poetry, 1985)

de la Fuente, Mario
  I Like You, Gringo, But! (autobiography, 1972)

De La Junta, Paco
  1983 Chicano Engagement Calendar: A Year of Poetry de Paco de la Junta
  (1982)

De León, Nephtalí
  5 Plays (drama, 1972)

Delgado, Abelardo
  Apathy Avenue (poetry, 1980)
  Chicano: 25 Pieces of a Chicano Mind (poetry, 1969)
  Bajo el so de Aztlán: 25 soles de Abelardo (poetry, 1973)
  Here Lies Lalo: 25 Deaths of Abelardo (poetry, 1977)
  It's Cold: 52 Cold Thought-Poems of Abelardo (1973)
  Letters to Louise (fiction, 1982)
  Reflexiones: 16 Reflections of Abelardo (poetry, 1976)
  Siete de Abelardo (poetry, 1979)
  Unos perros con metralla: 25 Perros of Abelardo (poetry, 1982)

Delgado, Holly
  The Junk City Journal (poetry, 1977)

Dinkel, Reynalda
  Con grato y dulce acento: A Book of Christmas in Poetry (1974)

Domínguez, Sylvia Maida
  La comadre Maria: una comedia (drama, 1973)

Elizondo, Sergio
  Libro para batos y chavalas chicanas (poetry, 1977)
  Muerte en una estrella (fiction, 1984)

Perros y antiperros: Una épica chicana (poetry, 1972)
Rosa, la flauta (short fiction, 1980)

Espinosa, Aurelio Macedonio
Conchita Argüello: Historia y novela Californiana (fiction, 1938)

Espinosa, Herberto
Viendo morir a Teresa y otros relatos (short fiction, 1983)

Estupinian, Rafael
A Toston: Reminiscences of a Mexican-American (poetry, 1973)

Flores, Gloria
And Her Children Lived (poetry, 1974)

Flores Peregrino, José
Mesqui + ierra (poetry, 1977)

Fuego, Laura del
Maravilla (fiction, 1988)

Gaitan, Marcela
Chicano Themes: Manita Poetry (1975)

Galarza, Ernesto
Barrio Boy: The Story of a Boy's Acculturation (fictionalized autobiography, 1971)
Kodachrome in Thyme (poetry, 1982)

Galvan, Roberto
Poemas en español (poetry, 1977)

Galvez, Javier
Encanto chicano (poetry, 1971)

Gamboa, Manuel
Born into Felony (poetry, 1977)
Divergencias (poetry, 1976)

Gamboa, Reymundo
Madrugada del 56: Selected Poems (1978)

Gamboa, Reymundo, and Ernesto Padilla
The Baby Chook and Other Remnants: Selected Poems (1976)

García, Andrew
Tough Trip Through Paradise, 1878-1879 (autobiography, 1967)

García, Arnoldo
Un macehual ed Madrid (poetry, 1981)

García, José
Castillos en el aire (poetry, 1925)
Sería rata! (poetry, 1930)

García, Lionel G.
Leaving Home (fiction, 1985)
A Shroud in the Family (fiction, 1987)

García, Luis
Beans (poetry, 1976)
Mister Menu (poetry, 1968)

García, Richard
Selected Poetry (1973)

García-Camarillo, Cecilio
Calcetines embotellados (poetry, 1982)
Carambola (poetry, 1982)
Doubleface (poetry, 1982)
Ecstasy and Puro Pedo (poetry, 1982)
Hang a Snake (poetry, 1982)
Winter Month (poetry, 1982)

Garza, Cheo
Capirotada (poetry, 1980)

Garza, Mario
Un paso más: Collected Poems (1976)

Gaspar, Tomás
North Side Story (poetry, 1978)

Gómez-Quiñones, Juan
5th and Grande Vista: Poems 1960-1973 (1974)

Gonzáles, Rodolfo "Corky"
I am Joaquin/Yo soy Joaquín: An Epic Poem (1967)

González, Beatriz
The Chosen Few (poetry, 1984)

González, Cásar A.
Unwinding the Silence (poetry, 1987)

González, David J.
A Journey to the Third World (poetry, 1979)

González, Genaro
Rainbow's End (fiction, 1988)

González, Rafael Jesús
El hacedor de huegos/The Maker of Games (poetry, 1977)

González, Ray
From These Restless Roots (poetry, 1986)

Hernandez, Alfonso
The False Advent of Mary's Child and Other Plays (1979)

Hernandez, Leo, and Marty Hernandez
Padre y hijo/Father and Son: Chicano Thoughts (poetry, 1974)

Hernandez Tovar, Inés
Con razon, Corazon (poetry, 1977)

Herrera, Juan Felipe
Exiles of Desire (poetry, 1985)
Rebozos of Love/We Have Woven/Sudor de Pueblos/On Our Backs (poetry, 1974)

Hinojosa, Rolando
Claros varones de Belken/Fair Gentlemen of Belken (fiction, 1986)
Dear Rafe (fiction, 1985)
Estampas del Valle y otras obras: Sketches of the Valley and Other Works (fiction, 1973)
Generaciones, notas y breachas (fiction, 1978)
Generaciones y semblanzas (fiction, 1977)
Klail City (fiction, 1987)
Korean Love Songs (poetry, 1978)

Mi querido Rafa (fiction, 1981)
Partners in Crime (fiction, 1985)
Rites and Witnesses (fiction, 1982)
The Valley (fiction, 1983)

Hruska y Cortes, Elías
This Side and Other Things (poetry, 1971)

Ibañez, Armando
Midday Shadows (poetry, 1980)

Islas, Arturo
Migrant Souls (fiction, 1990)
The Rain God: A Desert Tale (fiction, 1984)

Jaramillo, Cleofas M.
Romance of a Little Village Girl (autobiography, 1955)

Keller, Gary
Tales of El Huitlacoche (short fiction, 1984)

Lopez, Tomás
Chicano, Go Home: The Life of Alfonso Rodriquez (fiction, 1976)
The Aguila Family (fiction, 1980)

Luera, Yolanda
Solitaria (poetry, 1986)

Maldonado, Jesús María
Sal, pimienta y amor (poetry, 1976)

Mares, E. A.
The Unicorn Poem (1980)

Martínez, Lorri
Where Eagles Fall (poetry, 1982)

Martínez, Maria
Sterling Silver Roses (poetry, 1981)

Martínez, Max
The Adventures of the Chicano Kid and Other Stories (1982)
Monologue of the Bolivian Major: Cuento (short fiction, 1978)

Schooland (fiction, 1988)

Martínez, Ricardo
The Healing Ritual (fiction, 1983)

Martínez-Serros, Hugo
The Last Laugh and Other Stories (1988)

Medina, Roberto
Two Ranges (fiction, 1974)
Fabian no se muere: Novela de amor (fiction, 1978)

Melendez, Rudolph
Pachuco Mark (fiction, 1976)

Méndez, Miguel
Los criaderos humanos (épica de los desamparados) y Sahuaros (poetry, 1975)
Cuentos para niños traviesos/Stories for Mischievous Children (1979)
Peregrinos de Aztlán (fiction, 1974)
El sueno de Santa Maria de las Petras (fiction, 1986)
Tata Casehua y otros cuentos (short fiction, 1980)

Monreal, Art
L.A. and Other Tragedies (poetry, 1981)

Monreal, David Nava
The New Neighbor and Other Stories (1987)

Montalvo, José
A mi que! (poetry, 1983)
Pensamientos capturados: Poemas de José Montalvo (1983)

Montoya, José
El sol y los de abajo and other R.C.A.F. Poems (1972)

Mora, Pat
Borders (poetry, 1986)
Chants (poetry, 1984)

Mora, Ricardo
The Black Sun (poetry, 1973)

Moraga, Cherríe
  Giving up the Ghost (poetry, 1986)
  Loving in the War Years: Lo que nunca paso por sus labios (mixed genres, 1983)

Morales, Alejandro
  The Brick People (fiction, 1988)
  Caras viejas y nivo nuevo (fiction, 1975)
  Old Faces and New Wine (fiction, 1981)
  The Rag Doll Plagues (fiction, 1992)
  Reto en al paraiso (fiction, 1983)
  La verdad sin voz (fiction, 1979)

Moreno, Dorinda
  Le mujer es la tierra, la tierra de vida (poetry, 1975)

Morton, Carlos
  The Many Deaths of Danny Rosales and Other. Plays (1983)
  White Heroine Winter (poetry, 1971)

Muñoz, Art
  A Cop's Journal and Other Poems (poetry, 1984)
  In Loneliness (poetry, 1975)

Murguia, Alejandro
  Oración a la mano poderosa (poetry, 1972)
  Farewell to the Coast (poetry, 1980)

Muro, Amado
  The Collected Stories of Amado Muro (1979)

Navarro, J. L.
  Blue Day on Main Street (short fiction, 1973)

Niggli, Josephina
  Mexican Village (fiction, 1945)
  Step Down, Elder Brother: A Novel (1947)

Ochoa, Jesús B.
  A Soft Tongue Shall Break Hardness (poetry, 1973)

Ornelas, Berta
  Come Down from the Mound (fiction, 1975)

Ortega, Adolfo
 A Turn of the Hands (poetry, 1981)

Ortiz y Pino, José
 Curandero: A Cuento (short fiction, 1982)

Otero, Miguel Antonio
 My Life on the Frontier (autobiography, 1935)
 Otero: An Autobiographical Trilogy (1974)

Palomares, Jose Francisco
 Memoirs (autobiography, 1955)

Pérez, Reymundo
 Free, Free at Last (poetry, 1970)
 The Secret Meaning of Death (poetry, 1971)

Pineda, Cecile
 Face (fiction, 1985)
 Frieze (fiction, 1986)

Pino, Frank
 Paseos y peregrinaciones: Poemas (1978)

Ponce, Mary Helen
 Recuerdo: Short Stories of the Barrio (1983)
 Taking Control (short fiction, 1987)

Ponce-Montoya, Juanita
 Grief Work (poetry, 1978)

Portillo-Trambley, Estela
 Rain of Scorpions and Other Writings (short fiction, 1975)
 Sor Juana and Other Plays (1983)
 Trini (fiction, 1986)

Quinn, Anthony
 The Original Sin: A Self-Portrait (autobiography, 1974)

Quiñones, Naomi
 Sueño de colibri: Hummingbird Dream (poetry, 1985)

Quintana, Leroy V.
  Hijo del Pueblo: New Mexico Poems (1976)
  Sangre (poetry, 1981)

Ramírez, Orlando
  Speedway (poetry, 1979)

Ramos, Luis Arturo
  Siete veces el sueño (short fiction, 1976)

Ranck, Katherine Quintana
  Portrait of Dona Elena (fiction, 1982)

Rangel, Rubén
  Bajo la sombra de la maquinaria: Poemas (1980)

Rechy, John
  City of Night (fiction, 1963)
  The Fourth Angel (fiction, 1972)
  Numbers (fiction, 1967)
  Rushes (fiction, 1979)
  The Sexual Outlaw (fiction, 1977)
  This Day's Death (fiction, 1969)
  The Vampires (fiction, 1971)

Ríco, Armando
  Three Coffins for Nino Lencho (fiction, 1983)

Ríos, Alberto
  Elk Heads on the Wall (poetry, 1979)
  Whispering to Fool the Wind (poetry, 1982)

Ríos, Isabella
  Victuum (fiction, 1976)

Rivera, Marina
  Sobra (poetry, 1977)

Rivera, Tomás
  Always and Other Poems (1973)
  The Harvest Stories of Tomás Rivera (1989)
  This Migrant Earth (fiction, 1986)
  . . . y no se lo tragó la tierra (fiction, 1971)

Robles, Margarita Luna, and Juan Felipe Herrera
A Night in Tunisia (poetry, 1985)

Rocha, Rina G.
Eluder (poetry, 1980)

Rodríguez, Dennis
Pachuco (fiction, 1980)

Rodríguez, Joe
Oddsplayer (fiction, 1988)

Rodríguez, Richard
Hunger of Memory: The Education of Richard Rodríguez (autobiography, 1982)

Romero, Leo
Agua Negra (poetry, 1981)
Celso (poetry, 1985)
During the Growing Season (poetry, 1978)

Romero, Lin
Happy Songs, Bleeding Hearts (poetry, 1974)

Romero, Orlando
Nambe-Year One (fiction, 1976)

Royball, Rose Marie
From La Llorona to Envidia . . . A Few Reflections (poetry, 1973)

Rufus
The Last Taco in Pérez: A Comic Tragedy (drama, 1975)

Sagel, Jim
Hablando de brujas y la gente de antes: Poemas del Rio Chama (1981)
Los compleanos de Dona Agueda (poetry, 1984)
Tunomas Honey (short fiction, 1983)

Salas, Floyd
Lay My Body on the Line (fiction, 1978)
Tattoo the Wicked Cross (fiction, 1967)
What Now My Love? (fiction, 1969)

Salaz, Fernando
Cornerstone in Rhythm (poetry, 1981)
Un dia y una vida (poetry, 1977)

Salaz, Rubén Darío
Heartland: Stories of the Southwest (1977)

Salinas, Luis Omar
Afternoon the Unreal (poetry, 1980)
Crazy Gypsy (poetry, 1970)
Darkness Under the Trees/Walking Behind the Spanish (poetry, 1982)
I Go Dreaming Serenades (1979)
Prelude to Darkness (poetry, 1981)
The Sadness of Days (poetry, 1987)

Salinas, Raúl R.
Un Trip through the Mind Jail y Otras Excursiones: Poems (1980)
Viaje/Trip (poetry, 1973)

Sanchez, Pilar
Symbols (poetry, 1977)

Sánchez, Ricardo
Amsterdam cantos y poemas pistos (1983)
Brown Bear Honey Madness: Alaskan Cruising Poems (1982)
Canto y grito mi liberación (poetry, 1971)
Hechizospells (poetry, 1976)
Milhuas Blues and Gritos Norteños (poetry, 1984)
Selected Poems (1985)

Sánchez, Saúl
Desalojos (a la soledad) (poetry, 1982)
Hay plesha lichans tu di falc (short fiction, 1977)

Sanchez, Trinidad
Poems by Trinidad Sanchez (1984)

Santiago, Danny [Daniel James]
Famous All over Town (fiction, 1983)

Sapia, Yvonne
Valentino's Hair (poetry, 1987)

Sierra, Michael
  In Their Father's Time (poetry, 1984)

Silva, Beverly
  The Cat and Other Stories (1986)
  The Second Street Poems (1983)

Somoza, Joseph
  Backyard Poems (1986)

Soto, Gary
  Black Hair (poetry, 1985)
  Como arbustos de niebla (poetry, 1980)
  The Elements of San Joaquín (poetry, 1977)
  Father Is a Pillow Tied to a Broom (poetry, 1980)
  Lesser Evils: Ten Quartets (short fiction, 1988)
  Living up the Street: Narrative Recollections (short fiction, 1985)
  Small Faces (short fiction, 1986)
  The Tale of Sunlight (poetry, 1978)
  Where Sparrows Work Hard (poetry, 1981)

Tafolla, Carmen
  Curandera (poetry, 1983)

Talamantez, Luis
  Life Within the Heart Imprisoned (poetry, 1976)

Tapia, John Reyna
  Shadows in Ecstasy and Other Poems (1971)

Taylor, Sheila Ortiz
  Faultline (fiction, 1982)

Tejeda, Juan
  Enamorado en la guerra y reconcocido la tierra: Aztlán '76-77 (poetry, 1983)

Tenorio, Arthur
  Blessing from Above (fiction, 1971)

Teran, Heriberto
  Vida de elusiones (poetry, 1971)

Topete, Eutimio, and Jerry Gonzales
Recordar es vivir (autobiography, 1978)

Torres-Metzgar, Joshep V.
Below the Summit (fiction, 1976)

Tovar, Ines
Con razon corazon (poetry, 1977)

Trejo, Ernesto
The Day of the Venders (poetry, 1977)
El día entre las hojas (poetry, 1984)
Instrucciones y señales (poetry, 1977)
Los numbres propios (poetry, 1978)

Ulibarrí, Sabine R.
Amor y Ecuador (poetry, 1966)
Al cielo se sube a pie (poetry, 1966)
El Condor and Other Stories (short fiction, 1988)
El Gobernador Glu Glu y otros cuentos (short fiction, 1988)
Mi abuela fumaba puros y otros cuentos del Tierra Amarilla/My Grandmother Smoked Cigars and Other Stories (1977)
Primeros encuenteros (short fiction, 1982)

Ulica, Jorge
Crónicas diabólicas (1916-1926) de "Jorge Ulica"/Julico G Arce (short fiction, 1982)

Valdés, Gina
Puentes y fronteras: Coplas chicanas (poetry, 1982)
There Are No Madmen Here (fiction, 1981)

Valdez, Luis
Pensamientos Serpentino: A Chicano Approach to the Theatre of Reality (poetry, 1973)

Valdez, Luis, and El Teatro Campesino
Actos (drama, 1971)

Vallejo, Armando
Luna llena: Ocho años de poesia chicana: 1971-1979 (poetry, 1979)

Vásquez, Richard
 Another Land (fiction, 1982)
 Chicano (fiction, 1970)
 The Giant Killer (fiction, 1978)

Venegas, Daniel
 Las aventuras de Don Chipote, o cuando los pericos mamen (fiction, 1984)

Vigil, Evangelina
 The Computer Is Down (poetry, 1988)
 Nade y nade: A Collection of Poems (1978)
 Thirty an' Seen a Lot (poetry, 1982)

Villanueva, Alma
 Bloodroot (poetry, 1977)
 Crónica de mis anos peores (poetry, 1987)
 Life Span (poetry, 1984)
 Mother, May I? (poetry, 1978)
 The Ultraviolet Sky (fiction, 1987)

Villanueva, Tino
 Hay otro Voz: Poems 1968-1971 (1972)
 Shaking Off the Dark (poetry, 1984)

Villarreal, José Antonio
 Clemente Chacon (fiction, 1984)
 The Fifth Horseman (fiction, 1974)
 Pocho (fiction, 1959)

Villaseñor, Victor
 Macho! (fiction, 1973)
 Rain of Gold (nonfiction, 1991)

Villegas, Robert
 Credo for Future Man (poetry, 1980)
 The Resurrection: A Short Play (1978)

Viramontes, Helena Maria
 The Moths and Other Stories (1985)

Zamora, Bernice
 Restless Serpents (poetry, 1976)

b. Cuban American

Acosta, Ivan
  El Super (drama, 1982)

Arenas, Reinaldo
  Farewell to the Sea (fiction, 1986)
  Old Rosa: A Novel in Two Stories (1989)

Catalá, Rafael
  Caminos/Roads (poetry, 1972)

Fernández, Roberto G.
  La montana rusa (fiction, 1985)
  Raining Backwards (fiction, 1988)
  La vida es un special (fiction, 1985)

Fornes, Maria
  Plays (1986)
  Promenade and Other Plays (1987)

Hijuelos, Oscar
  The Mambo Kings Play Songs of Love (fiction, 1989)
  Our House Is the Last Word (nonfiction, 1983)

Medina, Pablo
  Arching into the Afterlife (fiction, 1991)
  Exiled Memories: A Cuban Childhood (nonfiction, 1990)

Muñoz, Elías Miguel
  Crazy Love (fiction, 1989)
  The Greatest Performance (fiction, 1991)

Padilla, Heberto
  Heroes Are Grazing in My Garden (fiction, 1981)
  Sent Off the Field (poetry, 1972)

Prida, Dolores
  Beautiful Senorita and Other Plays (1991)
  Coser y cantar (drama, 1981)

c. Puerto Rican

Algarín, Miguel
Body Bee Calling from the Twenty-first Century (poetry, 1982)
Mongo Affair (poetry, 1978)
On Call (poetry, 1980)
Time's Now/Ya es tiempo (poetry, 1985)

Algarín, Miguel, and Tato Laviera
Olu Clemente (drama, 1973)

Andreu Iglesias, Cesar, ed.
Memoirs of Bernardo Vega (autobiography, 1984)

Barreto, Lefty
Nobody's Hero (fiction, 1976)

Carrero, Jaime
Jet Neorriqueno: Neo-Rican Jet Liner (poetry, 1964)
Noo Jork (drama, 1974)
Pipo Subway no sabre reir (drama, 1973)
Requelo tiene un mensaje (fiction, 1970)

Cintrón, Humberto
Frankie Cristo (fiction, 1972)

Colón, Jesús
A Puerto Rican in New York and Other Sketches (memoirs, 1961)

Cotto-Thorner, Guillermo
Tropico en Manhattan (fiction, 1959)

Cruz, Nicky
The Lonely Now (fiction, 1971)
Run Baby Run (fiction, 1968)

Diaz Valcarcel, Emilio
Harlem todos los dias (fiction, 1979)

Espada, Martin
Trumpets from the Island of Their Eviction (poetry, 1988)

Esteves, Sandra Maria
  Tropical Rains (poetry, 1984)
  Yerba buena (poetry, 1980)

Figueroa, José A.
  East 100th Street (poetry, 1973)
  Noo Jork (poetry, 1981)
  Unknown Poets from the Full-Time Jungle (poetry, 1975)

González, José Luis
  En Nueva York y otras desgracias (fiction, 1973)
  Paisa (fiction, 1950)

Hernández-Cruz, Victor
  By Lingual Wholes (poetry, 1982)
  Mainland (poetry, 1973)
  Rhythm, Content and Flavor: Poems, Selected and New (1988)
  Snaps (poetry, 1968)
  Tropicalization (poetry, 1976)
  Red Beans (poetry, 1991)

Labarthe, Pedro Juan
  The Son of Two Nations: The Private Life of a Columbia Student (fiction, 1931)

Laguerre, Enrique
  El laberinto/The Labyrinth (fiction, 1959)

Laviera, Tato
  AmeRican (poetry, 1985)
  La Carreta Made a U-Turn (poetry, 1979)
  Enclave (poetry, 1981)
  Mainstream Ethics (poetry, 1988)

Manrique, Manuel
  Island in Harlem (fiction, 1966)

Marqúes, René
  La Carreta/The Oxcart (drama, 1955)

Marzán, Julio
  Translations Without Originals (poetry, 1986)

Meléndez, Jesús Papoleto
Street Poetry and Other Poems (poetry, 1972)

Mendez Ballester, Manuel
Encrucijada (drama, 1958)

Miraflores, Carmen de
Cantando bajito: Singing Softly (fiction, 1989)

Mohr, Nicholasa
El Bronx Remembered (fiction, 1975)
Going Home (fiction, 1986)
In Nueva York (fiction, 1977)
Nilda (fiction, 1973)
Rituals of Survival: A Woman's Portfolio (fiction, 1985)

Morales, Aurora Levins, and Rosario Morales
Getting Home Alive (poetry, 1986)

Ortiz Cofer, Judith
The Line of the Sun (fiction, 1988)
Searching for the Mainland (poetry, 1987)
Terms of Survival (poetry, 1987)

Ortiz Taylor, Sheila
Faultline (fiction, 1982)

Pietri, Pedro
Lost in the Museum of Natural History/Perdido en el Museo de Historia Natural (fiction, 1981)
The Masses Are Asses (drama, 1984)
Puerto Rican Obituary (poetry, 1973)
Traffic Violations (poetry, 1983)

Piñero, Miguel
La Bodega Sold Dreams (poetry, 1980)
Outrageous One-Act Plays (1986)
Short Eyes (drama, 1975)
The Sun Always Shines for the Cool; Midnight Moon at the Greasy Spoon; Eulogy for a Small-Time Thief (drama, 1984)

Rivera, Edward
Family Installments (fiction, 1982)

Ruiz, Richard
  The Hungry American (fiction, 1978)

Sierra Berdecia, Fernando
  Esta noche juega el joker (drama, 1939)

Soto, Pedro Juan
  Ardiente suelo, fria estacion/Hot Land, Cold Season (fiction, 1961)
  Spiks (fiction, 1956)

Thomas, Piri
  Down These Mean Streets (fiction, 1967)
  Savior, Savior, Hold My Hand (fiction, 1972)
  Seven Long Times (fiction, 1975)
  Stories from El Barrio (1978)

Torres, Edwin
  After Hours (fiction, 1979)
  Carlito's Way (fiction, 1975)

Vega, Ed
  The Comeback (fiction, 1985)
  Mendoza's Dreams (fiction, 1987)

Vivas, Jose Luis
  A vellon las esperanzas o Melania (fiction, 1971)

Zeno Gandia, Manuel
  La charca (fiction, 1894)
  El negocio (fiction, 1973)
  Los redentores (fiction, 1973)

C. Secondary Bibliography

1. Bibliographies and Literary Reference Works

Acosta-Belén, Edna, comp. "Puerto Rican Literature in the United States." In
  Redefining American Literary History, edited by A. LaVonne Brown Ruoff and
  Jerry W. Ward, Jr. (see 3B1). New York: Modern Language Association of
  America, 1990.
  Lists anthologies, primary and secondary works, and "Puerto Rican Literature,
  Originally Written in Spanish, Dealing with the Immigrant Experience."

Bleznick, Donald William. *A Sourcebook for Hispanic Literature and Language: A Selected, Annotated Guide to Spanish, Spanish-American, and Chicano Bibliography, Literature, Linguistics, Journals, and Other Source Materials.* 2d ed. Metuchen, N.J.: Scarecrow Press, 1983.
This enlarged edition has 1412 entries, mainly on Spanish and Spanish American literature. See sections 8, "Chicano Bibliography and Literature," and 15, "Other Useful References in the Hispanic Field."

Eger, Ernestina N., ed. *A Bibliography of Criticism of Contemporary Chicano Literature.* Berkeley, Calif.: Chicano Studies Library Publications, 1982.
Listings of criticism mostly since the "Chicano renaissance," or *florecimiento* (flowering), after 1960 or so. Sections on collections, bibliography, "La Chicana," theater, individual authors, and so on.

Eysturoy, Annie O., and José Antonio Gurpegui. "Chicano Literature: Introduction and Bibliography." *American Studies International* 28, no. 1 (April, 1990): 48-82.
This useful, up-to-date listing contains detailed, analytical introduction followed by bibliographical sections of suggested readings and primary and secondary sources.

Frankson, Marie Stewart. "Chicano Literature for Young Adults: An Annotated Bibliography." *English Journal* 79 (January, 1990): 30-38.
Contains useful annotations of fiction, poetry, drama, the oral tradition, anthologies, and biographies.

Kanellos, Nicolás, ed. *Biographical Dictionary of Hispanic Literature in the United States: The Literature of Puerto Ricans, Cuban Americans, and Other Hispanic Writers.* Westport, Conn.: Greenwood Press, 1989.
Short essays are followed by primary and secondary bibliographies. Does not cover Mexican-American authors.

Lomelí, Francisco A., and Carl R. Shirley, eds. *Chicano Writers: First Series.* Dictionary of Literary Biography 82. Columbia, S.C.: Bruccoli Clark Layman, 1989.
Contains useful critical essays on more than fifty Chicano writers, from Oscar Acosta and Leonard Adamé, to José Antonio Villarreal and Bernice Zamora. Appendices on Chicano history, language, other topics.

Lomelí, Francisco A., and Donald W. Urioste, comps. *Chicano Perspectives in Literature: A Critical and Annotated Bibliography.* Albuquerque, N.M.: Pajarito Publications, 1976.

A dictionary of writers and their works, with long annotations arranged alphabetically, by author, according to genre (poetry, novel, and so forth).

Martínez, Julio A., comp. *Chicano Scholars and Writers: A Bio-Bibliographical Directory*. Metuchen, N.J.: Scarecrow Press, 1979.
Data on more than five hundred writers and scholars "working in the fields of the humanities, the social sciences and education, as well as on Anglo-American and Latin-American scholars who have researched the Chicano experience." The directory is supplemented by a subject index (see "Chicano Drama," "Chicano Poetry," etc.).

_____, ed. *Dictionary of Twentieth-Century Cuban Literature*. Westport, Conn.: Greenwood Press, 1990.
Contains "ready reference information on contemporary Cuban creative writers on the island or in exile as well as essays on literary genres and movements," for example, "Literary Criticism Since 1900," "The Novel, 1900-1969."

Martínez, Julio A., and Francisco A. Lomelí, eds. *Chicano Literature: A Reference Guide*. Westport, Conn.: Greenwood Press, 1985.
Articles on Chicano poetry, literary criticism, the novel, and more, with bibliographies of primary and secondary works. Appendices: "Chronology of Chicano Literature," "Glossary," and "Bibliography of General Works."

McKenna, Teresa. "Chicano Literature." In *Redefining American Literary History*, edited by A. LaVonne Brown Ruoff and Jerry W. Ward, Jr. (see 3B1). New York: Modern Language Association of America, 1990.
This useful guide has listings of recent bibliographies and other aids to research, anthologies, primary and secondary works.

Ryan, Bryan, ed. *Hispanic Writers: A Selection of Sketches from Contemporary Authors*. Detroit: Gale Research, 1991.
Entries include biographical information, critical discussion of major works, and brief bibliographies.

Tatum, Charles M. *A Selected and Annotated Bibliography of Chicano Studies*. 2d ed. Lincoln: University of Nebraska Press, Department of Modern Languages and Literatures, 1979.
Sections include bibliographies, anthologies, "The Chicana," audiovisual materials, literature, criticism, and more.

Trejo, Arnulfo D. *Bibliografía Chicana: A Guide to Information Sources*. Detroit: Gale Research, 1975.
An early bibliography of general reference works, books in the humanities, social

sciences, history, and applied sciences. Under humanities, see "Literature" and listings for bibliography, biography, anthologies, etc.

Trujillo, Roberto G., comp. *Literatura Chicana: Creative and Critical Writings Through 1984*. Oakland, Calif.: Floricanto Press, 1985.
A bibliography of works "that include, in significant quantity, both creative and critical literary writings on the Chicano experience." Some 773 works are listed in fifteen sections, including poetry, novel, oral tradition, anthology, bibliographies, and video and sound recordings.

See also: Foster (1A4); Gonzales-Berry, Leal, "Multicultural Literature," Shirley (7C6); Lattin (7C5)

2. Interviews

Binder, Wolfgang. *Partial Autobiographies: Interviews with Twenty Chicano Poets*. Erlangen, Germany: Palm & Enke, 1985.
Interviews with Sandra Cisneros, Jim Sagel, Jimmy Santiago Baca, Gary Soto, Bernice Zamora, and fifteen other poets. Also includes bibliographies of primary and secondary materials.

Bruce-Novoa, Juan. *Chicano Authors: Inquiry by Interview*. Austin: University of Texas Press, 1980.
Interviews with contemporary Chicano writers: Alurista, Rudolfo A. Anaya, Ron Arias, Rolando Hinojosa, Tomás Rivera, Tino Villanueva, half a dozen others.

3. Drama

Huerta, Jorge A. *Chicano Theater: Themes and Forms*. Ypsilanti, Mich.: Bilingual Review/Press, 1982.
"By analyzing plays on varied topics relevant to the Chicano community, this book attempts to define Chicano theater, its major dramatists, and theater groups in an effort to reveal its diversity." Includes bibliography.

Kanellos, Nicolás, ed. *Hispanic Theatre in the United States*. Houston, Tex.: Arte Público Press, 1984.
Seven essays are contained in this slim volume, including the editor's "Overview of Hispanic Theatre in the United States."

_____. *A History of Hispanic Theatre in the United States: Origins to 1940*. Austin: University of Texas Press, 1990.

The purpose of this book is "to provide a basic starting point for further studies" in terms of the contributions of Hispanics. "The theatre was without a doubt the most popular and culturally relevant artistic form in Hispanic communities throughout the United States." Chapters on the most important centers of Hispanic theatrical activity: Los Angeles, San Antonio, New York, and Tampa.

_____. *Mexican American Theater: Legacy and Reality*. Pittsburgh: Latin American Literary Review Press, 1987.
Contains seven essays previously published in scholarly journals and anthologies.

_____, ed. *Mexican American Theatre: Then and Now*. Houston, Tex.: Arte Público Press, 1984.
A 1983 issue of *Revista Chicano-Riqueña* (11, no. 1) contains four vaudeville sketches, five "studies" (by Kanellos, Tomás Ybarra-Frausto, Jorge Huerta, others), and interviews with Luis Valdez and Rodrigo Duarte of El Teatro de la Esperanza.

_____. *Two Centuries of Hispanic Theatre in the Southwest*. Houston, Tex.: *Revista Chicano-Riqueña*, 1982.
Contains the program for the "Multi-Media Show on the History of Hispanic Theatre in the Southwest," which toured the Southwest in 1982.

Pottlitzer, Joanne. *Hispanic Theater in the United States and Puerto Rico*. New York: Ford Foundation, 1988.
Historical surveys and descriptions of current Hispanic theater activity are followed by a geographical directory of Hispanic theaters.

See also: 7B1c

4. Poetry

Bruce-Novoa, Juan. *Chicano Poetry: A Response to Chaos*. Austin: University of Texas Press, 1982.
A companion volume to the author's *Chicano Authors* (7C2, above). The poets interviewed in that collection are analyzed here in essays mapping out the contemporary poetry movement.

Candelaria, Cordelia. *Chicano Poetry: A Critical Introduction*. Westport, Conn.: Greenwood Press, 1980.
A "sustained, comprehensive, and systematic critical analysis" of Chicano poetry since 1967 (the date of Rodolfo "Corky" Gonzáles, *I Am Joaquin*), through Gary Soto, Bernice Zamora, and "The Flowering of Flor y canto" in the 1970's.

Sánchez, Marta Ester. *Contemporary Chicana Poetry: A Critical Approach to an Emerging Literature.* Berkeley: University of California Press, 1985.
Analyses of Alma Villanueva, Lorna Dee Cervantes, Lucha Corpi, and Bernice Zamora. Appendices contain sixty pages of Villanueva's poetry.

See also: 7B1d

5. Fiction

Lattin, Vernon E., ed. *Contemporary Chicano Fiction: A Critical Survey.* Binghamton, N.Y.: Bilingual Review/Press, 1986.
Sections on "Critical Overviews" (essays by Ramon Saldivar, José Armas, Marvin A. Lewis), "The Early Writers in English: Villarreal, Acosta, Barrio," "Tomás Rivera and the Spanish Language Novel," and "The Accomplished Voices" (essays on Rolando Hinojosa, Rudolfo Anaya, Ron Arias, etc.). "A Selected Bibliography of Criticism of the Chicano Novel" by Ernestina N. Eger.

Saldivar, Ramon. *Chicano Narrative: The Dialectics of Difference.* Madison: University of Wisconsin Press, 1990.
This study uses "narrative analysis, rhetoric, semiotics, and ideology as the basic coordinates of an interpretive model" of contemporary Chicano writers. Includes discussion of Américo Paredes, Tomás Rivera, Oscar Zeta Acosta, Rudolfo A. Anaya, Ron Arias, and Rolando Hinojosa.

See also: 7B1e

6. General Literary Studies

Anaya, Rudolfo A., and Francisco A. Lomelí, eds. *Aztlán: Essays on the Chicano Homeland.* Albuquerque, N.M.: Academia/El Norte Publications, 1989.
Contains essays on American Indian and Chicano myth, culture, and literature.

Armas, José, et al. eds. *Contemporary Chicano Literary Criticism.* Albuquerque, N.M.: Pajarito Publications, 1980.
From an issue of *De Colores* (5, nos. 1-2), this "volume of literary and cultural analysis" has essays on poetry, Luis Valdez, "On the Theoretical Bases of Chicano Literature," and more by Guillermo Hernandez, Vernon E. Lattin, others. Interview by Bruce-Novoa with Nash Candelaria.

Bruce-Novoa, Juan. *Retrospace: Collected Essays on Chicano Literature, Theory, and History.* Houston, Tex.: Arte Público Press, 1990.
Essays of a decade and a half by a leading scholar of Chicano literature.

Calderón, Héctor, and José David Saldívar, eds. *Criticism in the Borderlands: Studies in Chicano Literature, Culture, and Ideology*. Durham, N.C.: Duke University Press, 1991.
Includes a foreword, "Redefining American Literature," by Rolando Hinojosa and recent critical essays in four sections: "Institutional Studies and the Literary Canon," "Representations of the Chicana/o Subject: Race, Class, and Gender," "Genre, Ideology, and History," and "Aesthetics of the Border." Also includes "Selected and Annotated Bibliography of Contemporary Chicano Literary Criticism."

Chabram, Angie, and Rosa Linda Fregoso, eds. *Chicana/o Cultural Representations: Reframing Critical Discourses*. Special issue of *Cultural Studies* 4, no. 3 (1990). Contains theoretical essays that grew out of a panel at the 1989 National Association of Chicano Studies conference, "interrogating from a cultural studies perspective, Chicano Studies = community empowerment, and the notion of a singular Chicano cultural identity." Includes discussions of film, theatre, aesthetics.

Fabré, Genevieve, ed. *European Perspectives on Hispanic Literature of the United States*. Houston, Tex.: Arte Público Press, 1988.
Essays by Wolfgang Binder, Cordelia Candelaria, Francisco A. Lomelí, Marcienne Rocard, and others on nineteenth century Chicano autobiography, the Chicano novel, poetry, Rolando Hinojosa, Rudolfo Anaya, more.

García, Eugene E., et al., eds. *Chicano Studies: A Multidisciplinary Approach*. New York: Teachers College Press, 1984.
Section 3, "Literature and Folklore," includes "An Overview of Chicano Letters," "La Chicana in Literature," essays on Chicano theater, folklore, by Francisco A. Lomelí, María Herrera-Sobek, Jorge A. Huerta, and others.

García, John A., et al., eds. *The Chicano Struggle: Analyses of Past and Present Efforts*. Binghamton, N.Y.: Bilingual Review/Press, 1984.
This collection of essays on Chicano studies has a section entitled "Chicano Literature: Criticism and Analysis," with analyses of Evangelina Vigil, Tomás Rivera, Chicana writings, others.

Gonzales-Berry, Erlinda, ed. *Pasó por Aqui: Critical Essays on the New Mexico Literary Tradition, 1542-1988*. Albuquerque: University of New Mexico Press, 1989.
Fifteen essays on the historical development of the literature of the Southwest, Sabine Ulibarrí, Rudolfo Anaya, and so on, by Francisco A. Lomelí, Charles

Tatum, Bruce-Novoa, and other critics and scholars. See also "A Selected Bibliography of New Mexican Hispanic Literature" by Maria Teresa Marquez.

Hernández, Guillermo E. *Chicano Satire: A Study in Literary Culture.* Austin: University of Texas Press, 1991.
"Satire: An Introduction" is followed by analyses of Luis Valdez, José Montoya, and Rolando Hinojosa.

Jiménez, Francisco, ed. *The Identification and Analysis of Chicano Literature.* Binghamton, N.Y.: Bilingual Review/Press, 1979.
Essays by leading Chicano scholars are contained in sections on "Toward an Identification of Chicano Literature," "Origins, Background, and Development," "Critical Trends: An Overview," and "Critical Applications."

Leal, Luis, et al., eds. *A Decade of Chicano Literature (1970-1979): Critical Essays and Bibliography.* Santa Barbara, Calif.: Editorial La Causa, 1982.
Includes an overview by Tomás Rivera, essays on poetry (Carlota Cárdenas de Dwyer), the novel (Francisco A. Lomelí), theatre (Nicolás Kanellos), literary criticism (Carmen Salazar Parr), and other genres. Also contains "A Comprehensive Bibliography" compiled by Roberto G. Trujillo and Raquel de Gonzalez.

Lensink, Judy Nolte, ed. *Old Southwest/New Southwest: Essays on a Region and Its Literature.* Tucson: Tucson Public Library, 1987.
Papers from a 1985 conference include several on Chicano topics by Rolando Hinojosa-Smith, Tey Diana Rebolledo, Juan R. Garcia, and Rudolfo A. Anaya.

Lomelí, Francisco A., and Donald W. Urioste, eds. *Chicano Literature and Criticism.* Albuquerque, N.M.: Pajarito Publications, 1977.
This issue of *De Colores* (3, no. 4) contains essays by José Armas, Joseph Sommers, Juan Bruce-Novoa, others, on Chicano poetry, *Bless Me, Ultima*, "Critical Approaches to Chicano Literature," related topics.

Miller, Yvette Espinosa, et al., eds. "Special Issue of Chicano Literature." *Latin American Literary Review* 5, no. 10 (Spring-Summer, 1977).
The issue includes poetry by Tino Villanueva, Lorna Dee Cervantes; short fiction by Ron Arias, Rolando Hinojosa; articles on Chicano literature by Luis Leal, Rudolfo A. Anaya, others; and reviews of recently published literary works.

Mohr, Eugene V. *The Nuyorican Experience: Literature of the Puerto Rican Minority.* Westport, Conn.: Greenwood Press, 1982.
Analyses of books about New York by Piri Thomas, Nicholasa Mohr, other "personal, largely autobiographical" writers in "one of America's richest immigrant literatures."

"Multicultural Literature: Part IV." *ADE Bulletin* 91 (Winter, 1988): 30-62. Teresa McKenna, "A Chicano Literature Review and Pedagogical Assessment," and four essays on Puerto Rican literature. Includes an annotated bibliography by Edna Acosta-Belén.

Olivares, Julián. *International Studies in Honor of Tomás Rivera*. Houston, Tex.: Arte Público Press, 1986.
From an issue of *Revista Chicano-Riqueña* 13, nos. 3-4 (1985); has recollections and essays on Rivera and a section of essays on "Chicano and Hispanic Literature of the United States."

Robinson, Cecil. *Mexico and the Hispanic Southwest in American Literature*. Tucson: University of Arizona Press, 1977.
This early standard work has a chapter on "the fruitful new genre of Chicano literature."

——————. *No Short Journeys: The Interplay of Cultures in the History and Literature of the Borderlands*. Tucson: University of Arizona Press, 1992.
This posthumous collection of essays charts the dynamic interaction between Anglo and Hispanic cultures in the Southwest, including analyses of Rudolfo Anaya and Miguel Méndez.

Rocard, Marcienne. *The Children of the Sun: Mexican-Americans in the Literature of the United States*. Translated by Edward G. Brown, Jr. Tucson: University of Arizona Press, 1989.
This scholarly study, which was originally published in French in 1980, examines "the image of the Mexican-American in Anglo-American literature and both the oral and written literature of the Mexican minority . . . from the annexation in 1848 to 1974."

Rodríguez de Laguna, Asela, ed. *Images and Identities: The Puerto Rican in Two World Contexts*. New Brunswick, N.J.: Transaction Books, 1987.
Contains papers from a 1983 Rutgers University conference on "The Puerto Rican in Literature" by Piri Thomas, Juan Bruce-Novoa, Nicolás Kanellos, Charles Tatum, and other writers and scholars.

Romo, Ricardo, and Raymund Paredes, eds. *New Directions in Chicano Scholarship*. Santa Barbara: University of California Center for Chicano Studies, 1984.
Reprints essays from *New Scholar* 6 (1977) on folklore, bilingualism, literature (poetry, Felipe M. Chacón, etc.)

Shirley, Carl R., and Paula W. *Understanding Chicano Literature*. Columbia: University of South Carolina Press, 1988.

A brief but useful survey of the field, with chapters on major genres and "Literatura Chicanesca," plus "Chicano Literature: A Suggested Reading List" and annotated bibliography.

Sommers, Joseph, and Tomas Ybarra-Frausto, eds. *Modern Chicano Writers: A Collection of Critical Essays*. Englewood Cliffs, N.J.: Prentice-Hall, 1979.
In four sections: "A Conceptual Framework"; "The Narrative: Focus on Tomás Rivera"; "Poetry: Alurista, Villanueva, Lucero, Zamora, Montoya"; and "Theater: Focus on El Teatro Campesino."

Tatum, Charles M. *Chicano Literature*. Boston: Twayne, 1982.
This substantive study of "burgeoning" literature has chapters on historical background and "The Origins and Evolution of Chicano Literature from the 16th Century through the 1950s." Also chapters on Chicano theater, fiction, and poetry, concluding with "Overview—Past Achievements and Future Promise."

von Bardeleben, Renate, et al., eds. *Missions in Conflict: Essays on U.S.-Mexican Relations and Chicano Culture*. Tubingen, West Germany: Gunter Narr Verlag, 1986.
Twenty-six papers from a 1984 symposium by Jorge A. Huerta, Nicolás Kanellos, Wolfgang Binder, Juan Bruce-Novoa, and other scholars covering Chicano theater, poetry, and fiction.

See also: essays in Baker, Ruoff and Ward (3B1)

7. Latina Writers

Córdova, Teresa, et al., eds. *Chicana Voices: Intersections of Class, Race, and Gender*. Austin, Tex.: Center for Mexican American Studies, 1986.
The proceedings of the 1984 National Association for Chicano Studies conference include five essays in the "Language, Literature, and the Theatre" section.

Herrera-Sobek, María, ed. *Beyond Stereotypes: The Critical Analysis of Chicana Literature*. Binghamton, N.Y.: Bilingual Review/Press, 1985.
An introduction plus essays on prose (by Francisco A. Lomelí, Carmen Sazazar Parr, et al.) and poetry (Tey Diana Rebolledo, Marta E. Sánchez).

Horno-Delgado, Asunción, et al., eds. *Breaking Boundaries: Latina Writing and Critical Readings*. Amherst: University of Massachusetts Press, 1989.
Includes an introduction ("Toward a Critical Practice of Latina Writers"), essays in sections on Chicanas, Puertorriquenas, Cubanas, and "Latinoamericanas from Other Countries."

See also: *Auto/Biography Studies* (1B1); Cochran, Fisher, Moraga and Anzaldúa, and other anthologies listed in 3D2; Herrera-Sobek (7B1f); Gaspar de Alba and Sánchez (7C4)

NOTES

1. Annie O. Eysturoy and José Antonio Gurpegui, "Chicano Literature: Introduction and Bibliography," (7C1), pp. 48, 50.
2. Carl R. Shirley and Paula W. Shirley, *Understanding Chicano Literature* (1988), p. 183. (7C2)
3. As Eysturoy and Gurpegui do in their excellent "Chicano Literature: Introduction and Bibliography" noted above.
4. "The Evolution of Chicano Literature," in Baker, ed., *Three American Literatures* (4h), pp. 52-53.
5. Sources: Acosta-Belén, Eysturoy and Gurpegui, McKenna (in 7C1).

Chapter 8
ASIAN AMERICAN LITERATURE

A. A Brief Narrative History

The central problem for Asian American writers—and their readers—is that of identity. As the editors of one of the first anthologies of Asian American literature declared in the opening sentence of their introduction, "Asian Americans are not one people but several."[1] Chinese Americans and Japanese Americans have made up the bulk of the Asian American population since the nineteenth century, but the twentieth century has seen the addition of many Koreans, native Hawaiians, Philipinos, other Pacific Islanders, as well as Asian Indians, into that community. The entire face of Asian America has been changed in the last several decades by the addition of hundreds of thousands of immigrants from Southeast Asia. As with the Hispanic community, it is impossible to predict what Asian America—and therefore Asian American literature—will resemble even a decade from now.

Asian American culture is as diverse as the individual peoples it represents, but it is a culture that gets homogenized and misrepresented in mass culture and even in serious scholarship. The stereotypes of Asian Americans—the images of Charlie Chan, Fu Manchu, or Suzie Wong—are staples of popular culture in this country that further keep Asian Americans from gaining an individual identity. Granted, this is a problem all ethnic Americans face; American Indians, African Americans, and Mexican Americans have had to fight the images of the red savage, Uncle Remus, or the "Frito Bandito," respectively. The stereotypes surrounding Asian Americans, however, have been more insidious and more durable. Such racial representations not only reinforce negative qualities and assign a person to a group but, worse, in the case of Asian Americans, they give that group an identity they may not actually have. The clearest example comes from American history, when, in 1942, more than 100,000 Japanese Americans were rounded up and sent to internment camps across the United States. Their crime? They resembled America's enemy.

One of the major themes in Asian American literatures is in fact this dual identity, the conflict between an individual's ethnic heritage or roots in an ethnic Felipe community and culture and that person's individual identity. This theme fuels much of the best ethnic literature in America, but it has been particularly powerful in Asian American literature. (Witness the popularity of Chinese American Amy Tan's *The Joy Luck Club* in 1989 and *The Kitchen God's Wife* in 1991.) On one hand, this issue develops the tension between the desire for assimilation and the need for ethnic identity. On the other hand—and especially in Asian American literature—the theme reveals a conflict between generations, between the mothers and fathers who want to maintain cultural ethnicity and the children who want freedom to be more "American."

Perhaps this is one of the reasons that autobiography has always been one of the most popular genres of ethnic writing; it is the easiest place to work out the conflict.[2] Certainly it has been the most popular genre in Asian American literature, from early accounts of immigration and hardships in the nineteenth century through the Philippine American Carlos Bulosan's *America Is in the Heart* (1943), to Japanese Americans Daniel Inouye's *Journey to Washington* (1967) and Jeanne Wakatsuki Houston and James Houston's *Farewell to Manzanar* (1973).

As with so much of the ethnic literature under study here, in the recent renaissance of Asian American literature in the last several decades, other genres have emerged. The modern novel appeared in Japanese American John Okada's *No-No Boy* (1957) and continued in Korean American Richard Kim's *The Martyred* (1964) and Indian American Bharati Mukherjee's *Wife* (1975) through Amy Tan and Gus Lee's *China Boy* (1991). A similar case exists for the short story, in Japanese American Toshio Mori's *Yokohama, California* (1949) and Hisaye Yamamoto's *Seventeen Syllables: Five Stories of Japanese American Life* (1985), or Chinese American David Wong Louie's *Pangs of Love* (1991); the drama, in Chinese American Frank Chin (*The Year of the Dragon*, 1981) and David Henry Hwang (*M. Butterfly*, 1988); and the contemporary poetry of Japanese American Garrett Kaoru Hongo (*The River of Heaven*, 1988) and Janice Mirikitani (*Shedding Silence*, 1987). Asian American writers, in short, have become vital parts of all genres in the contemporary American literary scene. The numbers of younger writers emerging today—besides Lee, Louie, and Tan, Holly Uyemoto, Steven Lo, David Mura, Cynthia Kadohata—indicate that this trend will continue for some time.

The themes of autobiography, however—of dual identity, of cultural conflict and assimilation—also permeate Asian American creative literature, which raises a point that is crucial for all ethnic literatures: Without an understanding of individual ethnic histories, the apprehension of these ideas and issues in ethnic literature is virtually impossible. As Elaine H. Kim has phrased it, "An understanding of this social context is essential to understanding the literature."[3] To appreciate a writer like Maxine Hong Kingston, in other words, it is necessary to know the Chinese American history out of which she so brilliantly weaves her fictional/historical tapestry—or else her books become merely blurred photographs of life.

Fortunately, the most comprehensive history has recently appeared: Ronald Takaki's *Strangers from a Different Shore: A History of Asian Americans*.[4] Likewise, the best secondary literary studies have been published in the last few years: *Asian American Literature: An Annotated Bibliography* (1988) by King-Kok Cheung and Stan Yogi, and Elaine Kim's *Asian American Literature: An Introduction to the Writings and Their Social Context* (1982).[5]

At the same time—and as will be obvious from the lists of secondary works below—there has been a paucity of serious studies of Asian American literature. In fact, there have been fewer critical studies of Asian American literature than of any other major body of ethnic American literature. Much work remains to be done, especially when one considers the long lists of primary literature that have been produced by Asian Americans in the last century.

These works continue to be produced. The presence of Amy Tan, Maxine Hong Kingston, and others on recent best-seller lists demonstrates how much contemporary American literature depends on the contributions of Asian American writers. Similarly, new immigrants from Southeast Asia have other stories to tell which say much about recent history—not only about America's involvement in Vietnam, Laos, and Cambodia, but also about the enduring questions of ethnic identity, the clash of cultures and generations, the continuing power of the American Dream. Asian Americans have many more stories to tell.

B. A Selected List of Primary Works

1. Anthologies

a. General Collections

Berson, Misha, ed. *Between Worlds: Contemporary Asian-American Plays.* New York: Theatre Communications Group, 1990.
Includes short plays by David Henry Hwang, Jessica Hagedorn, Laurence Yep, and three other Asian American dramatists.

Bruchac, Joseph, ed. *Breaking Silence: An Anthology of Contemporary Asian American Poets.* Greenfield Center, N.Y.: Greenfield Review Press, 1983.
Fifty poets from the United States and Canada, including Diana Chang, Marilyn Chin, Garrett Kaoru Hongo, Janice Mirikitani, and Arthur Sze.

Chan, Jeffery Paul, et al., eds. *The Big Aiiieeeee! An Anthology of Chinese American and Japanese American Literature.* New York: Meridian, 1991.
This six-hundred-page collection has a long, angry introduction by Frank Chin ("Come All Ye Asian American Writers of the Real and the Fake"), selections of poetry, prose, and drama by Toshio Mori, Hisaye Yamamoto, Joy Kogawa, John Okada, David Wong Louie, and twenty other writers.

Chiang, Fay, et al., eds. *American Born and Foreign: An Anthology of Asian American Poetry.* New York: Sunbury Press Books, 1979.
An issue of *Sunbury—a poetry magazine—*(nos. 7-8) that contains dozens of contemporary poets arranged in topics such as "Working Mothers and Fathers," "Rituals," "Alienation," and "Relationships."

Chin, Frank, et al., eds. *Aiiieee!* Washington, D.C.: Howard University Press, 1974.
Still available in paperback in 1991, this early anthology has a long introduction to Chinese, Japanese, and Filipino American literatures (reprinted in Baker, *Three*

American Literatures, 3B1, pp. 197-228), plus excerpts from works by Carlos Bulosan, Frank Chin, John Okada, and eleven other writers.

Echoes from Gold Mountain: An Asian American Journal. Long Beach: California State University, Long Beach Asian American Studies, 1978.
The anthology reflects "the diversities of Asian America" as well as "a diverse cross-section of materials, points of view, ethnicity, and age" in poetry, prose, art works.

Gee, Emma, ed. *Counterpoint: Perspectives on Asian America*. Los Angeles: UCLA Asian American Studies Center, 1976.
This long anthology has sections on "Critical Perspectives" and "Contemporary Issues" (both containing essays on questions of history, education, and so forth). Also includes "Literature": pieces by Carlos Bulosan, Janice Mirikitani, Bienvenido N. Santos, Frank Chin, others.

Hongo, Garrett Kaoru, ed. *Asian-American Writers*. Special issue of *Greenfield Review* 6, nos. 1-2 (Spring, 1977).
Poetry, fiction, and essays by Alan Chong Lau, Bienvenido N. Santos, Frank Chin, and fifteen other participants to a 1976 Pacific Northwest conference.

Hsu, Kai-yu, and Helen Palubinskas, eds. *Asian-American Authors*. Boston: Houghton Mifflin, 1976.
One of the Houghton Mifflin Multi-Ethnic Literature series, this volume has sections on Chinese American (Pardee Lowe, Jade Snow Wong, Frank Chin, others), Japanese American (Daniel K. Inouye, Lawson Fusao Inada, Hisaye Yamamoto), and Filipino American (Jose Garcia Villa, Bienvenido N. Santos) literature. Each section is prefaced by a brief history and chronology.

Mar, Laureen, and Alan Chong Lau, eds. *Asian American: North and South*. Special issue of *Contact/II* 7, nos. 38-40 (1986).
This collection has poetry by fifty writers from Canada, the United States, and South America, as well as reviews of forty other works.

Tsutakawa, Mayumi, and Alan Chong Lau, eds. *Turning Shadows into Light: Art and Culture of the Northwest's Early Asian/Pacific Community*. Seattle: Young Pine Press, 1982.
Poems, stories, and essays by Carlos Bulosan, James Masao Mitsui, Garrett Kaoru Hongo, and other writers are contained in this regional ethnic anthology.

Wand, David Hsin-Fu, ed. *Asian-American Heritage: An Anthology of Prose and Poetry*. New York: Washington Square Press, 1974.
An early anthology containing stories by Richard Kim and others, as well as

poetry by Diana Chang and Jose Garcia Villa, two essays, five novel excerpts, and a selection of Samoan and Hawaiian "Oral Poetry"

b. Hawaiian

Chock, Eric, and Darrell H. Y. Lum, eds. *The Best of Bamboo Ridge: The Hawaii Writers' Quarterly.* Honolulu: Bamboo Ridge Press, 1986.
This special issue of *Bamboo Ridge* has introductions by the editors plus poetry and prose by Garrett Kaoru Hongo, Cathy Song, Ty Pak, and others who have appeared in the magazine since 1978.

c. Philippine

Cachapero, Emily, et al., eds. *Liwanag: Literary and Graphic Expressions by Filipinos in America.* San Francisco: Liwanag, 1975.
This "vehicle for Filipino-American artists dedicated to their respective art forms, old voices as well as new," includes selections by Jessica Tarahata Hagedorn and others.

Lumbera, Bienvenido, and Cynthia Nogales Lumbera, eds. *Philippine Literature: A History and Anthology.* Manila: National Book Store, 1982.
Most major writers are covered in this textbook spanning the history of Philippine literature, from the precolonial period (before 1564), through "Literature under Spanish Colonialism" (1565-1897) and "Literature under U.S. Colonialism" (1898-1945), to "Contemporary Literature" (1946-   ).

San Juan, E., Jr., ed. *Introduction to Modern Pilipino Literature.* New York: Twayne, 1974.
This anthology has a long introduction to Tagalog language and literature by Teodoro A. Agoncillo, sections of poetry and short fiction, and essays on the literature by Agoncillo and Epifanio de Los Santos Cristobal.

d. Chinese American

Hom, Marlon K. *Songs of Gold Mountain: Cantonese Rhymes from San Francisco Chinatown.* Berkeley: University of California Press, 1987.
This collection of vernacular rhymes written in the early 1910's has a long introduction, poems in both original Cantonese and in translation.

Lai, Him Mark, et al., eds. and trans. *Island: Poetry and History of Chinese Immigrants on Angel Island, 1910-1940*. San Francisco: Hoc Doi, 1980.
This remarkable volume has a long introduction (with photographs) by the editors and selections from the poetry written "on the barrack walls, recording the impressions of their voyage to America, their longing for families back home, and their outrage and humiliation at the treatment America accorded them." Among other qualities, the poems "express a vitality of indomitability never before identified with the Chinese Americans."

e. Japanese American

The Hawk's Well: A Collection of Japanese American Art and Literature. San Jose, Calif.: Asian American Arts Projects, 1986.
The primary aim of this anthology "is to introduce Japanese American artists and writers through a significant body of their work and to bring the art of Japanese America into a common theme with its evolving literature." Includes a short story by Yoshiko Uchida as well as poetry by Janice Mirikitani, three others.

Mirikitani, Janice, et al., eds. *Ayumi: A Japanese American Anthology*. Glenview, Ill.: Scott, Foresman, 1980.
A large, lavish collection of "inter-generation experiences of Japanese America." Prose and poetry by Issei (e.g., Shigeki Oka, Katsuma Sakai), Nisei (like James Masao Mitsui, Yasuo Sasaki), and Sansei and Yonsei (Garrett K. Hongo, Mirikitani, Francis Naohiko Oka, others).

f. Asian American Women

Hom, Sharon, et al., eds. *Without Ceremony: An Anthology of Work by Asian and Asian American Women*. New York: Ikon, 1988.
This special issue of *Ikon* 9 contains prose and poetry by Janice Mirikitani, Jessica Hagedorn, Fay Chiang, Nellie Wong, Diana Chang, and three dozen other women writers.

Lim, Shirley Geok-lin, et al., eds. *The Forbidden Stitch: An Asian American Women's Anthology*. Corvallis, Ore.: Calyx Books, 1989.
Contains introductions by the editors, poetry, prose, art, and reviews by Marilyn Chin, Nellie Wong, Diana Chang, Jessica Hagedorn, Mei-Mei Berssenbrugge, and many other artists.

Watanabe, Sylvia, and Carol Bruchac, eds. *Home to Stay: Asian American Women's Fiction*. Greenfield Center, N.Y.: Greenfield Review Press, 1990.

Stories by Maxine Hong Kingston, Amy Tan, Jessica Hagedorn, Hisaye Yama-moto, Bharati Mukherjee, and thirty other writers.

Wong, Diane Yen-Mei, et al., eds. *Making Waves: An Anthology of Writings By and About Asian American Women.* Boston: Beacon Press, 1989.
This large comparative collection organizes selections in seven thematic sections: immigration, war, work, generations, identity, injustice, and activism.

See also: anthologies by Anzaldúa, Blicksilver, Cochran, Faderman, Fisher, Haslam, Mirikitani, Moraga/Anzaldua, and others (3D2); Ling (8C2, below)

2. Individual Writers[6]

a. Chinese American

Berssenbrugge, Mei-Mei
 Fish Souls (poetry, 1972)
 Heat Bird (poetry, 1983)
 Random Possession (poetry, 1979)
 Summits Move with the Tide (poetry, 1974)

Chang, Diana
 Eye to Eye (fiction, 1974)
 The Frontiers of Love (fiction, 1956)
 The Gift of Love (fiction, 1978)
 The Horizon Is Definitely Speaking (poetry, 1982)
 The Only Game in Town (fiction, 1963)
 A Passion for Life (fiction, 1961)
 A Perfect Love (fiction, 1978)
 A Woman of Thirty (fiction, 1959)

Chang, Eileen
 Naked Earth (fiction, 1956)
 The Rice Sprout Song (fiction, 1955)
 The Rouge of the North (fiction, 1967)

Chang, Hsin-Hai
 The Fabulous Concubine (fiction, 1956)

Chao, Evelina
 Gates of Grace (fiction, 1985)

Chen, Su Hua Ling
Ancient Melodies (nonfiction, 1953)

Chen, Yuan-tsung
The Dragon's Village (fiction, 1980)

Cheng, Nien
Life and Death in Shanghai (autobiography, 1986)

Chennault, Anna
The Education of Anna (autobiography, 1980)
A Thousand Springs: The Biography of a Marriage (1962)

Chia, Cheng Sait
Turned Clay (poetry, 1982)

Chiang, Fay
In the City of Contradictions (poetry, 1979)
Miwa's Song (poetry, 1982)

Chiang, Monlin
Tides from the West (autobiography, 1947)

Chin, Frank
The Chickencoop Chinaman and the Year of the Dragon (drama, 1981)
The Chinaman Pacific and Frisco R. R. Co. (short fiction, 1988)
Donald Duk (fiction, 1991)

Chin, Marilyn
Dwarf Bamboo (poetry, 1987)

Ching, Frank
Ancestors: Nine Hundred Years in the Life of a Chinese Family (nonfiction, 1988)

Chiu, Tony
Port Arthur Chicken (fiction, 1979)

Chou, Cynthia
My Life in the United States (autobiography, 1970)

Chu, Louis N.
Eat a Bowl of Tea (fiction, 1961)

Chuang Hua
  Crossings (fiction, 1968)

Deng Ming-Dao
  Seven Bamboo Tablets of the Cloudy Satchel (1987)
  The Wandering Taoist (fiction, 1983)

Eaton, Edith [pseud. Sui Sin Far]
  Mrs. Spring Fragrance (short fiction, 1912)

Eaton, Winifred [pseud. Onoto Watanna]
  Cattle (fiction, 1924)
  The Diary of Delia (fiction, 1907)
  The Heart of Hyacinth (fiction, 1903)
  The Honorable Miss Moonlight (fiction, 1912)
  A Japanese Nightingale (fiction, 1901)
  Love of Azalea (fiction, 1904)
  Me. A Book of Remembrance (autobiography, 1915)
  Miss Nume of Japan: A Japanese-American Romance (fiction, 1899)
  Sunny-San (fiction, 1922)
  Tama (fiction, 1910)
  The Wooing of Wisteria (fiction, 1902)

Goo, Thomas York-Tong
  Before the Gods (autobiographical fiction, 1976)

Han Suyin [pseud. Rosalie Chou]
  Birdless Summer (autobiography, 1968)
  The Crippled Tree (nonfiction, 1975)
  Destination Chungking (fiction, 1942)
  The Enchantress (fiction, 1985)
  The Four Faces (fiction, 1963)
  A Many-Splendored Thing (fiction, 1952)
  A Mortal Flower (autobiography, 1966)
  The Mountain Is Young (fiction, 1958)
  My House Has Two Doors (autobiography, 1980)
  Till Morning Comes (fiction, 1982)

Hsaio, Ellen
  A Chinese Year (autobiography, 1970)

Hsia, Wei Lin
  The Poetry of English and Chinese (1978)

Hsiung, S. I.
  The Bridge of Heaven (fiction, 1943)
  The Story of Lady Precious Stream (fiction, 1950)
  Wang Pao-Chuan: Lady Precious Stream (drama, 1934)

Hwang, David Henry
  Broken Promises: Four Plays (1983)
  The Sound of a Voice (drama, 1984)

Jen, Gish
  Typical American (fiction, 1991)

Joe, Jeanne
  Ying-Ying: Pieces of a Childhood (autobiography, 1982)

Kingston, Maxine Hong
  China Men (biography, history, and fiction, 1980)
  Hawai'i One Summer (nonfiction, 1987)
  Tripmaster Monkey (fiction, 1989)
  The Woman Warrior: Memoirs of a Childhood among Ghosts (autobiography and fiction, 1976)

Kuo, Alexander
  Changing the River (poetry, 1986)
  New Letters from Hiroshima and Other Poems (1974)
  The Window Tree (poetry, 1971)

Kuo, Ching Ch'iu [pseud. Helena Kuo]
  I've Come a Long Way (autobiography, 1942)
  Peach Path (nonfiction, 1940)
  Westward to Chungking (fiction, 1944)

Kwan, Moon
  A Chinese Mirror: Poems and Plays (1932)

Lau, Alan Chong
  Songs for Jadina (poetry, 1980)

Lee, Chin-yang
  China Saga (fiction, 1987)
  Cripple Mah and the New Order (fiction, 1961)
  Days of the Tong Wars (fiction, 1974)
  Flower Drum Song (fiction, 1957)

Lover's Point (fiction, 1958)
Madame Goldenflower (fiction, 1960)
The Sawbwa and His Secretary: My Burmese Reminiscences (autobiographical fiction, 1959)

Lee, Gus
China Boy (fiction, 1991)

Lee, Li-Young
Rose (poetry, 1986)

Lee, Mary
The Guest of Tyn-y-Coed Cae: Poems and Drawings (1973)
Hand in Hand (poetry, 1971)
Tender Bough (poetry, 1969)

Lee, Mary Wong
Through My Windows (poetry, 1979)
Through My Windows, Book II (poetry, 1980)

Lee, Virginia
The House That Tai Ming Built (fiction, 1963)

Lee Yu-wha
"The Last Rite" and Other Stories (1979)

Lem, Carol
Don't Ask Why (poetry, 1982)
Grassroots (poetry, 1975)

Leong, George
A Lone Bamboo Doesn't Come from Jackson Street: History, Poetry, Short Story (1977)

Leong, Monfoon
Number One Son (short fiction, 1975)

Li, Ling-Ai
Life Is for a Long Time: A Chinese Hawaiian Memoir (1972)

Lim, Janet
Sold for Silver (autobiography, 1958)

Lim, Paul Stephen
   Some Arrivals, but Mostly Departures (short fiction, 1982)

Lim, Shirley [pseud. Geok-lin]
   "Another Country" and Other Stories (1982)
   Crossing the Peninsula (poetry, 1980)
   Modern Secrets (poetry, 1989)
   No Man's Grove (poetry, 1985)

Lin, Adet [under pseudonym Tan Yun]
   Flame from the Rock (fiction, 1943)

Lin, Adet, and Anor Lin
   Our Family (autobiography, 1939)

Lin, Adet, Anor Lin, and Meimei Lin
   Dawn over Chungking (autobiography, 1941)

Lin, Alice
   Grandmother Had No Name (autobiography, 1988)

Lin, Hazel Ai Chun
   House of Orchids (fiction, 1960)
   The Moon Vow (fiction, 1958)
   The Physicians (fiction, 1951)
   Rachel Weeping for Her Children, Uncomforted (fiction, 1976)
   Weeping Mary Tarry (autobiography, 1980)

Ling, Amy
   Chinamerican Reflections (poetry, 1984)

Lin Tai-yi [pseud. Anor Lin]
   The Eavesdropper (fiction, 1959)
   The Golden Coin (fiction, 1946)
   Kampoon Street (fiction, 1964)
   The Lilacs Overgrow (fiction, 1960)
   War Tide (fiction, 1943)

Lin Yutang
   Between Tears and Laughter (nonfiction, 1943)
   Chinatown Family (fiction, 1948)
   "Confucius Saw Nancy" and Essays About Nothing (1937)
   The Flight of the Innocents (fiction, 1964)

The Importance of Living (nonfiction, 1937)
A Leaf in the Storm: A Novel of War-Swept China (1941)
Looking Beyond (fiction, 1955)
Moment in Peking (fiction, 1939)
My Country and My People (nonfiction, 1937)
The Pleasures of a Nonconformist (nonfiction, 1962)
The Red Peony (fiction, 1961)
The Vermilion Gate: A Novel of a Far Land (1953)
The Vigil of a Nation (nonfiction, 1944)
With Love and Irony (nonfiction, 1940)

Liu, Aimee
Solitaire: A Narrative (autobiography, 1979)

Liu, Stephen
Dream Journeys to China (poetry, 1982)

Lo, Steven L.
The Incorporation of Eric Chung (fiction, 1989)

Lord, Bette Bao
Eighth Moon (nonfiction, 1964)
Spring Moon (fiction, 1981)

Louie, David Wong
Pangs of Love (short fiction, 1991)

Lowe, Pardee
Father and Glorious Descendant (autobiography, 1943)

McCunn, Ruthanne Lum
Sole Survivor (fiction, 1985)
Thousand Pieces of Gold (fiction, 1981)

Pei, Lowry
Family Resemblances (fiction, 1986)

Phou, Lee Yan
When I Was a Boy in China (autobiography, 1887)

Sledge, Linda Ching
Empire of Heaven (fiction, 1990)

Sze, Arthur
  Dazzled (poetry, 1982)
  Two Ravens (poetry, 1976)
  The Willow Wind (poetry, 1981)

Sze, Mai-Mai
  China (nonfiction, 1944)
  Echo of a Cry: A Story Which Began in China (autobiography, 1945)
  Silent Children (fiction, 1948)

Tan, Amy
  The Joy Luck Club (fiction, 1989)
  The Kitchen God's Wife (fiction, 1991)

Telemaque, Eleanor Wong
  It's Crazy to Stay Chinese in Minnesota (fiction, 1978)

Tsiang, H. T.
  And China Has Hands (fiction, 1937)

Tsui, Kitty
  Words of a Woman Who Breathes Fire: Poetry and Prose (1983)

Wang, David Rafael
  The Goblet Moon (poetry, 1955)
  The Intercourse (poetry, 1974)
  Rivers on Fire (poetry, 1974-1975)

Wei, Katherine, and Terry Quinn
  Second Daughter (autobiography, 1984)

Wing, Yung
  My Life in China and America (autobiography, 1909)

Wong, Jade Snow
  Fifth Chinese Daughter (autobiography, 1945)
  No Chinese Stranger (autobiography, 1975)

Wong, May
  A Bad Girl's Book of Animals (poetry, 1969)
  Reports (poetry, 1970)
  Superstitions (poetry, 1978)

Wong, Nanying Stella
Man Curving to Sky (poetry, 1976)

Wong, Nellie
The Death of the Long Steam Lady (poetry, 1986)
Dreams in Harrison Railroad Park (poetry, 1977)

Wong, Shawn
Homebase (fiction, 1979)

Wong, Su-ling, and Earl Herbert Cressy
Daughter of Confucius (autobiography, 1952)

Wu, K. C.
The Lane of Eternal Stability (fiction, 1962)

Yau, John
Broken Off by the Music (poetry, 1981)
Corpse and Mirror (poetry, 1983)
Crossing Canal Street (poetry, 1976)
Sometimes: Poems (1979)

Yee, Chiang
A Chinese Childhood (autobiography, 1952)
The Silent Traveller in Boston (nonfiction, 1959)
The Silent Traveller in New York (nonfiction, 1950)
The Silent Traveller in San Francisco (nonfiction, 1964)

Yeh, Chun-chan
Mountain Village (fiction, 1947)

Yen, Liang
Daughter of the Khans (autobiography, 1955)

Yep, Laurence
Seadeamons (fiction, 1977)

Yung, Wing
My Life in China and America (autobiography, 1909)

b. Japanese American

Ai
  Cruelty (poetry, 1973)
  Killing Floor (poetry, 1979)
  Sin: Poems (1986)

Fujita, June
  Poems in Exile (poetry, 1923)

Harada, Margaret N.
  The Sun Shines on the Immigrant (autobiography, 1960)

Hartmann, Sadakichi
  Buddha, Confucius, Christ: Three Prophetic Plays (1971)
  Drifting Flowers of the Sea and Other Poems to Elizabeth Walsh (1904)
  My Rubaiyat (poetry, 1913)
  Tanka and Haikai: Fourteen Japanese Rhythms (1915)
  White Chrysanthemums, Literary Fragments and Pronouncements (poetry, 1971)

Hatsumi, Reiko
  Rain and the Feast of the Stars (autobiography, 1959)

Hayakawa, Sessue Kintaro
  The Bandit Prince (fiction, 1926)

Hongo, Garrett K.
  Yellow Light (poetry, 1982)
  The River of Heaven (poetry, 1988)

Houston, Jeanne Wakatsuki
  Beyond Manzanar: View of Asian-American Womanhood (fiction and nonfiction, 1985)

Houston, Jeanne Wakatsuki, and James D. Houston
  Farewell to Manzanar (autobiography, 1973)

Ikeda, Patricia
  House of Wood, House of Salt (poetry, 1978)

Imura, Ernest Sakayuki
  Sunrise-Sunset: A Continuous Cycle of Living (poetry, 1976)

Inada, Lawson Fusao
Before the War: Poems as They Happened (1971)

Inouye, Daniel
Journey to Washington (autobiography, 1967)

Ishimoto, Shizue
Facing Two Ways: The Story of My Life (autobiography, 1935)

Itani, Frances
No Other Lodgings (poetry, 1978)

Kadohata, Cynthia
The Floating World (fiction, 1989)

Kaneko, Hizakazu
Manijiro, the Man Who Discovered America (biography, 1956)

Kawano, Doris
Harue, Child of Hawaii (novel, 1984)

Kikuchi, Charles
The Kikuchi Diary: Chronicle from an American Concentration Camp (autobiography, 1973)

Kikumura, Akemi
Through Harsh Winters: The Life of a Japanese Immigrant Woman (nonfiction, 1981)

Kitagawa, Daisuke
Issei and Nisei: The Internment Years (autobiography, 1967)

Kiyooka, Chiyono Sugimoto
Chiyo's Return (autobiography, 1935)

Kudaka, Geraldine
Numerous Avalanches at the Point of Intersection (poetry, 1979)

Masoaka, Mike, with Bill Hosokawa
They Called Me Moses Masaoka: An American Saga (autobiography, 1987)

Matsui, Haru [pseud. Ayako Ishigaki]
Restless Wave (autobiography, 1940)

Matsumoto, Toru, and Marion Lerrigo
   A Brother Is a Stranger (autobiographical fiction, 1946)

Matsuoka, Yoko
   Daughter of the Pacific (autobiography, 1952)

Mirikitani, Janice
   Awake in the River (poetry, 1978)
   Shedding Silence (poetry, 1987)

Mishima, Sumie Seo
   My Narrow Isle: The Story of a Modern Woman in Japan (autobiography, 1941)

Mitsui, James [Masao]
   Crossing Phantom River (poetry, 1978)

Miyakawa, Edward
   Tule Lake (fiction, 1979)

Miyamoto, Kazuo
   Hawaii: End of the Rainbow (fiction, 1964)

Mori, Toshio
   The Chauvinist and Other Stories (1979)
   Woman from Hiroshima (fiction, 1979)
   Yokohama, California (short fiction, 1949)

Mura, David
   After We Lost Our Way (poetry, 1989)
   Turning Japanese: Memoirs of a Sansei (nonfiction, 1991)

Murayama, Milton
   All I Asking for Is My Body (fiction, 1975)

Noda, Barbara
   Strawberries (poetry, 1979)

Noguchi, Yone
   The American Diary of a Japanese Girl (1901)
   From the Eastern Sea (poetry, 1910)
   The Story of Yone Noguchi Told by Himself (1914)

Oka, Francis Naohiko
Poems: Memorial Edition (1970)

Okada, John
No-No Boy (fiction, 1957)

Okimoto, Daniel
American in Disguise (autobiography, 1971)

Okubo, Mine
Citizen 13660 (nonfiction, 1946)

Osata, Sono
Distant Dances (autobiography, 1980)

Ota, Shelley Ayame Nishimura
Upon Their Shoulders: A Novel (1951)

Saiki, Patsy Sumi
Sachi, A Daughter of Hawaii (autobiography, 1977)

Sakai, Sueko
Chop Suey Collection of Facts and Fantasies (1973)

Sasaki, Yasuo
Village Scene/Village Herd (poetry, 1986)

Shirota, Jon
Lucky Come Hawaii (fiction, 1965)
Pineapple White (fiction, 1972)

Sone, Monica
Nisei Daughter (autobiography, 1953)

Sugimoto, Etsu Inaki
A Daughter of the Narikin (fiction, 1932)
A Daughter of the Nohfu (fiction, 1935)
A Daughter of the Samurai (fiction, 1925)
Grandmother O Kyo (fiction, 1940)

Takashima, Shizuyu
A Child in Prison Camp (fiction, 1974)

Tamagawa, Kathleen
Holy Prayers in a Horse's Ear (autobiography, 1932)

Tanaka, Ronald
The Shino Suite: Sansei Poetry, Opus 2 (1981)

Tasaki, Hanama
Long the Imperial Way (fiction, 1949)

Tsukiyama, Gail
Women of the Silk (fiction, 1991)

Uchida, Yoshiko
Desert Exile: The Uprooting of a Japanese American Family (autobiography, 1982)
Picture Bride: A Novel (1987)

Uyemoto, Holly
Rebel Without a Clue (fiction, 1989)

Watkins, Yoko Kawashima
So Far from the Bamboo Grove (autobiographical fiction, 1985)

Yamada, Mitsuye
Camp Notes (poetry, 1976)
Desert Run (poetry, 1989)

Yamamoto, Hisaye
Seventeen Syllables (short fiction, 1989)

Yoshida, Jim, and Bill Hosokawa
The Two Worlds of Jim Yoshida (autobiography, 1972)

c. Korean American

Cha, Theresa Hak Kyung
Dictee (prose, poetry, 1982)

Hyun, Peter
Man Sei! The Making of a Korean American (autobiography, 1986)

Kang, Younghill
 East Goes West: The Making of an Oriental Yankee (autobiography, 1937)
 The Grass Roof (autobiography, 1931)
 The Happy Grove (autobiography, 1933)

Kim, Chungmi
 Chungmi (poetry, 1982)

Kim, Richard
 The Innocent (fiction, 1968)
 Lost Names: Scenes from a Korean Boyhood (short fiction, 1970)
 The Martyred (fiction, 1964)

Kim Ronyoung
 Clay Walls (fiction, 1986)

Kim Yong Ik
 Blue in the Seed (fiction, 1964)
 The Diving Gourd (fiction, 1962)
 The Happy Days (fiction, 1960)
 Love in Winter (short fiction, 1963)
 The Shoes from Yan San Valley (short fiction, 1970)

New Il-Han
 When I Was a Boy in Korea (autobiography, 1928)

Pahk, Induk
 September Monkey (autobiography, 1954)

Pak, Ty
 Guilt Payment (fiction, 1983)

Song, Cathy
 Picture Bride (poetry, 1983)

d. Philippine American

Alvarez, Emigdio Enrique
 The Devil Flower (fiction, 1959)

Buaken, Manuel
 I Have Lived with the American People (autobiography, 1948)

Bulosan, Carlos
America Is in the Heart (autobiography, 1943)
If You Want to Know What We Are: A Carlos Bulosan Reader (fiction, nonfiction, 1983)
The Laughter of My Father (short fiction, 1944)

Carunungan, Celso Al
Like a Big Brave Man: A Novel (1960)

Castro, Fernando
Big White American (fiction, 1969)

Chock, Eric
Ten Thousand Wishes (poetry, 1978)

Concepcion, Marcelo de Gracia
Azucena (poetry, 1925)

Francia, Luis
Her Beauty Likes Me Well (poetry, 1979)

Gonzalez, Nestor Vincente M.
The Bamboo Dancers (fiction, 1964)
Children of the Ash-Covered Loam and Other Stories (1954) *Look, Stranger, on This Island Now* (short fiction, 1963)
Selected Stories (1964)
Seven Hills Away (short fiction, 1947)

Hagedorn, Jessica Tarahata
Dangerous Music (poetry, 1975)
Petfood and Tropical Apparitions (fiction, 1981)

Javellana, Steven
Without Seeing the Dawn (fiction, 1947)

Lim, Paulino, Jr.
"Passion Summer" and Other Stories (1988)

San Juan, E., Jr.
Godkissing Carrion: Selected Poems 1954-64 (1964)

Santos, Bienvenido N.
Dwell in the Wilderness: Selected Short Stories (1931-1941) (1985)

The Man Who (Thought He) Looked Like Robert Taylor (fiction, 1983)
Scent of Apples (short fiction, 1979)
What the Hell for You Left Your Heart in San Francisco (fiction, 1987)

Ty-Casper, Linda
    Awaiting Trespass (fiction, 1985)
    Dread Empire (fiction, 1980)
    "The Secret Runner" and Other Stories (1974)
    "The Transparent Sun" and Other Stories (1963)
    Wings of Stone (fiction, 1986)

Villa, Jose Garcia
    Appassionata: Poems in Praise of Love (1979)
    Footnote to Youth: Tales of the Philippines and Others (1933)
    Have Come, Am Here (poetry, 1942)
    Selected Poems and New (1958)
    Selected Stories (1962)
    Seven Poems (1948)
    Volume Two (poetry, 1949)

e. South and Southeast Asian American

Alexander, Meena
    House of a Thousand Doors (poetry, 1988)
    Nampally Road: A Novel (1991)
    The Storm (poetry, 1989)

Haing Ngor
    A Cambodian Odyssey (autobiography, 1987)

Larson, Wendy, and Tran Thi Nga
    Shallow Graves: Two Women and Viet Nam (poetry, 1986)

Law-Yone, Wendy
    The Coffin Tree (fiction, 1983)

Mukherjee, Bharati
    Darkness (short fiction, 1985)
    Jasmine (fiction, 1989)
    "The Middleman" and Other Stories (1988)
    The Tiger's Daughter (fiction, 1971)
    Wife (fiction, 1975)

Nguyen Ngoc Ngan
The Will of Heaven (autobiography, 1982)

Tran Van Dinh
Blue Dragon, White Tiger: A Tet Story (fiction, 1983)

Truong Nhu Tang, with David Chanoff and Doan Van Toai
A Vietcong Memoir (autobiography, 1985)

C. Secondary Bibliography

1. Bibliographies and Literary Reference Works

Cheung, King-Kok, and Stan Yogi, comps. *Asian American Literature: An Anno-
tated Bibliography.* New York: Modern Language Association of America, 1988.
This comprehensive bibliography has sections on reference works, anthologies,
journals, and secondary sources. Also includes annotated listings for Chinese
American, Japanese American, Filipino American, Korean American, South
Asian, and "Vietnamese and Other Southeast Asian American Literatures."

Kim, Elaine H., comp. "Asian American Writers: A Bibliographical Review."
American Studies International 22, no. 2 (1984): 41-78.
A detailed analytical overview of Asian American writers, plus bibliography.

Ling, Amy. "Asian American Literature." In *Redefining American Literary History,*
edited by A. LaVonne Brown Ruoff and Jerry W. Ward, Jr. New York: Modern
Language Association of America, 1990. (See 3B1)
Bibliographies, anthologies, primary works.

See also: Kim, "Multicultural Literature" (8C2)

2. General Literary Studies

Kim, Elaine H. *Asian American Literature: An Introduction to the Writings and
Their Social Context.* Philadelphia: Temple University Press, 1982.
The first and still the only comprehensive study of Asian American literature.
The analysis is organized by thematic chronology, from "Images of Asians in
Anglo-American Literature," through chapters on early Asian immigrant writers,
"Portraits of Chinatown," and "Japanese American Family and Community
Portraits," to "New Directions in Asian American Literature." Also contains a
useful bibliography.

Ling, Amy. *Between Worlds: Women Writers of Chinese Ancestry*. New York: Pergamon Press, 1990.
An "introduction, and a history, as well as my own readings of the full-length prose narratives (autobiographies, memoirs, fictionalized memoirs, and novels) written in English and published in the United States by women of Chinese or partial Chinese ancestry."

Meissenburg, Karin. *The Writing on the Wall: Socio-Historical Aspects of Chinese American Literature, 1900-1980*. Frankfurt: Verlag für Interkulturelle Kommunikation, 1987.
"The main object of this thesis is to show through Chinese American literature the various aspects and stages of the Chinese American experience in its diversity and unity." Includes analyses of Genny Lim, George Leong, Louis Chu.

"Multicultural Literature: Part III." Special section of the *ADE Bulletin* 80 (Spring, 1985): 29-45.
Contains Amy Ling's "Asian American Literature: A Brief Introduction and Selected Bibliography," Elaine H. Kim's "Asian American Literature and the Importance of Social Context," and Linda Ching Sledge's "Teaching Asian American Literature."

San Juan, E. *Toward a People's Literature: Essays in the Dialectics of Praxis and Contradiction in Philippine Writing*. Quezon City: University of the Philippines Press, 1984.
A materialist criticism of Philippine literature that includes essays on Carlos Bulosan, Jose P. Rizal, Juan C. Laya, Nick Joaquin, and other Philippine writers.

Simms, Norman. *Silence and Invisibility: A Study of the Literatures of the Pacific, Australia, and New Zealand*. Washington, D.C.: Three Continents Press, 1986.
Contains essays dealing with "methodological and theoretical problems perhaps even more than with the specific content of books written by men and women in the new nations of the Pacific region, from New Zealand Maori through Australian Aborigines to Pacific Islanders and the urban dwellers of the Southeast Asian peninsula."

Sumida, Stephen H. *And the View from the Shore: Literary Traditions of Hawai'i*. Seattle: University of Washington Press, 1991.
A multicultural literary history of two centuries of Hawaiian culture in "a fresh look at the vivid and various patterns within Hawaii's pastoral and heroic literary traditions."

See also: essays in Baker, Ruoff and Ward (3B1); Lumbera, San Juan (8B1c, above)

NOTES

1. Frank Chin et al., eds., *Aiiieee* (1974) (8B1a), p. vii. After saying this, the editors omitted several groups themselves, notably Korean Americans and Southeast Asians.

2. As Walter Ong has written, "All persons growing up with a double identity, ethnic or cultural or linguistic, live in some state of tension. But the tension is often easier to resolve at the social, political, and ideological level than at the level of the creative literary imagination." From the introduction to Baker, *Three American Literatures* (1982), p. 5. (See 3B1).

3. "Asian American Writers: A Bibliographical Review," p. 41 (see 8C1).

4. New York: Penguin, 1989. See 2C4 for a full description of this pivotal work.

5. Described below in 8C1 and 8C2, respectively.

6. Sources: Cheung and Yogi, Kim, Ling (8C1).

AMERICAN
ETHNIC
LITERATURES

INDEX

INDEX

INDEX

Ellison, Ralph 44, 73, 76, 77, 80, 89, 105, 110, 111, 114, 115, 120-123, 125
Emanuel, James A., and Theodore L. Gross, eds. 77
Empringham, Toni, ed. 138
Engeldinger, Eugene A., and Carol Fairbanks, comps. 108
English Journal 32
Equiano, Olaudah 81, 89
Erdoes, Richard, and Alfonso Ortiz, eds. 51
Erdrich, Louise 13, 48, 53-55, 59, 66, 68, 72
Espada, Martin 161
Espinosa, Aurelio Macedonio 147
Espinosa, Herberto 147
Esteves, Sandra Maria 162
Estupinian, Rafael 147
Ethnic Forum 10
Ethnic Reporter, The 11
Etulain, Richard W., comp. 42
Evans, James H., Jr. 110
Evans, Mari 77, 79, 89, 127
Everett, Percival 89
Explorations in Ethnic Studies 11
Eysturoy, Annie O., and José Antonio Gurpegui 165

Fabio, Sarah Webster 89
Fabré, Genevieve E. 107, 108, 170
Fabre, Michel 111
Faderman, Lillian, and Barbara Bradshaw, eds. 38
Faderman, Lillian, and Luis Omar Salinas, eds. 136
Fairbanks, Carol, and Eugene A. Engeldinger, comps. 108
Farmer, James 89
Fauset, Jessie Redmon 81, 89
Fawcett, James T., and Benjamin V. Carino, eds. 30
Feagin, Joe R. 21
Fernandez, Roberta 139, 140
Fernández, Roberto G. 160
Fessler, Loren W., ed. 30
Fiedler, Leslie, and Houston A. Baker, Jr., eds. 34
Fields, Mamie Garvin, with Karen Fields 89
Figueroa, José A. 162
Firmat, Gustavo Perez 138
Fisher, Dexter 34, 40, 72
Fisher, Dexter, and Robert B. Stepto, eds. 35
Fisher, Rudolph 89
Fitzpatrick, Joseph P. 28
Flipper, Henry Ossian 89
Flores, Gloria 147
Flores Peregrino, José 147

Fogel, Robert William 25
Foner, Eric 25
Fontenot, Chester J. 36, 126
Fontenot, Chester J., and Joe Weixlmann, eds. 126
Fornes, Maria 137, 160
Forrest, Leon 89, 121
Forster, Carol D., et al., eds. 6
Foss, Phillip, ed. 54
Foster, David William, ed. 9
Foster, Francis Smith 113
Fox, Robert Elliot 117
Francia, Luis 196
Franklin, John Hope 10
Franklin, John Hope, and Alfred A. Moss, Jr. 25
Franklin, V. P. 25
Frankson, Marie Stewart 165
Freedman, Morris, and Carolyn Banks, eds. 38
Fregoso, Rosa Linda, and Angie Chabram, eds. 170
Fuchs, Lawrence H. 18
Fuego, Laura del 147
Fujita, June 190
Fuller, Charles 90
Fuller, Hoyt 124

Gaines, Ernest J. 74, 80, 90, 115, 121, 126
Gaitan, Marcela 147
Galarza, Ernesto 147
Galvan, Roberto 147
Galvez, Javier 147
Gamboa, Manuel 147
Gamboa, Reymundo 147
Gamboa, Reymundo, and Ernesto Padilla 147
García, Andrew 148
García, Arnoldo 148
García, Eugene E. 170
García, John A. 170
García, José 148
García, Lionel G. 148
García, Luis 148
García, Richard 148
García-Ayvens, Francisco, comp. 133
García-Camarillo, Cecilio 148
Garza, Cheo 148
Garza, Mario 148
Garza, Roberto J., ed. 137
Gaspar, Tomás 148
Gates, Henry Louis, Jr. 10, 36, 42, 81, 82, 110, 121, 125, 127
Gates, Henry Louis, Jr., and Charles T. Davis, eds. 112
Gayle, Addison, Jr. 80, 81, 122, 126
Gee, Emma, ed. 178

207

INDEX